Introducing Interpreting Studies

'A first-rate introduction to the whole area of interpreting studies. *Introducing Interpreting Studies* is informed, authoritative and written in a clear and engaging style. A must for anyone involved in the teaching or study of interpreting and of value to anyone with an interest in interlingual and intercultural communication in today's world.'

Michael Cronin, *Dublin City University, Ireland*

'Franz Pöchhacker's textbook is a first, indispensable for students and teachers of interpretation. A solid foundation for further research.'

Alexandre Mikheev, *Monterey Institute of International Studies, USA*

A millennial practice which emerged as a profession only in the twentieth century, interpreting has recently come into its own as a subject of academic study. This book introduces students, researchers and practitioners to the fast-developing discipline of Interpreting Studies.

Written by a leading researcher in the field, *Introducing Interpreting Studies* covers interpreting in all its varied forms, from international conference to community-based settings, in both spoken and signed modalities.

The book first guides the reader through the evolution of the field, reviewing influential concepts, models and methodological approaches. It then presents the main areas of research on interpreting, and identifies present and future trends in Interpreting Studies.

Featuring chapter summaries, guides to the main points covered, and suggestions for further reading, Franz Pöchhacker's practical and user-friendly textbook is the definitive map of this important and growing discipline.

Introducing Interpreting Studies gives a comprehensive overview of the field and offers direction to those undertaking research of their own. The book is ideally complemented by *The Interpreting Studies Reader* (Routledge, 2002), a collection of seminal contributions to research in Interpreting Studies.

Franz Pöchhacker is Associate Professor of Interpreting Studies in the Department of Translation and Interpreting at the University of Vienna.

Introducing Interpreting Studies

Franz Pöchhacker

Routledge
Taylor & Francis Group

LONDON AND NEW YORK

First published 2004
by Routledge
2 Park Square, Milton Park, Abingdon, Oxon, OX14 4RN

Simultaneously published in the USA and Canada
by Routledge
270 Madison Ave, New York, NY 1006

Reprinted 2007

Routledge is an imprint of the Taylor & Francis Group, an Informa business

Typeset in Baskerville by
Keystroke, Jacaranda Lodge, Wolverhampton
Printed and bound in Great Britain
by The Cromwell Press, Trowbridge, Wiltshire

British Library Cataloguing in Publication Data
A catalogue record for this book is available from the British Library

Library of Congress Cataloging in Publication Data
A catalog record for this book has been requested

ISBN10: 0-415-26886-9 (cased)
ISBN10: 0-415-26887-7 (limp)

ISBN13: 978-0-415-26886-8 (cased)
ISBN13: 978-0-415-26887-5 (limp)

Contents

Figures

Acknowledgements

Building an academic discipline requires the committed efforts of many researchers, and it is only on the strength of the collective achievements of interpreting scholars past and present that this book has come to exist. By definition, then, I owe a great debt of gratitude to the entire community of scholars who have contributed to this field. Some of its most active members have, moreover, given generously of their time and expertise to read and comment on draft versions of one or several chapters. My sincere thanks go to Helle Dam, Daniel Gile, Nadja Grbić, Minhua Liu, Peter Mead, Barbara Moser-Mercer, Cynthia Roy, David Sawyer, Robin Setton and Graham Turner – colleagues whose cooperation has been invaluable, not only for their feedback on my text but for sharing its underlying aspirations. All of this is true also of that one special colleague and friend, who has known, encouraged, critiqued, and shepherded this project from the very beginning, when the idea of a companion volume to our *Interpreting Studies Reader* was first discussed, and the plan of writing it jointly fell victim to the constraints of time and distance. Thank you, Miriam (Shlesinger), for your unfailing inspiration, guidance and support!

Valuable assistance of many sorts, from swiftly providing requested information to sharing bibliographic material and granting me permission to use their work (over and above reprint permission from copyright holders as listed on the next page), has also been given by many colleagues, whom I would like to acknowledge here with gratitude: Barbara Ahrens, Bruce Anderson, Jesús Baigorri, Ivana Čeňková, Dennis Cokely, Ángela Collados Aís, Helle Dam, Daniel Gile, Rita Godijns, Nadja Grbić, Robert Ingram, Sylvia Kalina, Walter Keiser, Hella Kirchhoff, Ingrid Kurz, Regina Leven, Minhua Liu, Peter Mead, Bernd Meyer, Barbara Moser-Mercer, Jemina Napier, Anna-Lena Nilsson, Cynthia Roy, Robin Setton, Catherine Stenzl, Christoph Stoll, Birgit Strolz, Paolo Tosoratti, Joseph Tseng and Sergio Viaggio.

Fundamentally, this project has been nurtured by my understanding editors at Routledge, Louisa Semlyen and Christy Kirkpatrick and, if context is inseparable from cognition, by my dear fellow translatologists at work, and by Erika and the boys at home, whom I wish to thank and repay with love and attention for my engrossment in the writing of 'just this one more book'.

Franz Pöchhacker
Vienna, Easter 2003

Grateful acknowledgement is given to copyright holders and authors for permission to use the following material:

Figures 1.1, 1.5 and 10.1, adapted from F. Pöchhacker, *Dolmetschen. Konzeptuelle Grundlagen und deskriptive Untersuchungen*, copyright © 2000, Tübingen: Stauffenburg Verlag.

Figure 1.2, adapted from G. Garzone and M. Viezzi (eds), *Interpreting in the 21st Century: Challenges and Opportunities*, copyright © 2002, Amsterdam/Philadelphia: John Benjamins.

Figure 3.1, reproduced from S. Lambert and B. Moser-Mercer (eds), *Bridging the Gap: Empirical Research in Simultaneous Interpretation*, copyright © 1994, Amsterdam/Philadelphia: John Benjamins.

Figure 5.2, adapted from J. Tseng, *Interpreting as an Emerging Profession in Taiwan – a Sociological Model*, MA thesis, 1992, Fu Jen Catholic University.

Figure 5.3, adapted from R.W. Brislin (ed.), *Translation: Applications and Research*, copyright © 1976, New York: Gardner Press.

Figure 5.4, reproduced from D. Gile, *Basic Concepts and Models for Interpreter and Translator Training*, copyright © 1995, Amsterdam/Philadelphia: John Benjamins.

Figure 5.5, reproduced from C. Dollerup and A. Loddegaard (eds), copyright © 1992, Amsterdam/Philadelphia: John Benjamins.

Figure 5.6, adapted from R. M. Ingram, "Simultaneous interpretation of sign languages: Semiotic and psycholinguistic perspectives," *Multilingua* 4 (2), copyright © 1985, Amsterdam: Mouton Publishers.

Figure 5.7, adapted from H. Kirchhoff, "Das dreigliedrige, zweisprachige Kommunikationssystem Dolmetschen," *Le Langage et l'Homme* 31, copyright © 1976, Brussels: Institut Libre Marie Haps.

Figure 5.8, adapted from C. Stenzl, *Simultaneous Interpretation: Groundwork Towards a Comprehensive Model*, MA thesis, 1983, University of London.

Figure 5.9, adapted from S. Kalina, *Strategische Prozesse beim Dolmetschen*, copyright © 1998, Tübingen: Gunter Narr.

Figure 5.10, adapted from D. Seleskovitch and M. Lederer, *Interpréter pour traduire*, copyright © 1984, Paris: Didier Érudition.

Figure 5.11, reproduced from D. Cokely, *Interpretation: A Sociolinguistic Model*, copyright © 1992 by Dennis Cokely, Burtonsville, MD: Linstok Press.

Figure 5.12, reproduced from B. Englund Dimitrova and K. Hyltenstam (eds), *Language Processing and Simultaneous Interpreting*, copyright © 2000, Amsterdam/Philadelphia: John Benjamins.

Figure 5.13, reproduced from R. Setton, *Simultaneous Interpretation: A cognitive-pragmatic analysis*, copyright © 1999, Amsterdam/Philadelphia: John Benjamins.

Figure 10.2, reproduced from L. Bickman and D. J. Rog (eds), *Handbook of Applied Social Research Methods*, copyright © 1998 by Sage Publications, Inc. Reprinted by permission of Sage Publications, Inc.

Introducing *Introducing* . . .

In a mature discipline, textbooks are said to rewrite history so that the state of the art can be presented in a coherent manner (see Garnham 1994: 1123). In the young discipline of interpreting studies, which has yet to reach maturity, my task for this book was not so much rewriting but writing in the first place. There has in fact been no previous attempt by a single author to give a comprehensive and balanced account of this field that would include all its ramifications. The aim of providing students, research-minded teachers and practitioners of interpreting as well as scholars in related fields with a broad and accessible overview of interpreting studies as an academic field of study thus presupposes a newly developed 'vision' of the discipline.

Perspective

Inevitably, the vision of interpreting studies offered in this book is shaped by my individual perspective and some related constraints. Overall, interpreting is approached here from the perspective of 'Translation Studies', the field of my **academic socialization**. More specifically, this choice is linked to the genesis of this textbook as a companion volume to *The Interpreting Studies Reader* (Pöchhacker and Shlesinger 2002), which had in turn been conceived as a companion to *The Translation Studies Reader* (Venuti 2000). On the other hand, my **professional background** and experience (as an interpreter in international conference and media settings) is rather narrow compared to the breadth of the field to be covered. Indeed, it was only in the course of my work as a researcher that I came to be involved in the field of community-based interpreting and developed an appreciation for interpreting in signed language modalities. Though I have done my best to expand my horizon and interact with interpreting researchers in different domains of our emerging community, some of the latter might well regard me rather as an outsider, or 'immigrant', whereas in the opinion of others I may have ventured too far afield from my home turf. Eventually, I hope, such concerns will be allayed by the shared aspiration toward 'unity in diversity' for our field.

Another constraint relating to the perspective of this book is **language**. Being limited to a small number of working languages, I have been unable to give due consideration to the literature on interpreting in languages like Russian, Japanese and Chinese. This should be less of a problem in the years to come, as the growing use of English as a *lingua franca* helps us achieve more 'linguistic unity in diversity' for our field. However, this will not resolve the complex issue of terminological diversity and conceptual relativity, so acute in a discipline with an object as multi-faceted as interpreting, which has been described from many different perspectives. Since the space available in this textbook permits only a limited degree of definitional rigor, my use of basic concepts and terms – such as 'message', 'text', 'language', 'context' and 'culture', to name but a few – is often unspecified and aims at a broad 'common denominator' that would provide a starting point for further differentiation. With or without a definition, though, there should be no doubt in the reader's mind that conceptual choices of the kind underlying this book are invariably colored by a given analytical perspective. Hence the need to caution the would-be interpreting scholar right from the beginning against the temptation to accept 'reality' at face value, be it a definition for a concept – or a textbook for a discipline.

Much like the maker of a documentary, the writer of a textbook strives to give a meaningful account but cannot claim to know and represent what the state of affairs, or the state of the art, is 'really' like. The film-maker and the textbook author have to decide what to bring into view, what to foreground, in which light and from what angle. As much as the goal is to do justice to all the protagonists and everything contained in the 'script', the resulting picture is based on a great number of **choices**. Some of these may be painful (as in deciding what to leave out) and others creative (as in establishing new links and relations); all of them, however, are governed by the fundamental need to impose on the subject one's own sense of **coherence** and structure.

Structure and features

Turning to another metaphor which seems particularly appropriate here, this book is intended to be a 'map' of interpreting studies as a field of research. What is more, its individual parts and subdivisions can be viewed as mapping efforts in their own right, ultimately adding up to a multi-layered representation of the field. This section briefly describes the structure of the book, which consists of ten chapters organized into three parts. (The present section, and indeed these introductory pages as a whole, also serve as a small-scale model of the way individual chapters are structured. Following a short lead-in paragraph, each chapter has several 'sections', with numbered first-level subheadings (e.g. 3.1). Most sections are further subdivided into 'subsections', with numbered second-level subheadings (e.g. 3.1.1) after a short lead-in paragraph for the section.)

Part I: Foundations

Part I comprises five chapters which make up the 'synthetic' representation of the discipline. Chapter 1 reviews major **conceptual** distinctions to illustrate the breadth and complexity of the object of study and map out its theoretical terrain. The emphasis is on the construction of a coherent typological framework rather than on encyclopedic information about various forms of interpreting. A basic object-level familiarity with interpreting is thus presupposed. If needed, such knowledge would be readily available from the "Sources and further reading" listed at the end of the chapter.

Chapter 2 chronicles the **historical** "Evolution" of interpreting studies as a discipline. Responding to questions such as 'who?' 'when?' and 'where?', the chapter could be said to map the sociology and geography of the field and its institutional infrastructure. Chapter 3 reviews the major **disciplinary**, **theoretical** and **methodological** "Approaches" to interpreting, responding to the questions 'what?' and 'how?'. The account of guiding ideas and preferred methods then serves as a basis for a map of the discipline in terms of "Paradigms," or **research traditions**, in Chapter 4. Chapter 5, in turn, develops the theoretical foundations with regard to "Models" of interpreting at various levels of **modeling**.

Each of the five chapters in Part I begins with a list of the **main points** covered and ends with a "Summary" as well as a list of "Sources and further reading". In addition, some "Suggestions for further study" are provided as a prompt for reflecting on the chapter content with regard to geographical and linguistic contexts not covered in the text.

In order to avoid duplication and provide cross-references among major points covered in the various mapping dimensions, **text links**, mostly to information in particular subsections, are used throughout the book (e.g. » 3.1.1), creating interrelations within as well as between the different parts and chapters.

Part II: Selected topics and research

Building on the foundations laid in Part I by the 'synthetic' overview of interpreting studies in terms of concepts, developments, approaches, paradigms and models, the second part of the book is devoted to a more 'analytical' presentation of the **state of the art**. Under the broad headings of "Process" (Chapter 6), "Product and performance" (Chapter 7), "Practice and profession" (Chapter 8) and "Pedagogy" (Chapter 9), some of the prominent topics of research are introduced with reference to the relevant literature.

As much as readability would permit, some landmarks of empirical research are presented in the style of mini-abstracts, with special emphasis on aspects of research design such as the subjects, sample, techniques of data collection and analysis, and overall methodological strategy. Nevertheless, given the expanse of the territory to be covered, the review of selected research in Part II is even more reductionist than the mapping efforts in Part I, serving only as a 'roadmap', as it were, with hardly any room for a description of the scenery. It is designed to help locate various avenues and crossroads in the overall landscape of **research topics**; getting there, however, is only possible via the **literature** as such, listed as "Further reading" at the end of each chapter. The difficult choice of what to list, and what not, makes these thematic reviews highly prone to criticism from authors who may, rightly, feel that their work has been given short shrift. My hope is that they will nevertheless understand that such lack of coverage results not from a lack of appreciation but from the mandate to keep the book's bibliography to a manageable size (see below).

Part III: Directions

As a conclusion to the overview of interpreting studies provided in the two main parts of the book, Chapter 10 reviews the major trends and future perspectives of interpreting studies as a field of research. In addition to these "Directions" for the discipline, the final section of the book offers some basic orientation for those undertaking research of their own, directing them toward further useful resources as they take their first steps in contributing to the field.

Sources, authors, subjects

Given the need to keep the **bibliography** of this book reasonably concise, the list of references reflects a priority for widely cited 'classics', for particularly innovative and illustrative examples of recent work, and, overall, for publications which may be more readily accessible, both in linguistic and material terms, to the readers of this book. Many of the resulting gaps can be filled by resorting to *The Interpreting Studies Reader* (Pöchhacker and Shlesinger 2002). Moreover, the list of **Internet sites** following the bibliography includes electronic gateways to comprehensive and updated collections of bibliographic information, not to mention access to journals, research groups, and professional as well as academic associations. The two-part **index**, finally, permits a focus on individual members of the interpreting studies community and their work ("Author index") and serves as an effective tool to access key concepts and topics ("Subject index") across the structural subdivisions of the book.

Function

The fact that this book is organized by thematic considerations rather than typological criteria which have long divided the field into separate domains points to the underlying vision of the discipline to be introduced. While recognizing that interpreting studies is characterized by an overwhelming degree of diversity and difference, this textbook reaffirms linkages, relations, and common ground in various dimensions. While this may be of little worth to researchers and teachers who specialize in one domain or another, the added value of this **integrated approach** for the discipline as a whole would seem to justify the focus on 'unity in diversity'.

Aside from the function of this book for the interpreting studies community at large, its design and thematic scope should make it obvious how it can be used as a textbook, ideally in conjunction with *The Interpreting Studies Reader*, all chapters of which are cited repeatedly in the text. Ideally, teachers of introductory courses or modules on interpreting theory would consider this book essential reading for their students. If this could be the case irrespective of professional domain, the ambition for this book would be amply fulfilled.

Part I

Foundations

1   Concepts

This initial chapter introduces some basic concepts and distinctions relating to interpreting as the object of interpreting studies. The set of types and terms presented here will serve as a broad foundation for what will be presented in the course of this book.

The **main points** covered in this chapter are:

- the conceptual roots of 'interpreting'
- the definition of interpreting
- the relationship between interpreting and translation
- the social settings and interaction constellations in which interpreting takes place
- the major parameters underlying typological distinctions
- the complex interrelationships among various 'types' of interpreting
- the mapping of theoretical dimensions and domains of interpreting practice and research

---

1.1 Conceptual roots

Interpreting is regarded here as **translational activity**, as a special form of 'Translation'. (The capital initial is used to indicate that the word appears in its generic, hyperonymic sense.) Interpreting is an ancient human practice which clearly predates the invention of writing – and (written) translation. In many Indo-European languages, the concept of interpreting is expressed by words whose etymology is largely autonomous from that of (written) translation. Expressions in Germanic, Scandinavian and Slavic languages denoting a person performing the activity of interpreting can be traced back to Akkadian, the ancient Semitic language of Assyria and Babylonia, around 1900 BC (see Vermeer 1992: 59). The Akkadian root *targumānu*, via an etymological sideline from Arabic, also gave rise to the 'autonomous' English term for interpreter, **dragoman**.

The English word 'interpreter', in contrast, is derived from Latin *interpres* (in the sense of 'expounder', 'person explaining what is obscure'), the semantic roots of which are not clear. While some scholars take the second part of the word to be derived from *partes* or *pretium* ('price'), thus fitting the meaning of a 'middleman', 'intermediary' or 'commercial go-between' (see Hermann 1956/2002), others have suggested a Sanskrit root. Be that as it may, the Latin term *interpres*, denoting someone 'explaining the meaning', 'making sense of' what others have difficulty understanding, is a highly appropriate semantic foundation for 'interpreter' and 'interpreting' in our current understanding.

These etymological roots of the verb '**to interpret**' make for a semantically tense relationship with the terms 'translation' and 'translate': While one can capitalize on the polysemy of 'interpret' to argue for a meaning-based, rather than word-based, conception of Translation (» 3.2.6), it has also been common to stress the distinction between the more general hermeneutic sense and a narrowly construed translational sense of the word. This is particularly striking in the legal sphere, where lawyers view it as their prerogative to 'interpret' (the law) and expect court interpreters to 'translate' (the language) (» 7.4.1). Rather than semantic quibbling, this constitutes a fundamental challenge to our understanding of what it means to translate and/or interpret, and many parts of this book, beginning with the following section, will be devoted to attempts at finding an appropriate response.

1.2 Interpreting defined

Within the conceptual structure of Translation, interpreting can be distinguished from other types of translational activity most succinctly by its **immediacy**: in principle, interpreting is performed 'here and now' for the benefit of people who want to engage in communication across barriers of language and culture.

1.2.1 Kade's criteria

In contrast to common usage as reflected in most dictionaries, 'interpreting' need not necessarily be equated with 'oral translation' or, more precisely, with the 'oral rendering of spoken messages'. Doing so would exclude interpreting in signed (rather than spoken) languages (» 1.4.1) from our purview, and would make it difficult to account for the less typical manifestations of interpreting mentioned further down. Instead, by elaborating on the feature of immediacy, one can distinguish interpreting from other forms of Translation without resorting to the dichotomy of oral vs written. This is what Otto **Kade**, a self-taught interpreter and translation scholar at the University of Leipzig (» 2.3.1), did as early as the 1960s. Kade (1968) defined interpreting as a form of Translation in which

- the source-language text is presented only once and thus cannot be reviewed or replayed, and
- the target-language text is produced under time pressure, with little chance for correction and revision.

Kade chose to label the semiotic entities involved in Translation as 'texts' (» 7.1), for which one could substitute expressions like 'utterances' (in the broad sense), 'acts of discourse', or 'messages', subject to an appropriate definition. Whatever the terms, his definition elegantly accommodates interpreting from, into or between signed languages and also accounts for such variants of interpreting as 'sight translation' (» 1.4.2), 'live subtitling' or even the on-line (written) translation of Internet chats. This vindicates the general characterization of interpreting as an **immediate** type of translational activity, performed 'in real time' for immediate use. A definition relying on Kade's criteria, foregrounding the immediacy of the interpreter's text processing rather than real-time communicative use, could thus be formulated as follows:

> Interpreting is a form of Translation in which a **first and final rendition in another language** is produced on the basis of a **one-time presentation** of an utterance in a source language.

The criteria of ephemeral presentation and immediate production go some way toward covering our need for conceptual specification. Making our concept of interpreting hinge on the generic notion of Translation, however, leaves us exposed to the more general uncertainty of how to define that term. While the study of interpreting does not presuppose an account of Translation in all its variants and ramifications, our choice to define interpreting as a form of Translation implies that no interpreting scholar can remain aloof to the underlying conceptual issues. As George Steiner (1975: 252) put it, with reference to the German word for 'interpreter'. "Strictly viewed, the most banal act of interlingual conveyance by a *Dolmetscher* involves the entire nature and theory of translation."

1.2.2 Interpreting as Translation

Given the expansive and varied theoretical territory of Translation, as covered in reference works like the *Encyclopedia of Translation Studies* (Baker 1998), there is a plethora of approaches on which we might draw to enrich our account of interpreting as a form of Translation. Since different scholars will define and characterize their object of study in accordance with their particular aims, experiences and interests, the basic question regarding the nature of Translation has drawn widely discrepant answers. To illustrate the spectrum of choice, let us take a look at four answers to the question 'What is Translation?' and consider their theoretical implications.

Translation is:

(a) a process by which a spoken or written utterance takes place in one language which is intended or presumed to convey the same meaning as a previously existing utterance in another language (Rabin 1958)

(b)   the transfer of thoughts and ideas from one language (source) to another (target), whether the languages are in written or oral form . . . or whether one or both languages are based on signs (Brislin 1976a)

(c)   a situation-related and function-oriented complex series of acts for the production of a target text, intended for addressees in another culture/language, on the basis of a given source text (Salevsky 1993)

(d)   any utterance which is presented or regarded as a 'translation' within a culture, on no matter what grounds (Toury 1995)

Definition (a) foregrounds the defining relationship between the source and target utterances and stipulates 'sameness of meaning' as an essential ingredient. It also introduces, albeit implicitly, human agents and attitudes in terms of 'intentions' and 'expectations'. Definition (b) describes Translation as a process of 'transfer' acting on 'ideas' in the medium of 'language'. Definition (c) introduces a number of descriptive features, such as 'situation', 'function', 'text' and 'culture', and stresses the target orientation of the translational product. The target orientation is carried to the extreme in definition (d), in which the theorist relinquishes any prescriptive authority and accepts as Translation whatever is treated as such in a given community.

All four definitions accommodate interpreting, but each foregrounds different conceptual dimensions. And whatever is stipulated as an essential feature of Translation (i.e. notions like transfer, ideas, sameness, intention or culture) will carry over to our definition of interpreting and will have to be accounted for in subsequent efforts at description and explanation. We are free of course to formulate an altogether diffferent definition of our own, but it would seem foolish to reinvent the wheel of Translation in order to move on with the study of interpreting. We could certainly mine the various definitions of Translation for basic conceptual ingredients, such as

–   an **activity** consisting (mainly) in
–   the **production** of **utterances** (**texts**) which are
–   presumed to have a **similar meaning and/or effect**
–   as **previously existing** utterances
–   in **another language and culture**.

These terms can be adapted and refined in different ways. The notion of 'activity', for instance, could be specified as a 'service', possibly qualified as 'professional', for the purpose of 'enabling communication' and for the benefit of 'clients' or 'users'. Similarly, we could specify 'production' (and 'communication') as taking place in a given 'situation' and 'culture', and we could elaborate and differentiate such key concepts as 'culture', 'language', 'utterance' and 'meaning'. No less significant than terminological refinements, however, are the ways in which our conceptual framework reflects some key areas of theoretical controversy. These include:

- the scope of the interpreter's task ('mainly' production);
- the perspective on the translational process (target-oriented 'production' rather than source-dependent 'transfer'); and
- the normative specification of the translational product (the assumption of 'similarity' in 'meaning' or 'effect').

Whichever of these options one might wish to pursue, the definitional scaffolding set up in these terms should provide sufficient support to interpreting scholars seeking to conceptualize their object of study as a form of Translation. It should be clear, though, even – or especially – in a textbook, that any definition of one's object of study is necessarily relative to a set of underlying theoretical assumptions. In the words of Gideon Toury (1995: 23):

> Far from being a neutral procedure, establishing an object of study is necessarily a function of the *theory* in whose terms it is constituted, which is always geared to cater for certain needs. Its establishment and justification are therefore intimately connected with the *questions* one wishes to pose, the possible *methods* of dealing with the objects of study with an eye to those questions – and, indeed, the kind of *answers* which would count as admissible.

In this relativistic perspective, there can be no such thing as an objective definition fixing, once and for all, the 'true meaning' or 'essence' of what we perceive or believe something to be like. This 'non-essentialist', postmodern approach to meaning has been reaffirmed by leading scholars as part of the "shared ground" in Translation studies (Chesterman and Arrojo 2000). Its theoretical and methodological consequences will become clear in subsequent sections of this book (» 3.2.1, » 3.3.1, » 5.1.2) In the present, foundational chapter, we will return to the concept of interpreting and review ways in which it can be further distinguished with regard to various criteria.

1.3 Settings and constellations

If we approach the phenomenon of interpreting from a historical perspective, the most obvious criterion for categorization and labeling is the **social context of interaction**, or **setting**, in which the activity is carried out. In its distant origins, interpreting took place when (members of) different linguistic and cultural communities entered into contact for some particular purpose. Apart from such contacts *between* social entities in various **inter-social settings**, mediated communication is also conceivable *within* heterolingual societies, in which case we can speak of interpreting in **intra-social settings**.

1.3.1 Inter-social and intra-social settings

Some of the first mediated contacts between communities speaking different languages will have served the purpose of trading and exchanging goods, of 'doing business', which would give us **business interpreting** as a 'primeval' type of interpreting. In one of the earliest publications discussing different types of interpreting, Henri van Hoof (1962) mentions **liaison interpreting** as a form of interpreting practiced mainly in commercial negotiations. More than thirty years later, Gentile *et al.* (1996) took advantage of the generic meaning of 'liaison', denoting the idea of 'connecting' and 'linking up', and extended the term 'liaison interpreting' to a variety of interpreting settings across the inter- vs intra-social dimensions.

Where the representatives of different linguistic and cultural communities came together with the aim of establishing and cultivating political relations, they will have relied on mediators practicing what is usually called **diplomatic interpreting**. When relations turned sour, or maybe before they were even pursued, armed conflict would have necessitated mediated communication in a military setting. Such **military interpreting**, as in talks with allies, truce negotiations or the interrogation of prisoners, thus bears a historical relation to the diplomatic kind.

As societies became increasingly comprehensive and complex, we can conceive of multi-ethnic socio-political entities (such as the empires of Roman times or Spain's Golden Age) in which communication between individuals or groups belonging to different language communities necessitated the services of interpreters. Following the establishment of institutions for the enforcement of laws and the administration of justice, particularly in newly conquered or colonized territories, interpreters were enlisted to ensure that even those not speaking the language of the authorities could be held to account. Hence, **court interpreting**, for which specific legal provisions were enacted in sixteenth-century Spain, is a classic example of interpreting in an *intra-social* institutional context. In many jurisdictions, what is commonly labeled 'court interpreting' includes tasks like the certified translation of documents as well as interpreting in quasi-judicial and administrative hearings. One can therefore distinguish between the broader notion of **legal interpreting**, or **judicial interpreting**, and **courtroom interpreting** in its specific, prototypical setting.

Apart from the legal sphere, interpreting to enable communication between 'heterolingual' segments of a multi-ethnic society emerged only more recently in the context of egalitarian states committed to the 'welfare' of all their citizens and residents. Once the principle of 'equal access' came to be seen as overriding expectations of linguistic proficiency, the intra-social dimension of interpreting became increasingly significant. In the US, for instance, legislation in the 1960s designed to give deaf persons equal access to the labor market gave a strong impetus to the development of interpreting services for users of signed language (» 1.4.1, » 2.1.2). With the focus of such efforts at the 'social rehabilitation' of the deaf placed on employment training and education in general, sign language interpreting in educational settings (**educational interpreting**) went on to become one of the most significant types of intra-social interpreting.

The issue of access, first to the labor market and then to a variety of public institutions and social services, was also at the heart of new communication needs arising in the context of (im)migration. While countries like Sweden and Australia responded as early as the 1960s to the demand for interpreting services to help immigrants function in the host society, others have been slow to address such intra-social communication needs. It was only in the 1980s and 1990s, in the face of mounting communication problems in public-sector institutions (health-care, social services), that 'interpreting in the community' (**community-based interpreting**) acquired increasing visibility. Thus **community interpreting**, also referred to as **public service interpreting** (mainly in the UK) and **cultural interpreting** (in Canada), emerged as a wide new field of interpreting practice, with **healthcare interpreting (medical interpreting, hospital inter-preting)** and **legal interpreting** as the most significant institutional domains.

An interpreting type whose linkage to the intra-social sphere is less obvious is **media interpreting**, or **broadcast interpreting** (often focused on **TV interpreting**), which is essentially designed to make foreign-language broad-casting content accessible to media users within the socio-cultural community. Since spoken-language media interpreting, often from English, usually involves personalities and content from the international sphere, media interpreting appears as rather a hybrid form on the inter- to intra-social continuum. On the other hand, the community dimension of the media setting is fully evident when one considers broadcast interpreting into signed languages. By the same token, court interpreting can also be located in the international sphere, as in the case of war crimes tribunals.

As indicated, the activity of interpreting has evolved throughout history in a variety of settings, from first-time encounters between different tribes to institutionalized inter-social 'dealings' as well as in intra-social ('community') rela-tions. We can therefore posit a spectrum which extends from inter- to intra-social spheres of interaction and reflects an increasing institutionalization of contacts and communication. Some of the contexts for which there is historical evidence of the interpreting function are illustrated in Figure 1.1 along the inter- to intra-social

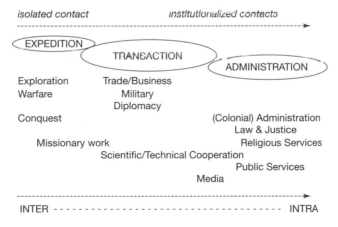

Figure 1.1 Interpreting in different spheres of social interaction

spectrum. Selected settings are grouped under the catchwords 'expedition' (= isolated *inter-social*), 'transaction' (= institutionalized *inter-social*) and 'administration' (= institutionalized *intra-social*), with the progression from the upper left to the lower right corner of the diagram indicating, ever so roughly, developments and shifts in relative importance over time.

1.3.2 *Constellations of interaction*

In addition to the categorization of interpreting types by social context and institutional setting, further significant distinctions can be derived from the situational constellation of interaction. In an early sociological analysis, R. Bruce W. Anderson (1976/2002) modeled the prototypical constellation of interpreting as 'three-party interaction' (» 5.3.1), with a (bilingual) interpreter assuming the pivotal mediating role between two (monolingual) clients. This is commonly referred to as **bilateral interpreting** or **dialogue interpreting**. While the former foregrounds the (bi)directionality of mediation (» 1.4.3), the latter highlights the mode of communicative exchange. Either term is closely associated, if not synonymous, with what was previously introduced as '**liaison interpreting**' (« 1.3.1). All of these terms are in contrast with interpreting in multilateral communication, as in conferences attended by delegates and representatives of various nations and institutions, hence **conference interpreting**.

Interpreting for international conferences and organizations, in many ways the most prominent manifestation of interpreting in our time, did not emerge as a recognized specialty until the early twentieth century, when official French–English bilingualism in the League of Nations ushered in *de facto* multilingualism in international conferencing. **International conference interpreting**, which was to find its apotheosis in the policy of linguistic equality of the European Union, has spread far beyond multilateral diplomacy to virtually any field of activity involving coordination and exchange across linguistic boundaries. Thus it is no longer associated with a particular institutional setting or context (though one could arguably retain the traditional term **parliamentary interpreting** for conference interpreting as practiced in the Belgian, Canadian or European parliaments). What is distinctive about conference interpreting is that it takes place within a particular format of interaction ('conference'). It is often set in an international environment, though there is usually a significant 'local' market for conference interpreting services mainly between English and the national language.

Combining the analytical criteria of setting and constellation against the background of the 'spheres of (inter)action' modeled in Figure 1.1, we can conceive of interpreting as a conceptual spectrum extending from **international** (conference) to intra-social (**community**) interpreting. While it is tempting – and often efficient – to juxtapose conference and community interpreting, it is important to understand the difference between focusing either on the level of socio-cultural communities and their members/representatives or on the format of interaction (e.g. a multilateral conference or face-to-face dialogue). Figure 1.2 attempts to illustrate this dual spectrum, in which liaison/dialogue interpreting holds more

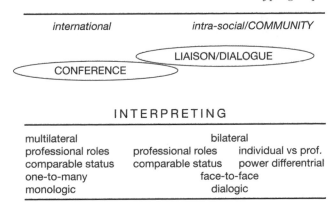

Figure 1.2 Conceptual spectrum of interpreting

of the middle ground, with reference to some characteristics which are usually or typically associated with either end of the spectrum.

While the descriptive features are neither exhaustive nor suggestive of all-or-nothing distinctions, they do capture some typical differences across different parts of the conceptual spectrum. In particular, the nature of community interpreting is best understood by bearing in mind that one of the parties involved is an **individual** human being, speaking and acting on his or her own behalf. Even so, the dual distinction between 'international vs community-based' and 'conference vs liaison/dialogue interpreting' is only one way of categorizing major (sub)types of interpreting. The following section will introduce additional parameters and interpreting types in order to sharpen awareness of the diversity and complexity of the phenomenon under study.

1.4 Typological parameters

Apart from the broad classification of interpreting types by settings and constellations, there are additional and rather clear-cut criteria for a more systematic inventory of types and subtypes of interpreting, among them: language modality, working mode, directionality, technology, and professional status.

1.4.1 Language modality

In most of the literature on the subject, the term 'interpreting' is used generically as implying the use of spoken languages, in particular Western European languages as used in international conferences and organizations. The more explicit term **spoken-language interpreting** gained currency only with the increasing need for a distinction vis-à-vis **sign language interpreting**, popularly known also as 'interpreting for the deaf'. Since deaf and hearing-impaired people may actually rely on a variety of linguistic codes in the visual rather than the acoustic medium, it is more accurate to speak of **signed-language interpreting** (or **visual**

language interpreting). This allows for the significant distinction between interpreting from or into a sign language proper (such as American Sign Language, British Sign Language, French Sign Language, etc.), that is, a signed language which serves as the native language for the **Deaf** as a group with its own cultural identity (hence the distinctive capital initial), and the use of other signed codes, often based on spoken and written languages (e.g. Signed English). Working from and into such secondary (spoken-language-based) sign systems is referred to as **transliteration**, and sign language interpreters or transliterators will be used depending on the language proficiency and preferences of the clients.

Interpreting into a signed language is sometimes referred to, loosely, as 'signing' ('voice-to-sign interpreting' or 'sign-to-sign interpreting') as opposed to 'voicing' or 'voice-over interpreting' ('sign-to-voice interpreting'). A special modality is used in communication with the deaf-blind, who monitor a signed message, including **fingerspelling**, by resting their hands on the signer's hands (**tactile interpreting**).

1.4.2 Working mode

As in the case of language modality, the way in which interpreting was originally practiced did not require terminological qualification until the emergence of a new working mode. It was only in the 1920s, when transmission equipment was developed to enable interpreters to work simultaneously, that it became meaningful to distinguish between **consecutive interpreting** (after the source-language utterance) and **simultaneous interpreting** (as the source-language text is being presented). It may be interesting to note that simultaneous interpreting was initially implemented as **'simultaneous consecutive'**, that is, the simultaneous transmission of two or more consecutive renditions in different output languages. Recently, another hybrid form, which could be labeled **'consecutive simultaneous'**, has become feasible with the use of highly portable digital recording and playback equipment (» 8.5.2).

Since consecutive interpreting does not presuppose a particular duration of the original act of discourse, it can be conceived of as a continuum which ranges from the rendition of utterances as short as one word to the handling of entire speeches, or more or less lengthy portions thereof, 'in one go' (Figure 1.3). Subject to the individual interpreter's working style – and memory skills – and a number of situational variables (such as the presentation of slides), the consecutive

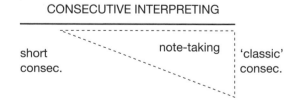

Figure 1.3 Continuum of consecutive interpreting

interpretation of longer speeches usually involves **note-taking** as developed by the pioneers of conference interpreting in the early twentieth century (» 2.1.1, » 2.2.1). Hence, consecutive interpreting with the use of systematic note-taking is sometimes referred to as '**classic**' **consecutive**, in contrast to **short consecutive** without notes, which usually implies a bidirectional mode in a liaison constellation.

For sign language interpreters, whose performance in the visual channel leaves little room for activities requiring additional visual attention, note-taking is less of an option, and they work in the short consecutive or, typically, the simultaneous mode. It should be pointed out in this context, however, that the distinction between consecutive and simultaneous interpreting is not necessarily clear-cut. Since neither voice-over interpreting nor signing cause interference in the acoustic channel, sign language interpreters are free to start their output before the end of the source-language message. Indeed, even spoken-language liaison interpreters often give their (essentially consecutive) renditions as simultaneously as possible.

Whereas the absence of acoustic source–target overlap makes simultaneous interpreting (without audio transmission equipment) the working mode of choice for sign language interpreters, spoken-language interpreting in the simultaneous mode typically implies the use of electro-acoustic transmission equipment. Only where the interpreter works right next to one or no more than a couple of listeners can he or she provide a rendition by **whispered interpreting**, or '**whispering**' (also known by the French term *chuchotage*), which is in fact done not by whispering but by speaking in a low voice ('*sotto voce*'). This is also possible with portable transmission equipment (microphone and headset receivers) as used for guided tours. Nevertheless, simultaneous interpreting with full technical equipment (» 8.6.1) is so widely established today that the term '**simultaneous interpreting**' (frequently abbreviated to **SI**) is often used as shorthand for 'spoken-language interpreting with the use of simultaneous interpreting equipment in a sound-proof booth'.

A special type of simultaneous interpreting is the rendition of a written text 'at sight'. Commonly known as '**sight translation**', this variant of the simultaneous mode, when practiced in real time for immediate use by an audience, would thus be labeled more correctly as '**sight interpreting**'. In sight translation, the interpreter's target-text production is simultaneous not with the delivery of the source text but with the interpreter's real-time (visual) reception of the written source text. If the interpreter is working 'at sight' without the constraints of real-time performance for a (larger) audience, sight interpreting will shade into the consecutive mode or even come to resemble 'oral translation', with considerable opportunity for 'reviewing' and correction. A special mode of (spoken-language) simultaneous interpreting is **SI with text** in the booth. Since authoritative input still arrives through the acoustic channel, with many speakers departing from their text for asides or time-saving omissions, this variant of the simultaneous mode is not subsumed under sight interpreting but rather regarded as a complex form of SI with a more or less important sight interpreting component.

Some of these distinctions, which are represented graphically in Figure 1.4, do not hold to the same degree across language modalities. As already mentioned, signing (i.e. voice-to-sign, sign-to-sign or **text-to-sign interpreting**) is feasible in the simultaneous mode without special equipment. In contrast, sign-to-voice interpreting may be performed with or without a microphone and a booth. The latter, though, applies only to cases where a monologic source speech in sign language needs to be interpreted into several (spoken) languages, requiring the use of simultaneous interpreting equipment to maintain separate channels. In text-to-sign interpreting, the interpreter may need to alternate between reception (reading) and production (signing), thus bringing sight translation closer to the (short) consecutive mode.

1.4.3 Directionality

While the interpreting process as such always proceeds in one direction – from source to target language – the issue of direction is more complex at the level of the communicative event. In the prototype case of mediated face-to-face dialogue (« 1.3.2, » 5.3.1), the interpreter will work in both directions, that is, 'back and forth' between the two languages involved, depending on the turn-taking of the primary parties. **Bilateral interpreting** is thus typically linked with the notions of 'liaison interpreting' and 'dialogue interpreting', but it may equally occur in conference-type interaction, where interpreters may work in a 'bilingual booth', or are said to provide 'small retour' (i.e. interpret questions and comments back into the language chiefly used on the floor).

Although it is common practice in conference interpreting, there is no special label for 'one-way' or one-directional interpreting at the level of the communicative event. Relevant distinctions are rather made with reference to the individual interpreter's combination of working languages, classified by AIIC, the

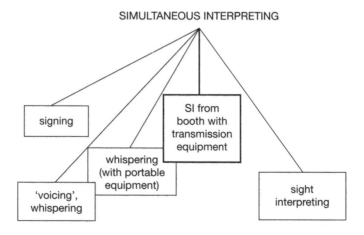

Figure 1.4 Forms of simultaneous interpreting

International Association of Conference Interpreters (» 2.1.1), as A-, B- or C-languages (A = native or best 'active' language; B = 'active' language commanded with near-native proficiency; C = 'passive' language allowing 'complete understanding'). The western tradition of conference interpreting has favored simultaneous interpreting from B- or C-languages into an interpreter's A-language. **A-to-B interpreting**, or **retour interpreting** ('return interpreting'), though widely practiced on the 'local', or private market, has not been equally accepted for simultaneous interpreting in international organizations. In contrast, sign language interpreters, most of whom are not native signers, typically practice simultaneous interpreting as A-to-B interpreting and consider B-to-A, that is, sign-to-voice interpreting, the more challenging direction.

An issue which actually constitutes a parameter in its own right, but can be linked to the present directional context, is the directness with which the source-to-target transfer at a particular communicative event is effected. Where the language combination of the interpreters available does not allow for 'direct interpreting', recourse is made to **relay interpreting**, that is, indirect interpreting via a third language, which links up the performance of two (or more) interpreters, with one interpreter's output serving as the source for another. Relay interpreting in the simultaneous mode was standard practice in what used to be the Eastern bloc countries, where Russian served as the *pivot* language in the multilingual Soviet Empire. The Russian relay system and its reliance on A-to-B interpreting as the standard directional mode were shunned by proponents of the western tradition. For some UN and EU working languages, however, the combination of A-to-B and relay interpreting has played an important role, often with English serving as the *pivot* language, and is likely to become more prominent in an enlarged European Union.

1.4.4 Use of technology

The use of technical equipment was discussed earlier in connection with simultaneous interpreting (« 1.4.2), where it essentially functions to avoid the mixing of source- and target-language messages in the acoustic channel. Obviously though, electronic transmission systems for sounds and images also serve more generally to overcome spatial distances and 'connect' speakers (including interpreters) and listeners who are not 'within earshot' or, in the case of signing, within the range of view. Apart from their common use *in situ*, that is, in conference halls or in noisy conditions, electro-acoustic and audiovisual transmission systems are therefore employed in particular to reach far beyond a given location. In what is generally called **remote interpreting**, the interpreter is not in the same room as the speaker or listener, or both. The oldest form of remote interpreting, proposed as early as the 1950s, is **telephone interpreting (over-the-phone interpreting)**, which became more widely used only in the 1980s and 1990s, particularly in intra-social settings (healthcare, police, etc.). The development of video(tele)phony is of particular significance for **videophone interpreting** for the deaf and hard-of-hearing. Telephone interpreting is usually performed with standard telecommunications equipment in the bilateral consecutive mode, but there have also been efforts, particularly in the US, to introduce a specially designed audio switching system for (bilateral) **remote simultaneous interpreting** for use in healthcare settings. For international and multilateral conferences, the use of video-conferencing technology, in various transmission channels, has made audiovisual remote (conference) interpreting and **tele-interpreting** the focus of attention, and this area can be expected to remain among the most dynamically evolving domains of interpreting in the future.

No less future-oriented than technology-driven forms of remote interpreting (which, despite complaints about the 'dehumanization' of interpreting, continue to rely on specially skilled human beings) are attempts at developing **automatic interpreting** systems on the basis of machine translation software and technologies for speech recognition and synthesis. While such **machine interpreting** should be within the interpreting scholar's purview, the prospects for 'fully automatic high-quality interpreting' remain doubtful at best.

1.4.5 Professional status

Whereas the parameters and interpreting types introduced so far relate to the way in which interpreting is performed, yet another crucial distinction relates to the level of skill and expertise with which the human agent performs the task. Most of the literature on interpreting presupposes a certain – and, more often than not, rather high – professional status of the activity and its practitioners. In other words, the unmarked form of 'interpreting' often implies **professional inter-preting**, and 'interpreters' are regarded as 'professionals' with special skills – also in the usage of this book. Historically, it is of course difficult to clearly separate professional interpreting from what we might call **lay interpreting** or **natural interpreting**, that is, interpreting done by bilinguals without special training for the task.

The issue of "natural translation" has been championed since the 1970s by Canadian translatologist Brian Harris, who postulated that "translating is coextensive with bilingualism", that is, that all bilinguals have at least some translational ability (Harris and Sherwood 1978: 155). Similarly, Toury (1995) put forward the somewhat less radical notion of a "native translator," stressing the role of bilingualism as a basis for learning how to interpret (and translate). Both proposals point to the merit of studying the process by which a bilingual without special training acquires and applies interpreting skills, and Harris as well as Toury agree that there exist socio-cultural translational norms which shape interpreting practices and determine the skill levels required for the activity to be recognized as such.

"The translating done in everyday circumstances by people who have had no special training for it" (Harris and Sherwood 1978:155) has presumably been common practice throughout history. Today, too, communication with speakers of other languages often remains heavily dependent on the efforts of natural interpreters, the most significant example in community settings being bilingual children, of immigrants or deaf parents, interpreting for their family. On the whole, it was only when task demands exceeded what 'ordinary' bilinguals were expected to manage that the job of interpreter was given to people who had special knowledge (of the culture involved or of the subject matter) and skills (in memorizing and note-taking or simultaneous interpreting) as well as other qualifications, such as moral integrity and reliability (» 8.4.1). Even so, the criteria for deciding what or who is professional or not in interpreting are not always hard and fast, and the issue of the professional status of (various types of) interpreting and interpreters needs to be considered within the socio-cultural and institutional context in which the practice has evolved (» 2.1).

1.5 **Domains and dimensions**

The typological distinctions introduced in the course of this chapter indicate the multi-faceted nature of interpreting as an object of study. This concluding section will present an overall view of this diversity and complexity by aligning a number of conceptual dimensions and parameters which relate to major domains of interpreting practice. The resulting 'map' of the territory of interpreting studies should provide some useful orientation for our subsequent *tour d'horizon* of the field.

The best-known and most influential attempt at charting the territory of the discipline concerned with the study of translational activity is the survey of translation studies by James S Holmes (1972/2000), usually represented graphically as the 'map' of Translation studies (see Toury 1995: 10, Munday 2001: 10). Holmes was not primarily concerned with interpreting, which he posited far down in his branch structure as oral (vs written) human (vs machine) Translation in the "medium-restricted" theoretical domain. To put interpreting more visibly on the map, Heidemarie Salevsky (1993) proposed an analogous branch structure for the discipline of interpreting studies, with theoretical subdomains based on a list of situational variables (see Salevsky 1993: 154): varieties of interpreting (consecutive vs simultaneous); the medium (human, machine, computer-aided interpreting); language combinations; culture combinations; area/institution (interpreting in court, in the media, etc.); text relations (text type, degree of specialization, etc.); and partner relations (source-text producer vs target-text addressee).

In a synthesis of these mapping efforts and the discussion in sections 1.3 and 1.4 above, we can adopt the following set of eight dimensions to map out the theoretical territory of interpreting studies: (1) **medium**; (2) **setting**; (3) **mode**; (4) **languages (cultures)**; (5) **discourse**; (6) **participants**, (7) **interpreter**; and (8) **problem**. These conceptual dimensions are used in Figure 1.5 to illustrate the broad spectrum of phenomena to be covered by theoretical and empirical research on interpreting.

While Figure 1.5 is primarily designed to exemplify the varied nature of interpreting in the horizontal dimensions, the vertical arrangement of the dimensions is such as to suggest major subdomains of interpreting practice and

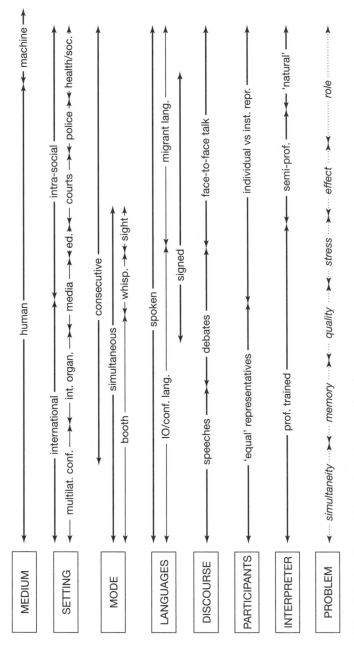

MEDIUM ——— human ———————— machine

SETTING — international ————— intra-social
multilat. conf. —— int. organ. —— media —— ed. —— courts —— police —— health/soc.

MODE ——————— consecutive
———— simultaneous
—— booth —— whisp. —— sight

LANGUAGES ——— spoken
—— IO/conf. lang. —— migrant lang.
signed

DISCOURSE —— speeches —— debates —— face-to-face talk

PARTICIPANTS — 'equal' representatives — individual vs inst. repr.

INTERPRETER —— prof. trained —— semi-prof. —— 'natural'

PROBLEM — simultaneity —— memory —— quality —— stress —— effect —— role

Figure 1.5 Domains and dimensions of interpreting theory

research. Thus, on the left-hand side of the diagram, the features listed for the various dimensions add up to the domain of international conference interpreting, whereas a vertical cross-section on the right-hand side suggests some of the main features of community-based interpreting. Given the many facets of the diverse phenomena to be covered, the diagram cannot amount to a combinatorial map of features. On the whole, however, the interplay of the first seven dimensions serves to highlight some of the key factors in the various prototypical domains. As indicated by the use of dotted lines, the problem-oriented dimension shown at the bottom of Figure 1.5 represents not a continuum of descriptive features but a set of examples of major research concerns to date, as explored more fully in Part II of this book.

Summary

This chapter has laid the conceptual foundations for our survey of interpreting studies by defining the object of study and reviewing its typological ramifications. Acknowledging a basic dependence on theoretical approaches to the generic concept of Translation, interpreting was characterized as an *immediate* form of translational activity, performed for the benefit of people who want to engage in communication across barriers of language and culture. Defined as a form of Translation in which a first and final rendition in another language is produced on the basis of a one-time presentation of a source-language utterance, the concept of interpreting was differentiated according to *social* contexts and institutional *settings* (inter-social vs intra-social settings) as well as situational *constellations* and formats *of interaction* (multilateral conference vs face-to-face dialogue). In addition to the continuum between the prototypical domains of *international conference interpreting* and *community-based dialogue interpreting*, including *court* or *legal interpreting* and *healthcare interpreting*, a more detailed typology of interpreting practices was drawn up by applying the parameters of language modality (*signed-* vs *spoken-language interpreting*), working mode (*consecutive* vs *simultaneous interpreting*), directionality (*bilateral, B/C-to-A, A-to-B* and *relay interpreting*), use of technology (*remote interpreting, machine interpreting*), and *professional status* ('natural' vs *professional interpreting*). Finally, a conceptual orientation to the complex interplay of domains and dimensions was offered in the form of a 'map' of the theoretical territory of research on interpreting.

Sources and further reading

On the terms 'interpreter' and 'interpreting' in English and other languages, see Mead (1999). There are few publications specifically devoted to a comprehensive conceptual analysis of interpreting. The pioneering "taxonomic survey" of interpreting put forward by Harris in the mid-1990s has remained unpublished. For typological discussions with reference to community interpreting, see e.g. Gentile *et al.* (1996) and papers in Carr *et al.* (1997). For reference, see the articles on interpreting in the *Encyclopedia of Translation Studies* (Baker 1998), the *Dictionary of Translation Studies* (Shuttleworth and Cowie 1997) or, for German, the *Handbuch Translation* (Snell-Hornby *et al.* 1998). For interpreting in various social contexts through history, see Bowen (1995). Most monographs recommended for a deeper understanding of various domains of professional practice focus only on a particular type of interpreting. These include: for conference interpreting, Herbert (1952), Seleskovitch (1978a), Jones (1998); for court interpreting, González *et al.* (1991), Laster and Taylor (1994), Mikkelson (2000); for community interpreting/liaison interpreting, Gentile *et al.* (1996), Erasmus (1999), Wadensjö (1998, ch. 3); for sign language interpreting, Frishberg (1990), Stewart *et al.* (1998).

Suggestions for further study

–   What is the etymology and current meaning of words for 'interpreter' and 'interpreting' in other languages?
–   How is the distinction between 'translation' and 'interpreting' made in other languages, in dictionaries, academic writings and in the profession(s)?
–   Do other languages offer a lexical distinction between 'interpreting', or 'interpretation', in the translational sense and in the sense of exegesis or explanation?
–   What forms and types of interpreting are conceptually salient in other languages and national contexts, and how are they differentiated and interrelated?

2   Evolution

This chapter chronicles the development of research on interpreting to date. Highlighting the crucial role of professionalization in the emergence of this field of study, this historical sketch briefly reviews the professional underpinnings of the discipline and then traces its evolution from profession-based writings to theory-based research, with special emphasis on the sociology of the field and its academic infrastructure. Thus the 'making' and the 'make-up' of interpreting studies will be profiled in response to questions like 'who?', 'when?' and 'where?'.

The **main points** covered in this chapter are:

- the evolution of professional standards for interpreting as a specialized occupation
- the beginnings of research on interpreting
- the academic institutionalization of the discipline
- the leading representatives and centers of interpreting research
- the diversification and integration of interpreting studies since the 1990s
- the state of the discipline at the beginning of the twenty-first century

---

2.1 Socio-professional underpinnings

Although interpreting is an ancient human practice, it appears that, through the ages, up to the twentieth century, it was usually considered too 'common' and unspectacular to deserve special mention. Nevertheless, there is some fascinating evidence of the role and status of interpreters in history, including: the Ancient Egyptian honorific "overseer of dragomans" claimed by the princes of Elephantine in the third millennium BC (see Hermann 1956/2002), and the interpreter depicted in the relief of General Haremhab's Memphite tomb dating from 1546 BC (see Delisle and Woodsworth 1995: 279); the scores of salaried interpreters in the service of the far-flung Roman Empire; the early conference interpreters/translators serving ecclesiastic authorities at the Lateran Council in AD 649; the decisive role of Doña Marina ('la Malinche') in helping Hernán Cortés take possession of the

Aztec empire; the laws enacted in the sixteenth century by the Spanish Crown to regulate interpreting practices in its colonies; the French and Austrian 'language boys' in Constantinople initiated as interpreters into diplomacy with the Ottoman empire; the French 'resident interpreters' serving as key traders and negotiators with native Canadian tribes in the seventeenth century; and the pivotal role of Professor Mantoux interpreting in the peace negotiations after World War I.

Thus interpreting has long been practiced in various regions and periods in history with at least some degree of remuneration, legal standards or special know-how, if not training. On the whole, however, it has not been associated with a fixed (professional) status and 'job definition'. In a longstanding tradition, a distinction can be made between culturally hybrid 'dragomans' (« 1.1), serving as local intermediaries in a variety of roles (including those of guide, adviser, trader, messenger, spy or negotiator), and the nation's own trusted 'interpreter-secretaries' involved in the conduct of its affairs of state. It was from the latter sphere that the first major wave of professionalization took shape early in the twentieth century.

2.1.1 International conference interpreting

The brilliant example of Paul Mantoux interpreting for the Allied leaders at the Paris Peace Conference in 1919 marks a fundamental turning point in the modern history of international interpreting: the transition from 'chance interpreters' (i.e. more or less bilingual individuals who happen to be on hand) to the corps of specially skilled professionals working at the **League of Nations** and its affiliate, the International Labour Office (ILO), in Geneva. The first specific **training initiatives**, for note-taking in consecutive interpreting, as well as the earliest piece of scientific **research** on interpreting and interpreters (Sanz 1931), are associated with this context (» 2.2.1). As the communication needs in international politics and trade expanded, new institutions for systematic training in linguistic and translational skills, distinct from those preparing linguists for the diplomatic service, were set up. The very first such school in twentieth-century Europe was a college for business translators/interpreters founded in **Mannheim**, Germany, in 1930 and subsequently transferred to the University of Heidelberg. In the early 1940s, **schools** for the training of (translators and) interpreters (T/I schools, 'interpreter schools') were also established at the universities of Geneva and Vienna, soon to meet new training needs in the wake of the successful introduction of simultaneous interpreting, which, though pioneered as early as the mid-1920s, was put to its crucial test at the **Nuremburg Trial** (1945–6) and subsequently adopted by the United Nations.

Fostered by an expanding professional market and rising numbers of graduates, national as well as international **professional organizations** of (translators and) interpreters were set up in the early 1950s. Alongside the International Federation of Translators (FIT), designed as an umbrella organization to represent T/I professionals via affiliated national associations of translators and interpreters, the International Association of Conference Interpreters (**AIIC**) was set up in 1953 as a professional body with worldwide individual membership. Based on a **code**

of ethics and **professional standards** adopted in 1957, AIIC proved highly successful in regulating interpreters' working conditions and establishing a high profile for the profession on an international scale. In the face of a US anti-trust action in the 1990s which challenged fee arrangements and working conditions, AIIC held its ground on the latter. It maintains its influence in collective bargaining with international organizations and plays a significant role in the area of training (» 2.1.3, » 9.5.2) as well as in research on vital aspects of the profession (» 7.5.1, » 8.6). Still, the fact that the essentially self-regulating international profession has, to some extent, been brought under national jurisdiction and curtailed in its power is to a certain extent indicative of professional developments in other domains of interpreting. Indeed, beyond or, rather, below the level of international organizations and conferences, the struggle for professionalization has typically been set in a territorial context subject to national legislation and local institutional constraints.

2.1.2 Interpreting in the community

Compared to the 'wave' of professionalization that swept conference interpreting to high international prestige after the 1950s, the professionalization of interpreting in community-based settings appears more like a pattern of ripples. The type of intra-social interpreting with the strongest historical roots is interpreting in courts of law. Nevertheless, despite sixteenth-century precedents in legislation, interpreting in the courtrooms of most national jurisdictions was not linked to particular professional standards until late in the twentieth century, often with continued reliance on 'chance interpreters'. There are some early **legal provisions** for the appointment and even testing of 'sworn translators-interpreters' (e.g. in Denmark), as well as **associations** of court interpreters dating back to the 1920s, but little evidence of systematic training (» 2.1.3, » 9.1.2). In the US, a major impetus for the establishment of professional interpreting **standards** in (federal) courts came from the 1978 Court Interpreters Act, which established mechanisms for **testing and certification**, ushering in a wave of professionalization efforts at federal and state levels (» 8.3).

The significance of legal provisions governing the use of interpreters is also evident in the professionalization of American sign language interpreters. Prompted by legislation in the 1960s which authorized the use and remuneration of interpreters for the vocational rehabilitation of deaf and hearing-impaired persons, providers of education and rehabilitation services for the **deaf** met with interpreters in 1965 and founded a national organization of interpreters, subsequently known as the Registry of Interpreters for the Deaf, or **RID** (» 8.1.2). It was this professional body that, much like AIIC, succeeded in establishing standards of professional practice and ethics for its (several thousand) members, and enforcing these through its own system of evaluation and **certification**. A cornerstone for these efforts was the RID **Code of Ethics**, which became a much emulated model for subsequent attempts by spoken-language community interpreters to codify their professional standards.

Sharing the mission of facilitating 'access' to public services, but serving (im)migrants rather than deaf and hearing-impaired citizens, spoken-language community interpreting was pioneered by countries with an explicit **immigration** policy, such as Australia and Sweden, where telephone interpreting and on-site healthcare and social service interpreting were launched around 1970. While such interpreting services were subsequently adopted also in North America and Europe (e.g. in France, the Netherlands and the UK), Australia remains unique for its National Accreditation Authority for Translators and Interpreters (NAATI), which gives **accreditation** to training courses and administers tests for the recognition of different levels of vocational linguistic qualifications in more than forty languages.

Aside from legal interpreting, which is often viewed as a separate professional domain, progress in the professionalization of community interpreting has been achieved mainly in the field of healthcare. In the US, in particular, anti-discriminatory legislation has been used to promote the employment of skilled medical interpreters, thus providing a basis for the creation of **professional organizations** (» 8.3). On the whole, though, the great diversity of institutional settings, demographic and political circumstances, and regulatory environments in different countries have made the development of community-based inter-preting as a profession highly uneven and dispersed. It was only by the mid-1990s that community interpreting became the topic of international cooperation and exchange. Even so, much of the common ground of community interpreters worldwide has consisted in the lack, rather than the existence, of professional standards, remuneration and training, and those promoting harmonization at the national and international levels – such as the US National Council for Interpretation in Health Care (NCIHC), the European Federation of Sign Language Interpreters (EFSLI), or the European association of community inter-preting agencies 'Babelea' – have found it difficult to achieve substantial progress. With public-sector institutions often unable, or unwilling, to pay for professional interpreting services, there are few incentives for engaging or investing in higher-level **training**. Indeed, little training for interpreters working in community settings is offered at an academic level (» 9.1.2). This lag in the academization of the profession is one of the crucial differences between conference and community interpreting, and has profound implications for the development of research, as discussed further below.

2.1.3 Academization

Aside from the role of AIIC as a worldwide body enforcing standards of profes-sional performance and remuneration, the high status enjoyed by conference interpreters since the 1950s is largely due to a strong market (with financially potent institutional clients) and **university-level training**. The latter has been strongly shaped by the profession, in particular by the 'school policy' of AIIC adopted in 1959. T/I schools undertaking to observe its criteria (e.g. that interpreting courses be designed and taught by practicing conference interpreters) joined together in the early 1960s to form **CIUTI**, the Conference of University-level Translator and Interpreter Schools, as a select group of recognized institutions. Though foregrounding their university affiliation, CIUTI schools (including Geneva, Heidelberg, Paris, Trieste and Vienna) had a distinctly **vocational profile**, and many long retained a separate organizational status, as reflected in designations like *École (Supérieure)*, *Institut Supérieur, Hoger Instituut, Scuola Superiore* or *Escuela Universitaria*.

In this institutional context, pioneering professionals produced the first textbooks of interpreting (Herbert 1952, Rozan 1956, van Hoof 1962, Seleskovitch 1968), and (conference) interpreter training programs throughout the 1970s and 1980s foregrounded the professional rather than the academic dimension of higher education. Ever since the 1980s, though, there has been a trend in many institutions toward what Mackintosh (1999: 73) calls "a more theory-friendly curriculum": CIUTI has come to stress the dual identity of interpreter (and translator) education as being both oriented towards professional practice and guided by **academic research**; more and more interpreter trainers have been taking an interest in research (to enhance their teaching or their academic career opportunities, or both); interpreting students have become increasingly exposed to theoretical analysis and reflection; some T/I schools have been more closely integrated with research-oriented departmental structures; and many students have completed **graduation theses** devoted to interpreting research. Most importantly, interpreting has increasingly become accepted as a subject worthy of doctoral research, and there has been a steady output of **PhD theses**, whose role in fueling the development of interpreting studies as an academic discipline can hardly be overestimated.

Notwithstanding this evolution of (conference) interpreting – and interpreting research – in the academic environment, a tension between the vocational and academic orientations of T/I schools is often felt by professionals, teaching staff and administrators alike. A striking example is the (failed) attempt by German authorities in the 1990s to demote the venerable Department of Translation and Interpreting at the University of Heidelberg to the level of a polytechnic (*Fachhochschule*). Against this background, the newly harmonized structure for higher education within the expanding European Union (i.e. 3- or 4-year bachelor's programs followed by master's programs) is likely to have a decisive impact on the academic status of interpreter education – for sign languages and community-based settings as well as for international conference interpreting – and thus on the future of interpreting studies as an academic discipline. On the one hand, the undergraduate option may facilitate the creation of degree-level programs in previously neglected domains (such as the BA program in court and healthcare interpreting launched in the late 1990s at Magdeburg, Germany); on the other hand, greater reliance on BA programs for T/I training might lead to more graduates directly entering the job market rather than working toward an MA degree with an advanced professional as well as a strong academic component. The history of education and research in the field of sign language interpreting in the US may be a paragon in this regard: while the education of sign language interpreters was promoted vigorously in the 1970s, with a number of federally sponsored training programs created at universities throughout the country, most instruction remains limited to post-secondary certificate and undergraduate degree courses. Meanwhile, it has been the graduate-level degree course at **Gallaudet University** in Washington DC that has proved seminal to the promotion of research on sign language interpreting. Even so, those undertaking PhD research have had to rely on fields like (socio)linguistics and education for an academic home base.

Whatever social and professional developments may shape the future of interpreting, it should be understood that interpreting studies as a field of academic pursuit, and the concerns of scholars and researchers to date, have been intricately linked with the field's socio-professional underpinnings since the early twentieth century. Having foregrounded the academization of interpreter training as the critical link between professionalization and the emergence of autonomous research, we can now go on to review the 'making' and 'make-up' of the discipline with regard to its authors, centers, milestone events and publications.

2.2 Breaking ground: professionals and psychologists

The recognition of interpreting as a profession implies that there is a body of specialized knowledge and skills which is shared by its practitioners. This professional expertise, which is initially developed through experience and reflection, needs to be externalized and made explicit, both for (re)presenting the profession to others in society and in support of the training of future practitioners. Hence the important role of publications which describe and add to the collective experience and disseminate the specialized knowledge of the profession.

2.2.1 Pioneers in Geneva and elsewhere

The earliest and probably best-known profession-building monograph on (conference) interpreting is *The Interpreter's Handbook (Manuel de l'interprète)* by Jean **Herbert**, which originally appeared in 1952 in three languages and was subsequently published in several others. Dedicated to "Paul Mantoux, the first Conference Interpreter," the 100-page booklet by one of the pioneers of the profession and first Chief Interpreter of the United Nations has an essentially pedagogical orientation. More specifically didactic is the booklet on note-taking in consecutive interpreting by Jean-François **Rozan** (1956), a colleague of Herbert's at the *École d'Interprètes* in **Geneva**. Even before these now classic works in the interpreting literature, essays by leading interpreter personalities, such as André **Kaminker** and Günther **Haensch**, were published in *L'interprète*, the bulletin of the Geneva school's alumni association. Indeed, *L'interprète* stands out as the field's first specialist periodical, appearing years before *Babel*, published by FIT, and *Lebende Sprachen*.

These early authors naturally focused on describing the conference interpreter's task as well as the abilities and skills required. Interest in the latter has been shared by many psychologists, and as early as 1931, Jesús **Sanz**, a Spanish psychologist, published a conference paper, in French, on the work and abilities of conference interpreters in a specialist journal in Barcelona (» 8.4.1).

The study by Sanz (1931), who had raised issues like cognitive abilities, stress factors, and training needs, remained largely unknown. Indeed, Roger **Glémet**, another leading interpreter and teacher at the Geneva school, began his much-quoted contribution to an early volume on *Aspects of Translation* by suggesting that "no one twenty years ago would have imagined that Conference Interpreting could become a subject for a serious paper" (1958: 105). Nevertheless, it had already figured as the subject of a master's thesis, completed by Eva **Paneth** at the University of **London** in 1957. Paneth, who had trained informally as a conference interpreter at A.T. Pilley's Linguists' Club in London, had collected observational data both on interpreting in practice and, in particular, on training methods at several interpreter schools in Europe (see Paneth 1957/2002). Yet her pioneering thesis, some passages of which were subsequently retracted in response to criticism from AIIC, remained an isolated example, and it was only a dozen years later that the first academic theses on interpreting were completed at the University of Heidelberg.

Further profession-building publications appeared in the course of the 1960s, mainly in Europe, but also in **Japan** (e.g. Fukuii and Asano 1961). In the same year as **van Hoof**'s (1962) comprehensive monograph on interpreting, a seminal article on conference interpreting, by Danica **Seleskovitch** (1962), was published in *Babel*. Seleskovitch, one of the co-founders of AIIC and its long-time Executive Secretary, went on to describe the theory and practice of international conference interpreting in a book which was originally published in 1968, appeared in English ten years later (Seleskovitch 1978a), and was deemed worth translating into German as late as 1988. In 1968, when *L'interprète dans les conférences internationales* first appeared (and Patricia **Longley** published a similar volume in London), interpreters and interpreting also formed the topic of a special workshop at the European Forum **Alpbach**, a high-level conference held annually in an Alpine village in Austria. As reflected in the ten-page typewritten minutes (Alpbach 1968), the small group of research-minded conference interpreters meeting at Alpbach together with a specialist in medical science discussed issues like mental processes and input variables, skills testing, machine interpreting, stress and fatigue, ethics, and client expectations. Most of these profession-based concerns were to emerge, sooner or later, as significant lines of research in interpreting studies.

2.2.2 Experimental psychologists

During the 1960s, interpreting again attracted the attention of specialists in psychology. Pierre **Oléron**, a distinguished French psychologist who published extensively on deaf intelligence and education, is credited with the first experimental study of simultaneous interpreting (Oléron and Nanpon 1965/2002). Based on observational and experimental data, the authors carried out measurements of the time delay (décalage) between the original and the interpreter's output

(» 6.2.3) and found simultaneous interpreting to be a highly complex operation involving a number of rather elusive qualitative variables.

The first PhD thesis on simultaneous interpreting was completed in 1969 by Henri C. **Barik** in the Department of Psychology of the University of North Carolina at Chapel Hill. Barik analyzed experimentally generated interpretation data (» 4.3) for qualitative-linguistic features, in particular various types of 'errors' (» 7.2.2), as well as quantitative-temporal characteristics, such as pausing and time lag (» 6.2.2, » 6.2.3). He shared these latter research interests with British psycholinguist Frieda **Goldman-Eisler** (1967, 1972/2002), who studied simultaneous interpreters' output as a form of spontaneous speech and focused on pausing as a 'window' on the process of language production. Another PhD thesis in psychology, on the feasibility of acquiring the skill of simultaneous listening and speaking through practice, was completed in 1969 at the University of Vienna by Ingrid Pinter, who was also an interpreter by training and later became a prolific author on interpreting under her married name **Kurz**. The issue of divided attention (» 6.2.1) was also among the topics studied by David **Gerver**, the leading representative of psychological interpreting research until his untimely death in 1981. In his 1971 PhD thesis at Oxford University, Gerver presented experiments on the impact of noise (» 6.6.1) and input speed (» 6.6.3) as well as on interpreters' memory performance (» 6.4.1). Based on his findings, he also formulated the first information-processing model of simultaneous interpreting (» 5.4.3). In 1977 Gerver co-organized an interdisciplinary symposium on interpreting research in **Venice** which brought together experts from a variety of scientific disciplines (including linguistics, cognitive psychology, sociology and artificial intelligence) as well as interpreter personalities such as Herbert and Seleskovitch. The proceedings volume of that milestone event (Gerver and Sinaiko 1978), though long out of print, remains one of the richest and most comprehensive collections of papers on interpreting to date and the discipline's most important 'classic'.

2.3 Laying academic foundations

While scientists like Barik, Gerver and Goldman-Eisler were discovering (simultaneous) interpreting as an *object* of research in the late 1960s, a few personalities with a professional background in interpreting were also working towards establishing the study of interpreting (and translation) as a *subject* in academia.

2.3.1 Kade and the 'Leipzig School'

The most influential pioneer in the German-speaking area was Otto **Kade**, a teacher of Czech and Russian and self-taught conference interpreter, who spearheaded interpreter (and translator) training at the University of **Leipzig** from the late 1950s. In his doctoral dissertation, defended in 1964, Kade (1968) established the conceptual and theoretical groundwork for the systematic study of translation and interpreting, for which he coined the German hyperonym

Translation. While as an educator he conducted a special training course for conference interpreters and introduced graduates into professional practice, Kade the scholar was appointed professor in 1969 and went on to complete a post-doctoral thesis in the 1970s. Though interpreting was not the primary concern for Kade and his colleagues of the so-called 'Leipzig School' of linguistically oriented translation studies, their few articles on the subject (e.g. Kade 1967, Kade and Cartellieri 1971) proved seminal to subsequent work such as that done in Germany by Hella **Kirchhoff** (» 5.3.2, » 5.4.2) in Heidelberg and Heidemarie **Salevsky** in (East) Berlin (» 4.5).

2.3.2 Chernov and the 'Soviet School'

In training as well as research activities, the 'Leipzig School' maintained close ties with the 'Soviet School' of interpreting research, as represented chiefly by Ghelly V. **Chernov** at the Maurice Thorez Institute of Foreign Languages in **Moscow**. In the late 1960s, between two six-year stints as an interpreter at the United Nations in New York, Chernov engaged in a research effort in cooperation with psychologist Irina **Zimnyaya** and conducted an experiment on the role of predictive understanding in simultaneous interpreting (» 6.3.2). While Chernov, who was appointed full professor in 1981, was not the only Russian author to publish a monograph on interpreting (see also Shiryayev 1979), his work (e.g. Chernov 1978, 1979/2002) clearly stands out as the most influential in the Russian literature on interpreting.

2.3.3 Seleskovitch and the 'Paris School'

Kade and Chernov, the two 'eastern' practitioners whose research interests had launched them to professorial positions, had a highly prominent western counterpart in Danica **Seleskovitch**, a self-taught conference interpreter working for the European Coal and Steel Community as well as freelance (« 2.2.1). Seleskovitch started teaching in the late 1950s, published a seminal book in 1968, and completed a doctoral thesis on note-taking in consecutive interpreting in 1973 (see Seleskovitch 1975/2002). At her academic home base, the *École Supérieure d'Interprètes et de Traducteurs* (**ESIT**) of the University of **Paris** III/Sorbonne Nouvelle, she managed to establish a doctoral program in "*traductologie*" as early as 1974, thus "conquering the bastion of the Sorbonne", as she reportedly put it in her 1990 retirement speech. The theoretical and methodological approach to the study of interpreting and translation established at ESIT (» 4.2) proved fertile ground for a number of doctoral dissertations on interpreting, most notably by Karla **Déjean le Féal**, Mariano **García-Landa** and Marianne **Lederer**, all completed in 1978. The thesis by Lederer was published as a book in 1981 and added greatly to the conceptual edifice of the so-called 'Paris School' (» 4.2). Seleskovitch and Lederer went on together, publishing a volume of collected papers in 1984 and a comprehensive presentation of the ESIT approach to interpreter training (Seleskovitch and Lederer 1989/1995).

With scholarly exchange and research cooperation limited even within the domain of conference interpreting, it is not surprising that sign language interpreting and liaison interpreting, which also emerged as objects of research in the late 1970s, remained outside the Paris-dominated mainstream for the time being. Both the proceedings of the Venice conference (Gerver and Sinaiko 1978) and the seminal collection edited by Richard **Brislin** (1976b) contained papers on these 'other' areas of interpreting alongside those by Seleskovitch, apparently without generating any interaction. In particular, the appeal by Robert **Ingram** (1978) for sociological and social psychological studies of interpreters and their roles seems to have made as little impact as his admonition that "no description (practical or theoretical) of interpretation which fails to take account of sign language interpretation can be regarded as complete" (1978: 109). It was not until the late 1980s that a *rapprochement* between the Paris-led conference interpreting community and the domain of sign language interpreting made itself felt: French Sign Language interpreting became the topic of a doctoral thesis (by Philippe Séro-Guillaume) as well as a course language at ESIT; Seleskovitch was the invited speaker at the 1991 RID Convention, and published a keynote statement in the 1992 edition of the RID *Journal of Interpretation*, on whose Board of Editors she served in the 1990s; an English version of *Pédagogie raisonnée* (Seleskovitch and Lederer 1989) was published in 1995 by the RID; and Seleskovitch guest-edited a special issue of the Canadian T/I journal *Meta* (42:3, 1997) on sign language interpreting.

2.4 Renewal and new beginnings

During the heyday of the Paris School, other types of interpreting, though gaining increasing recognition as fields of professional practice and/or objects of research, largely remained in the shadow of conference interpreting. Nevertheless, in the 1980s, a process of diversification was under way that would soon make itself felt in the literature.

2.4.1 Diversification

The only domain of interpreting beyond international conferences and organizations that gained wider visibility in the course of the 1980s was **legal interpreting**, which had previously been dealt with mainly from the perspective of the legal system. A doctoral thesis on judicial interpreting in Germany was completed by Christiane **Driesen** at ESIT in 1985, and groundbreaking empirical research on interpreting in the courtroom appeared in the late 1980s, including the 1989 MA thesis by conference interpreter Ruth **Morris** at the Hebrew University of Jerusalem. *Parallèles*, the journal published by the Geneva school, made court interpreting the subject of a special issue (No. 11, 1989), which also featured a six-page bibliography. Even so, with attention often focused on famous international trials, and AIIC voicing demands for an emancipation of court interpreting along the lines of international conference work, interpreting scholars in Europe had not yet come to fully embrace the distinct realities of legal interpreting in the community.

For the interpreting community in Canada and the US, in contrast, the 1980s were the crucial decade for court interpreting (see Harris 1997: 1). Following a colloquium organized by T/I scholars at the University of **Ottawa** (Roberts 1981), major professionalization efforts, with some networking between North American interpreting scholars, gradually came to be reflected in the literature (e.g. Hammond 1988, Repa 1991). In other community-based domains, and other regions, professional profiles had to be created largely from scratch. In the UK, a professionalization initiative for the field of **community interpreting** (in medical, social as well as legal settings) resulted in the publication of a seminal handbook (Shackman 1984) and further profession-building initiatives and publications by the country's leading organizations of 'professional linguists', the **Institute of Linguists** and the Institute for Translation and Interpreting (**ITI**). There and elsewhere, the literature on interpreting in various institutional settings received considerable input from **service providers** themselves, as reflected in a number of papers on "working with interpreters" by medical and legal experts (e.g. Marcos 1979, Putsch 1985). Further afield, linguists and anthropologists studying language use in intercultural communication came to investigate the performance of (untrained) bilingual mediators practicing **natural interpreting** (e.g. Kaufert and Koolage 1984, Knapp-Potthoff and Knapp 1986, 1987). Their efforts were to remain in the shadow of mainstream research on professional interpreting until the following decade, when they were revived in the context of the interactionist discourse-analytical paradigm (» 4.6).

With a considerable headstart in its professionalization, **sign language interpreting** in the US and Canada had matured sufficiently by the mid-1980s to generate not only handbooks laying down the field's body of specialized knowledge (e.g. Frishberg 1990) and a large body of profession-based and training-oriented writings, but also PhD theses and research-oriented debate (see the bibliography by Patrie and Mertz 1997). For lack of an academic infrastructure of their own, pioneering US scholars like Dennis **Cokely** and Cynthia B **Roy**, whose dissertations were not published until the following decade (Cokely 1992a, Roy 2000a), turned to sociolinguistics as a disciplinary framework, while endeavoring also to take account of research findings from the field of spoken-language conference interpreting.

2.4.2 Reorientation

With few exceptions, such as Etilvia **Arjona** (e.g. 1984), the community of conference interpreting researchers remained largely aloof to the varied 'new beginnings' of professional writing and research in other domains during the 1980s. Meanwhile, the field came to experience a substantial renewal within its own ranks. A methodological reorientation was foreshadowed in the MA theses by Catherine **Stenzl** and Jennifer **Mackintosh**, both completed in 1983 at the University of **London**, and in a number of innovative papers by Daniel **Gile** in the early 1980s.

These research-minded interpreters expressed a keen interest in more scientific studies on interpreting, as had been launched around 1970, most notably by Gerver. Their cause, promoted also in the framework of the AIIC Research Committee, happened to be shared by a number of individual interpreting scholars, also – and not least – in Eastern Europe. Experimental PhD theses were published, such as those by Andrzej **Kopczyński** (1980), Heidemarie **Salevsky** (1987) and Ivana **Čeňková** (1988), reviving and following up on the pioneering work of authors like Barik, Chernov and Kade. In the 'West', an approach rooted in cognitive psychology was promoted, among others, by Barbara **Moser-Mercer** (Geneva/Monterey) and Sylvie **Lambert** (Monterey/Ottawa), who reaffirmed the view of interpreting as cognitive information processing (» 3.2.5). A good illustration of the renewal taking shape in interpreting research toward the mid-1980s is the special issue on conference interpreting published in the thirtieth anniversary volume of *Meta* (30:1, 1985). Interspersed among the leading representatives of the Paris School, authors like Gile, Lambert, Mackintosh and Moser-Mercer are represented in that collection with papers highlighting the cognitive-psychological reorientation.

A landmark event in this development was the international symposium on conference interpreter training organized in late 1986 by the T/I school (SSLMIT) of the University of **Trieste**. It was at that meeting that many science-minded interpreter educators openly called into question some of the hallowed positions championed by the Paris School, and resolved to study them within a more rigorous framework of empirical research. Expressing the buoyant mood felt at that meeting, Jennifer Mackintosh, speaking at the close of the **Trieste Symposium**, suggested the beginning of "'The Trieste Era' in interpretation studies" (Gran and Dodds 1989: 268). Indeed, the Trieste School rose to a pivotal position in the field of interpreting research on several grounds. One was its **interdisciplinary approach** to the neurolinguistic foundations of (simultaneous) interpreting (» 4.4, » 6.1.2). No less important was the launching, in 1988, of a medium for continued networking and exchange – *The Interpreters' Newsletter*. The publication quickly outgrew the function suggested by its name and turned into a (roughly annual) specialized journal of interpreting research. With the publication of the proceedings of the Trieste Symposium (Gran and Dodds 1989) and other events and publications (e.g. Gran and Taylor 1990), often in close cooperation with Gile (e.g. 1990a), Trieste clearly became a hub and rallying point for empirical research, particularly with a neuropsychological as well as a text-linguistic orientation. At the same time, 1990 saw the retirement of Seleskovitch from university, marked by the publication of a *festschrift* and an international symposium, and may thus be regarded as the point of transition from the Paris-led to the Trieste era.

The reorientation which took place in the course of the 1980s within the community of interpreting scholars could be described as a 'vertical' development, with empirical research probing ever more deeply into the cognitive processes underlying interpreting performance. At the same time, the 1980s were also a decade in which the field embarked on a process of 'horizontal' development, of diversification and opening up to interpreting domains beyond international conferences and organizations. An excellent illustration of the widening scope of the emerging discipline around 1990 is a volume compiled by David and Margareta **Bowen**, of Georgetown University, which features contributions on the history of (diplomatic) interpreting and on (conference) interpreter training as well as on the newly emerging concerns of court interpreting, community interpreting and media interpreting. Although Bowen and Bowen (1990) failed to include the domain of sign language interpreting (as pointed out in a critical review by Gile), the breadth and variety of approach of the book make it a harbinger of the disciplinary integration that was to emerge in the course of the 1990s.

2.5 Consolidation and integration

At the Trieste Symposium, a number of participants stated that interpreting as an academic subject, however interdisciplinary in its theoretical and methodological approach, should be regarded as a discipline in its own right. It was not obvious, though, where in academia interpreting scholars might stake out their claim to an autonomous field of study. The answer found in the early 1990s proved to be based on the common conceptual and institutional ground shared by interpreting and translation.

2.5.1 Linking up

An ideal opportunity for the interpreting research community to promote its dual aspiration to interdisciplinarity and an academic home base of its own arose at the "Translation Studies Congress" held at the University of **Vienna** in September 1992. The theme of that international event, "Translation Studies – An Interdiscipline", attracted leading scholars of translation and interpreting alike. The plenary address on interpreting was given by Daniel Gile, who appealed for a process of "opening up" toward other disciplines in what he referred to as "interpretation studies" (Gile 1994a). Gile's use of a distinct disciplinary label was paralleled by Salevsky's in a programmatic paper, delivered several weeks later at an international conference in Prague, whose title featured the name of the discipline as "Interpreting Studies" (see Salevsky 1993). Designating the field in analogy with the term coined by Holmes (1972/2000) in his seminal paper on "The Name and Nature of Translation Studies" reinforced the identity of interpreting studies as a (sub)discipline within the broader field of **Translation studies** (» 3.1.1).

Benefiting from the emerging socio-academic infrastructure of Translation studies, interpreting scholars such as Gile gave visibility to their specialty within the European Society for Translation Studies (**EST**), which had been founded at the close of the Vienna Congress. Gile also became a key associate of the CE(T)RA summer school in translation studies at the University of Leuven. A number of young scholars who participated in that program, particularly during Gile's turn as CERA Professor in 1993, went on to complete doctoral theses on interpreting.

In particular, a group of Danish interpreters teaching at the **Aarhus** School of Business, including Helle **Dam**, Friedel **Dubslaff** and Anne **Schjoldager**, took up the torch: they edited a thematic issue on interpreting research for their school's journal, *Hermes. Journal of Linguistics* (No. 14, 1995), and, in early 1997, made Aarhus the venue for an international CE(T)RA-inspired **research training** seminar for PhD students of interpreting (» 9.5.4).

Gile was also a driving force in several other networking and publishing initiatives in the 1990s. In early 1991 he launched the International Interpretation Research and Theory Information Network (IRTIN, subsequently shortened to **IRN**). Now designated as **CIRIN** (Conference Interpreting Research Information Network), Gile's network publishes an informal semi-annual *Bulletin* with bibliographic updates and other relevant information. Thanks to Gile's active role as an information broker, conference interpreting researchers throughout the world have shared and gained access to a wealth of bibliographic information, including references to unpublished theses and works published in languages like Chinese, Czech, Finnish and Japanese. Research-minded interpreters in Japan, including Masaomi **Kondo** and Akira **Mizuno**, proved highly motivated to join the networking effort, having founded their own Interpreting Research Association in late 1990. The Japanese association went on to publish its own semi-annual journal, *Tsûyakurironkenkyû*, which featured an all-English special issue on the occasion of the 1999 AILA Congress in Tokyo (*Interpreting Research* 8:2, 1999). In 2000, the association was officially registered as the Japan Association for Interpretation Studies (**JAIS**), and the journal renamed *Tsûyaku Kenkyû / Interpretation Studies*.

Increased international networking in interpreting studies also manifested itself in the publication, in 1992, of a special issue of *The Interpreters' Newsletter* on Japanese interpreting research as well as a special issue of *Target*, the *International Journal of Translation Studies*, devoted to *Interpreting Research*. Guest-edited by Daniel Gile, *Target* **7:1** (1995) provides a panorama of the field in the mid-1990s, including a profile of leading researchers and their affiliations; papers on methodological issues and on the implications of research on sign language interpreting; and essays on the evolution and state of interpreting research at Trieste, in Eastern Europe and in Japan. An even more ambitious and far-reaching attempt at a broad-based stocktaking of interpreting research was the "International Conference on Interpreting" organized in 1994 in **Turku**, Finland, in cooperation with Gile and representatives of the Trieste School. Though foregrounding interdisciplinarity and the research paradigms of neurolinguistics and cognitive psychology, the conference also addressed key professional concerns (e.g. 'quality') and conceptual issues (e.g. 'culture') associated in particular with liaison interpreting and with court and media settings. While this broader scope is not reflected in the title of the Turku Conference proceedings (Gambier *et al.* 1997), which document keynote speeches as well as the interactive workshops on topics like research policy, training, and quality in conference interpreting (see also Tommola 1995), the fact that 'non-conference interpreting' was represented at all, not least in the keynote paper by Per **Linell** (1997), clearly reflects the growing scholarly interest in community-based interpreting at the time.

2.5.2 *The Critical Link*

In 1995, community-based interpreting had its own milestone event – the "First International Conference on Interpreting in Legal, Health, and Social Service Settings", held at **Geneva Park** near Toronto, Canada. Though still grappling with basic professional issues, community interpreting presented itself there as a buoyant field, as reflected in the rich volume of proceedings (Carr *et al.* 1997). Like the participants at the 1986 Trieste Symposium, the practitioners and scholars attending the landmark conference at Geneva Park were united in the belief that the field needed some sustained channels for international exchange and cooperation. Indeed, the title of the conference, "**The Critical Link**/Un maillon essentiel", lived on as a semi-annual *Newsletter* coordinated by Diana **Abraham** in the Ministry of Citizenship of Ontario, Canada. She and a group of committed educators and scholars, in particular Brian **Harris** and Roda **Roberts** of the University of Ottawa, moved to institutionalize "The Critical Link" as a conference series, the second and third editions of which were held with undiminished vitality in Vancouver in 1998 (Roberts *et al.* 2000) and in Montreal in 2001. In early 2003, *The Critical Link* was launched as "A Quarterly Journal dedicated to interpreting in the social, health care and legal sectors", with plans to make it available on the Web.

Despite the heterogeneity of community-based settings and a general lack of national, let alone international standards, the Critical Link community has displayed a keen awareness of the common ground shared between community-based spoken-language and signed-language interpreters as well as between those working in legal, healthcare and other settings in a great variety of circumstances throughout the world. As regards leadership, apart from the Critical Link community's driving forces in Canada, educators and researchers like Holly **Mikkelson** (Monterey, USA) and Cecilia **Wadensjö** (Linköping, Sweden) emerged as influential authorities on the strength of their professional experience and academic achievements. Mikkelson and Wadensjö also played an important role in the integration process of interpreting studies by forming part of key initiatives of the mainstream interpreting research community in the 1990s. One of these – a major landmark in the institutional development of interpreting studies – was the launching, in 1996, of the first international refereed journal devoted solely to interpreting. Initiated by Barbara Moser-Mercer, *Interpreting: International Journal of Research and Practice in Interpreting* reflected a strong cognitive-science orientation, not least by the composition of its original editorial team. Nevertheless, the journal (published by John Benjamins Co. of Amsterdam) endeavored to cover the breadth of interpreting modes and settings, and has featured several contributions on community interpreting, first and foremost by Mikkelson (e.g. 1996, 1998). Wadensjö, in turn, was part of the group of instructors at the "Aarhus Seminar on Interpreting Research" in 1997, where she presented her discourse-based approach to the study of interpreting in dialogic interaction (» 4.6). In addition, Wadensjö was a major source of inspiration and a key contributor to the special issue on *Dialogue Interpreting* guest-edited by Ian **Mason** for *The Translator* (5:2, 1999).

By the time the third landmark conference on interpreting to take place in Italy (after Venice 1977 and Trieste 1986) was held at the T/I school of the University of Bologna at **Forlì** in late 2000, the converging developments outlined above were clearly making themselves felt. Although only a 'local' initiative when compared to the multi-center cooperation underlying the 1994 Turku Conference, the Forlì Conference exceeded the latter in scope and diversity. Participants experienced a comprehensive overview of the field, with the concerns of sign language interpreters and mediators in courtroom and healthcare settings being voiced alongside those of interpreters working in EU institutions and the UN as well as in the media. The Forlì Conference convincingly lived up to its theme of *Interpreting in the 21st Century* (Garzone and Viezzi 2002, Garzone *et al.* 2002) and gave a bright finish to the formative decade of interpreting studies as a discipline.

2.6 Interpreting studies in the twenty-first century

Though the turn of the millennium is a rather arbitrary, and Eurocentric, marker, it does coincide with some significant developments in interpreting studies, both in its European 'heartland' and beyond, which are likely to shape the prospects for further progress of the discipline in the course of the new century.

2.6.1 Old issues, new horizons

As interpreting studies became increasingly diversified in the course of the 1990s, there was no longer a main center or hub for the discipline as a whole. Not only did the T/I school of the University of **Bologna** join Trieste in promoting the field (see Mead 2001), but new (and old) institutions came to play a more active role in interpreting research. Most prestigiously, the T/I school in **Geneva** (« 2.2.1) launched PhD-level programs in interpreting, built on a "consensus to align research on interpretation and interpreter training with mainstream cognitive science" (Moser-Mercer and Setton 2000: 51). This 'Geneva doctrine' rests on the possible convergence between approaches from cognitive psychology and linguistics as pursued by Moser-Mercer and Robin **Setton**. The former, who had championed interdisciplinary, scientific research on interpreting for many years, as reflected in particular in the **Ascona workshops** of 1997 and 2001 (*Interpreting* 2:1/2, 1997 and 5:2, 2000/01), has put the emphasis on cognitive psychology; Setton, in contrast, sought to build on the foundations of the Paris School with a new conception of linguistics informed by Relevance Theory, that is, cognitive pragmatics (» 5.4.3).

Interpreting researchers at the T/I school of the University of **Granada**, such as Ángela **Collados Aís** (1998/2002), also developed PhD courses and issued a flurry of publications. An international conference on **quality** in interpreting, organized by the Granada team at Almuñécar in 2001, featured leading members of the conference interpreting research community and attracted contributions from scholars working in many different contexts (see Collados Aís *et al.* 2003). More so than at the T/I conference at the University of **Vigo** in 1998 (Álvarez

Lugrís and Fernández Ocampo 1999), in which interpreting research had been highly visible, participants had indeed come to Spain from far and wide. Apart from heightened interest in East European countries like Poland and Slovenia in the face of EU enlargement, the Almuñécar Conference included contributions by a number of Chinese scholars, from Guangdong, Hong Kong, and Taipei, reflecting the growing momentum of interpreting research in the Far East.

Various universities in the Republic as well as the People's Republic of **China** have hosted international T/I conferences (e.g. Hung 2002), and papers on interpreting have been published in the journals of the respective professional associations of translators and interpreters. With the launch of PhD programs in T/I, a greater number of monographs and collective volumes in Chinese are also likely to appear – and to confront the interpreting studies community with a formidable linguistic barrier. The same applies to publications on interpreting in **Korea**, where T/I research and **training** have been promoted with great zeal. International conferences on T/I studies have been organized by Sookmyung Women's University and, in particular, by the Graduate School of Interpretation and Translation at Hankuk University of Foreign Studies in **Seoul**. In 1999, the Korean Society of Conference Interpretation, founded by Jungwha **Choi**, started publishing the journal *Conference Interpretation and Translation*, whose inaugural issue featured papers by several 'western' conference interpreting scholars associated with the Paris School (« 2.3.3). While subsequent issues also reflected other schools of thought (e.g. Moser-Mercer and Setton 2000), Choi, who completed a doctoral dissertation at ESIT in 1986, joined Lederer to launch *Forum*, an international journal of interpreting and translation published (in English and French) by Presses de la Sorbonne Nouvelle. Developments in the Far East are thus giving an impetus to the evolution of interpreting studies as a global discipline – by foregrounding previously neglected **linguistic issues** and socio-cultural contexts while at the same time reviving the heritage of profession-oriented theoretical approaches which had underpinned the emergence of the field in Europe.

2.6.2 'Success story' – to be continued

Judging from the review of landmark events and pioneering initiatives in the evolution of interpreting studies up to the turn of the millennium, the discipline could well be made out as a 'success story of the 1990s' (to adapt a phrase used to characterize translation studies in the 1980s). And yet one could also list a number of problems and weaknesses which continue to plague this young academic field. Despite considerable progress with academization, the community of interpreting scholars remains rather small, and its research output, while steady, is relatively modest. Even focusing on the more established domain of conference interpreting research, Gile (1998, 2000), for one, has found the discipline wanting in both quantitative and qualitative terms, and pointed to a lack of motivated scholars with adequate research training.

The extension of research interest toward the varied domain of liaison or dialogue interpreting in the community (including natural interpreting), while implying a loss of professional luster, may help redress the perceived lack of conceptual and methodological sophistication in interpreting studies. Interpreting practices in community-based settings have proved an attractive topic to non-interpreter specialists in fields like linguistics, sociology, and discourse studies. Indeed, some of the research that has been claimed as most influential in the area of community interpreting – such as the work of Susan **Berk-Seligson** (1990) and Robert **Barsky** (1996) – was not set in the disciplinary context of interpreting studies at all. While this may well pose a challenge to the young discipline's emerging identity as an autonomous academic field, the phenomenon as such is certainly not new: one could hardly imagine the history of conference interpreting research without the impetus provided by psychologists like Barik and Gerver. Nor is the issue of disciplinary integration vs fragmentation unique to interpreting studies: Translation studies as a whole is clearly subject to dynamic forces resulting from the multi-faceted nature of its object and from the diversity of (inter)disciplinary lines of approach (see Munday 2001: 190).

Without seeming unduly optimistic, one may claim that the prospects for interpreting studies early in the twenty-first century could hardly be more favorable: the discipline is accepted within the wider field of Translation studies (as reflected in conference programs, membership in EST, and the Routledge *Encyclopedia*) and at the same time respected as one of its subareas "whose volume and degree of specialization demand separate coverage" (Venuti 2000: 2); cooperation and exchange within the field are increasing, facilitated by English as the *lingua franca* as well as unprecedented levels of access to electronic means of communication; more and more scholars with a background in conference interpreting, many of them based in Europe, are taking an interest in community-based domains (e.g. at the Fourth – and first European – Critical Link Conference held in Stockholm in 2004); technology-driven developments in the interpreting profession generate new needs for research (» 10.2.2); and the discipline has its own journals and identity-building publications, such as *The Interpreting Studies Reader* (Pöchhacker and Shlesinger 2002) and the present textbook, which celebrate the rich body of ideas and findings on interpreting to date. All of this gives ample reason to assume that the evolution of interpreting studies, in both sociology and substance, is set to continue, and the field is earning broader recognition for playing its part in the concert of academic disciplines.

Summary

Against the background of the *twentieth-century professionalization* of interpreting, with particular regard to the increasing *academization of training*, this chapter has reviewed several stages in the evolution of interpreting studies, roughly indicating who did what, and what happened when, and where. Following the groundbreaking efforts of *pioneer conference interpreters and psychologists* in the 1950s and 1960s, *academic foundations* for the field were laid in the 1970s, especially at ESIT in Paris under the leadership of Danica Seleskovitch. Even during the heyday of the so-called *'Paris School'* in the early 1980s, the field experienced both an internal *reorientation* toward more rigorous scientific investigation and a growing *diversification* of its professional domain. Around 1990, when the *Trieste School* established itself as the new hub of activity in (interdisciplinary) conference interpreting research, such previously marginal domains as *court interpreting* and *sign language interpreting* gained visibility as fields of professional practice and objects of research. In the early 1990s, interpreting scholars such as Daniel Gile forged closer links with Translation studies and its newly emerging socio-academic infrastructure, and engaged in increased international *networking and cooperation*, as reflected in various research training initiatives, conferences and publications. Later in the 1990s, *community interpreting* became prominent as an area in dire need of training and research, particularly through the *Critical Link* conference series in Canada. Through the efforts of such educators and researchers as Holly Mikkelson and Cecilia Wadensjö, the community-based domains came into closer contact with the mainstream (conference) interpreting research community, leading toward a growing consolidation and integration of interpreting studies as a discipline. This momentum is fueled not least by heightened interest and activity in interpreting research and interpreter training in the *Far East*, substantially broadening the discipline's horizon at the turn of the millennium.

Sources and further reading

Sources on interpreting in history and the history of the profession(s) are introduced in the first section of Chapter 8 (» 8.1). For further information on various professional domains, see the sources and further reading at the end of Chapter 1. Website addresses of relevant professional organizations, academic institutions, and collections of bibliographic information are provided at the end of the book following the Bibliography.

For the development and status of interpreting studies as an academic discipline, see Gambier *et al.* (1997), Gile (1988, 1994a, 1995a, 2000), Pöchhacker (2000a), Salevsky (1993), Seleskovitch (1991) and the Special Issue of *Target* (7:1, 1995) on *Interpreting Research*. For a concise introduction to the discipline and biographical mini-sketches of leading authors, see the *Reader*.

Suggestions for further study

– What is the status of various interpreting domains in countries and regions other than those referred to in this chapter?

–   What is the academic status of interpreting and interpreter education, and how has it been changing over the years?

–   What is the status of academic research on interpreting (publications, PhD programs, etc.)?

–   When and where does the interpreting literature in languages other than English reflect evidence of interaction between various domains of the profession, and between interpreters and specialists in other academic disciplines?

3   Approaches

Against the background of the academic institutionalization and 'sociology' of interpreting studies (Chapter 2), we now turn to the ideas and lines of inquiry which make up the substance of this discipline. This chapter will thus review the major disciplinary, conceptual, and methodological approaches that can be and have been taken to study the phenomenon of interpreting.

The **main points** covered in this chapter are:

- the disciplinary perspectives from which inquiry into interpreting has been launched
- the key ideas which inform past and present thinking about interpreting
- the conceptual relations of the central ideas, or 'memes', in interpreting studies
- the interplay of theory and methodology, and major methodological orientations
- the research strategies and techniques that have been applied to the study of interpreting

---

3.1 Disciplinary perspectives

The field of interpreting studies, which began to form a (sub)disciplinary identity of its own in the 1990s, has been strongly shaped by conceptual and methodological approaches from other, more established disciplines. Taking stock of its central ideas and theoretical frameworks therefore presupposes an awareness of the disciplinary perspectives from which the phenomenon of interpreting has been seen and studied.

3.1.1 Interpreting in Translation studies

Having positioned interpreting studies within the wider field of Translation studies, we would naturally assume that the fundamental ideas and research approaches of the 'parent' discipline also inform inquiry into the translational activity of interpreting. And yet research on interpreting has been sourced from translation studies only to a very limited degree. Translation scholars have mostly defined their object in the narrower sense, as limited to the written medium, and have seen little need to fit their models and methods to interpreting. Indeed, the number of those who have adopted a comprehensive conception of Translation, including all and any translational activity, is very small. Scholars such as Holmes, Toury and Vermeer, who have sought, in principle, to account for interpreting in their theories, have tended to neglect it in their research practice. Understandably, perhaps, considering the strongly profession-based tradition and, at times, defensive attitude of the mainstream (conference) interpreting research community, and considering the elusive nature of the phenomenon, so much less convenient to study than language fixed in writing. The scant attention from translation scholars was matched by interpreting researchers' lack of interest in potentially relevant work on written translation. The notion of equivalence is a case in point. While it has occupied a central position in the discourse on translation for decades (see Munday 2001, ch. 3; Venuti 2000: 121f), many interpreting researchers have worked with such notions as accuracy or errors on the tacit and apparently unproblematic assumption of source–target equivalence. It was only in the early 1990s that influential approaches to (written) translation began to be explored in the field of interpreting.

The tenuous links between translation theory and research on interpreting may also be due to the fact that scholars investigating written translation are anything but a close-knit community. Notwithstanding Snell-Hornby's (1988) seminal attempt to reconcile the various linguistic and literary approaches, often linked to genre-based domains, translation studies in the mid-1990s was still, in the eyes of Toury (1995: 23), "a remarkably heterogeneous series of loosely connected paradigms". It was only towards the end of that decade that efforts to reaffirm the common ground shared by the translation studies community gathered momentum – some of which carried over to the interpreting studies community as well. A position paper on "Shared Ground in Translation Studies" published by Chesterman and Arrojo (2000) in *Target* drew numerous constructive responses, including two by leading authors in interpreting studies. This suggests that, at least at the fundamental levels of **epistemology** and **methodology**, basic insights and ideas about Translation may now be feeding more directly into interpreting studies and enriching its **theoretical foundations** (» 3.2.2). On the whole, however, the evolution of research on interpreting to date has been shaped much more decisively by approaches from other than its sibling discipline.

3.1.2 Psycho / linguistic approaches

Of the long list of disciplines, sub- and inter-disciplines which have some bearing on the study of interpreting, the most prominent is clearly the field of **psychology** (« 2.2), whose conceptual and methodological approaches have been brought to bear particularly on the study of (simultaneous) conference interpreting. Like any prospering discipline, psychology has undergone some major reorientations and 'paradigm shifts' (» 4.1), and these carried over also to psychological research on issues relating to interpreting: interest in 'verbal behavior' at the level of conditioned reflexes was displaced by a focus on the cognitive workings inside the 'black box'; the psycholinguistic concern with lexical and grammar-processing skills gave way to the study of strategic discourse processes; and the analysis of constructed laboratory tasks lost ground to the study of real-world fields of expertise. While it is not possible here to offer a more detailed discussion of the underlying conceptual and methodological changes and their implications, it should be understood that there is no such thing as *a* (single) psychological approach which could be brought to bear on the study of interpreting. Rather, research on aspects relating to interpreting has been linked to many different subfields of psychology, including **cognitive psychology**, **educational psychology**, **psycholinguistics** and **neuropsychology**, which are in turn highly interdisciplinary in nature. Authors such as Barik, Goldman-Eisler and Gerver (« 2.2.2, » 6.2) as well as Sylvie Lambert (» 6.4.1) and Franco Fabbro (» 6.1.2) are but a few cases in point.

Complex subdivisions, interdisciplinary overlap, and major paradigm shifts also characterize the second broadly labeled field which is commonly viewed as a logical source for interpreting studies – **linguistics**. In the 1960s, when interest in a scientific account of translation and interpreting rose, linguists could still be seen as mainly concerned with the study of phonology, lexis and grammar of language as a system (as *langue*, in Saussure's terms). In subsequent decades, the linguistics community sprouted such subdomains as **contrastive linguistics**, **sociolinguistics** and **text linguistics** and a variety of specific applications (e.g. **clinical linguistics**, **forensic linguistics**) and methodologies (e.g. **computational linguistics**, **corpus linguistics**), all of which have informed the study of interpreting in one way or another (» 7.1). Of particular relevance has been the interface between linguistics and the psychology of language, which has given rise to various cognitive linguistic approaches, including the relevance-theoretical account known as **cognitive pragmatics** (» 4.4.2).

As early as the mid-1970s, an interdiscipline labeled **cognitive science** had emerged from a convergence of interest between linguists, psychologists, philosophers of language and researchers in artificial intelligence. Their work on 'natural language processing' had a major impact on the field of **text linguistics**, particularly as conceived by Robert de Beaugrande (1980). As linguists extended their scope of analysis to 'language beyond the sentence', 'text' as language used orally or in writing in communicative interaction became the object of both structural description and pragmatic (i.e. user-oriented) analysis (see Beaugrande and Dressler 1981). In a closely related development, the focus on 'discourse' gave rise to the even wider framework of **discourse studies**, which proved highly attractive to communication-oriented researchers in anthropology, linguistics, philosophy, psychology and sociology. Indeed, the notion of 'discourse' has come to be used in such a variety of fields as to defy a standard definition. Compared to the text-linguistic approach, with which it shares a concern for the structural and procedural features of communicative language use (see van Dijk 1997a), linguistic **discourse analysis** goes further in extending the focus to situated interaction in society (see van Dijk 1997b). Given their primary interest in face-to-face conversational exchanges, approaches in discourse studies such as **conversation analysis** (ethnomethodology) and (sociolinguistic) **pragmatics** have thus served as important foundations for studies of liaison or dialogue interpreting since the mid-1980s (» 4.6).

3.1.3 Socio/cultural approaches

Sociolinguistic approaches to discourse constitute a broad area of overlap between what I have distinguished here as 'psycho/linguistic' and 'socio/cultural' perspectives. Nevertheless, approaches to communication from disciplines like **sociology** and **cultural anthropology**, which have played a relatively modest role in interpreting studies to date, can be viewed as distinct by virtue of their foregrounding of the interactional as well as cultural dimensions. **Interactional sociolinguistics**, for instance, which combines anthropological, sociological and linguistic perspectives on the interplay between language, culture and society, highlights the way role relationships and expectations as well as social, cultural and other prior knowledge shape meanings in communication. By the same token, the **ethnography of communication** and the variegated field of **intercultural communication** rest on the view that the set of assumptions and beliefs referred to as 'culture' guide the way people think and (inter)act. These theoretical and methodological frameworks, which emerged around 1960 in the US, spearheaded by anthropologists like John Gumperz, Dell Hymes and Edward T. Hall, are of obvious relevance to the mediation of communication across cultures. And yet, having come to the fore in the 1970s (e.g. Gumperz and Hymes 1972), as the interpreting research community was coming to grips with the mental mechanics of (conference) interpreting, these socio-cultural perspectives were largely eclipsed by approaches from cognitive science until they were brought to bear on the emerging domain of interpreting in non-conference settings. An exception to the neglect of sociological concerns was the work of R.B.W. Anderson (1976/2002), who pointed to the research potential of issues like situational constellations and role conflict as well as the power and relative status of participants with regard to social class, education and gender. Another singular source of influence from sociology was Erving Goffman (e.g. 1981), whose analysis of face-to-face interaction and participation in discourse strongly inspired the work of Wadensjö (» 5.3.1) and became a cornerstone in the study of dialogue interpreting (» 4.6). At a broader level, key notions of the sociology of Pierre Bourdieu, such as habitus, field, and symbolic capital, have proved attractive to Translation scholars studying the profession and its institutional status in society. More broadly still, an exploration of the power and cultural status of interpreters in history has been suggested from the perspective of **cultural studies**. The call by Michael Cronin (2002) for a "cultural turn" in interpreting studies probably marks the most distant horizon in the current landscape of interpreting studies.

All the disciplinary perspectives reviewed above, from the broad and variegated domains of psychology and linguistics to the more specialized frameworks for the study of language use in social interaction, have contributed to research on the phenomenon of interpreting, either by specialists in these fields taking a direct interest in the subject or by supplying conceptual and methodological tools for use by scholars of interpreting. Clearly, then, there is an impressive variety of disciplinary vantage points which have shaped the view of interpreting as an object of study. The following section takes stock of these various conceptions in terms of the 'memes', or recurring ideas, in interpreting studies.

3.2 Memes of interpreting

The notion of 'memes' is used here in analogy with Andrew Chesterman's (1997) account of *Memes of Translation*. The socio-biological concept of 'meme', which was introduced in the mid-1970s, refers to ideas, practices, creations and inventions that have spread and replicated, like genes, in the cultural evolution of mankind. Applying this fundamental theoretical framework specifically to the evolution of thinking about translation, Chesterman highlights memes as metaphors elucidating the concept of 'translation', as particular ways of 'seeing' and theorizing about the phenomenon.

3.2.1 'Ways of seeing'

The first step in the process of research is to see a phenomenon, or 'problem', and perceive it as an object of inquiry. This, in the broadest sense, corresponds to **theory** as used by Chesterman (1997: 1f) with reference to the Greek etymology of the word: *theoria*, meaning both 'a looking at', 'a viewing' and 'contemplation', 'speculation'. Taking a look at something is a deliberate activity that necessarily proceeds from a given 'point of view', which thus constrains what is seen, and how. In what follows we will review what interpreting has seemed to be like to those who have reflected on the phenomenon from various disciplinary vantage points.

In the case of translation as well as interpreting, some ideas about the phenomenon are so broad and pervasive as to constitute "supermemes" (Chesterman 1997: 7). These supermemes of interpreting – **process(ing)** and **communicative activity** as well as supermemes relating to **Translation** in general – will be introduced first to serve as a gateway to the subsequent presentation of five more specific memes of interpreting.

3.2.2 Interpreting as Translation

In line with the conceptualization underlying this book (« 1.2.2), interpreting can be viewed most fundamentally as Translation. Since much of the ground at this level is covered by Chesterman's account of memes, it will suffice here to introduce his five supermemes and reflect briefly on the degree to which they permeate also the conceptual space of interpreting.

The five ideas which Chesterman (1997) elevates to the status of supermemes of translation are: the **source–target** metaphor, the idea of **equivalence**, the myth of **untranslatability**, the **free-vs-literal** dichotomy, and the idea that all **writing is** a kind of **translating**. The last-mentioned item reflects Chesterman's focus on (written) translation rather than Translation as a hyperonym and need not concern us much further. (A somewhat parallel idea will be discussed later in the sense of 'all understanding is interpreting'.) The remaining four supermemes of translation are easily shown to be present, though not always made explicit, in theoretical approaches to interpreting as well. Most pervasively perhaps, the free-vs-literal dichotomy, in terminological guises like 'meaning-based' vs 'form-based interpreting' or 'interpreting proper' vs 'transcoding', will also appear in the following discussion of memes. The issue of untranslatability would appear to be of more concrete concern to interpreters than to translators, given the real-time performance constraints which define the activity of interpreting. Nevertheless, except for some references to forms of expression which have commonly been considered unsuitable to interpreting, like poetry or wordplay, the issue of untranslatability has received little attention in interpreting studies and has essentially been left to the philosophers of translation. By the same token, the idea of equivalence as a major translation-theoretical problem is largely absent from the discourse of interpreting, though it seems to have been a tacit assumption underlying much work on 'accuracy' and 'errors' in conference interpreting research. The source–target metaphor, finally, is practically a *sine qua non* for interpreting, given the situational immediacy linking the two acts of discourse. As in translation, proceeding from source to target in interpreting suggests a process of transfer which moves something from one side to the other. Unlike translation theorists, though, who have focused mainly on the linguistic 'objects' involved in the transfer, interpreting researchers have foregrounded the idea of a 'process', which can safely be called the most influential supermeme in interpreting studies to date.

3.2.3 Process(ing) vs communicative activity

While the notion of 'process' can also be construed much more broadly (see Linell 1997: 50), its use in the discourse on interpreting has largely been confined to the more specific sense of **processing** operations transforming an input into an output. Gile (1994b: 40) has represented this conception of a process advancing from one point to another, from start to finish, as "a process P acting on an input I and producing an output O" (Figure 3.1).

The generic process structure can be instantiated for various types of input and output. Most typically, the interpreting process has been conceptualized as a process acting on 'verbal material', as a transfer of words and structures from a source language to a target language. The notion of **verbal transfer** can thus be

Figure 3.1 The process(ing) supermeme (from Gile 1994b: 40)

seen as a very common (sub)meme of the process supermeme (» 3.2.4), even though it has mostly been espoused by non-interpreters and served as an antithesis for interpreters forming their own ideas. Interpreting as verbal processing has been studied both from a linguistic point of view, with regard to particular lexical and structural input–output correspondences, and from a psychological vantage point, with regard to measuring various performance aspects of this verbal processing task (» 6.2.3). As psychologists turned from observing verbal behavior to speculating about the mental operations taking place in the 'black box', researchers' attention shifted from the verbal input–output relation to the mental process as such. Drawing on advances in information theory and cognitive psychology, interpreting was conceptualized as a set of information processing operations rather like those in a digital data processing device (i.e. a computer). The human processor was assumed to perform a number of cognitive skills, such as speech recognition, memory storage and verbal output generation, the combination of which would account for the complex task of interpreting. This concern with **cognitive information processing skills** is clearly the most widespread meme in interpreting studies to date (» 3.2.5).

A supermeme of interpreting which is largely complementary to the idea of process(ing) is the notion of interpreting as a **communicative activity** performed by a human being in a particular situation of interaction. In this more 'naturalistic' perspective, interpreting is seen as a combined listening and speaking activity to enable communication. Strongly shaped by the views of practitioners in the formative decades of the conference interpreting profession, the overall idea of the interpreter's communicative activity found its most poignant expression in the meme of **making sense**, which conceptualizes the interpreter's task as grasping the intended meaning ('sense') of an original speaker and expressing it for listeners in another language (» 3.2.6). In subsequent theorizing, the idea of interpreters performing a communication service appears to have been taken for granted, as too basic to merit much further attention and development. Thus the communicative-activity supermeme, notwithstanding its latent existence, received explicit theoretical attention only as scholars of Translation were widening their scope of analysis in the 1980s and, more importantly perhaps, as previously neglected types of interpreting were emerging as challenging objects of study. This gave rise to two more (sub)memes of the communicative-activity supermeme, which are in fact closely related: **text/discourse production** (» 3.2.7) and **mediation** (» 3.2.8). The former is largely shaped by theories of text, discourse and translation, while the latter is closely linked to the sociology of interaction, and both share a concern with the cross-cultural dimension of mediated communication.

The five memes of interpreting which have been introduced in this section under the umbrella of the process(ing) and communicative-activity supermemes will be discussed in more detail in the following subsections, with particular regard to their prevalence in particular periods and disciplinary contexts.

3.2.4 *Verbal transfer*

The most "primitive" conception of interpreting – and of Translation in general (see Chesterman 1997: 20f) – is that of a process in which words in one language are converted into words in another language. The underlying assumption of what St Jerome captured in the phrase "*verbum exprimere e verbo*" is that words contain meanings and serve as the elementary building blocks of a language. Thus a speech made up of words in one language would be reassembled by the interpreter using target-language words with corresponding meanings, and the ease or difficulty of the task would essentially depend on the nature of the verbal material. It is this conception which formed the basis of the dichotomy between translation and interpreting set up by the German theologian Friedrich Schleiermacher in the early nineteenth century. Distinguishing between the (written) "translation" of scholarly and artistic works on the one hand, and oral as well as written translational activity in the world of commerce ("interpreting") on the other, Schleiermacher held that the language used in transacting business was so straightforward as to make interpreting "a merely mechanical task that can be performed by anyone with a modest proficiency in both languages, and where, so long as obvious errors are avoided, there is little difference between better and worse renditions." (Schleiermacher 1813/1997: 227)

The idea of interpreting as a **language-switching** operation performed more or less naturally by any bilingual was also held by Julius Wirl (1958), a professor of English at the Vienna School of Business who was one of the first linguists to theorize about the practice of interpreting. Basing his explanation on the phenomena of automaticity and inter-idiomatic relations, Wirl (1958) claimed that in the truly bilingual and thus perfect linguistic mediator, the two languages were inter-convertible at all times, thus enabling the interpreter to perform the task as an automatic reflex rather than an act of volition.

The assumption that bilingualism would express itself in the facility of switching from a word in one language to its 'other-language equivalent' also formed the underpinning of experimental research on the **verbal behavior** of bilinguals in the 1950s. Shaped by contemporary psychological approaches, bilingualism researchers measured the degree of automaticity of **word-translation** tasks in terms of their bilingual subjects' response times to the verbal stimuli (see W.E. Lambert 1978). Four decades later, the experimental designs of some cognitive-psychological and neurolinguistic studies on bilingual processing (e.g. de Groot 1997), though set within a more profound understanding of the interpreting process, were at least reminiscent of the word-based transfer view.

The verbal-transfer meme also thrived in association with the information-theoretical mathematical model of communication advanced in the late 1940s by Claude Shannon and Warren Weaver. Based on the analogy of electrical signal transmission, Translation was viewed as a combined decoding and encoding operation involving the switching of linguistic code signals. The translator/interpreter as a special type of 'transmitter' between a 'source' and a 'receiver' was thus seen as 'switching signals' of one information-bearing 'code' to those of another. This serial conception of linguistic **code-switching**, or **transcoding**, became firmly rooted as one of the most powerful metaphors of Translation among psychologists and linguists alike. In early psycholinguistic experiments, for instance, the focus was on the extra time required by the 'code-switching operation' in simultaneous interpreting in comparison to the monolingual repetition of verbal input known as 'shadowing' (» 6.2.3). In a similar vein, Goldman-Eisler (1967: 125) positioned simultaneous interpreting at an intermediate level of complexity between reading aloud and spontaneous speech, and described it as "translation entailing generative acts concerned with lexical and syntactic decisions."

With regard to such recoding of not only lexical but also grammatical structures, German, with its distinct structural features among contemporary European conference languages, appeared to pose a particular challenge, and became a target for syntax-oriented studies of simultaneous interpreting. In the late 1960s, scholars at the University of Leipzig who saw linguistics as the most promising scientific framework for the study of translational phenomena (« 2.3.1) sought to identify not only **lexical equivalence** relations but also **syntactic regularities** and correspondence rules determining the "optimum moment" (i.e. 'start-up distance') in simultaneous interpreting (see Kade and Cartellieri 1971). Nevertheless, Kade and his associates also realized that the interpreter's processing of the "chain of linguistic signs" could be overridden by knowledge-based anticipation (» 6.7.3), as studied in the 1974 MA thesis by Nanza Mattern and reported by Wolfram Wilss (1978). It had thus emerged by the late 1960s that the (simultaneous) interpreting process could not be explained as a direct linguistic transfer of lexical units and syntactic structures but was obviously mediated by some form of cognitive representation or memory.

3.2.5 Cognitive information processing skills

Whereas behaviorist psychologists had scorned any theorizing about internal processes in favor of observing behavioral responses, cognitive psychologists hypothesized various **mental structures and procedures** responsible for the processing of verbal data, mostly by drawing on analogies with digital data processing (**computing**) as a metaphor of the human information processing system. Within this conceptual framework, Gerver (1971: viii) defined the interpreting task as "a fairly complex form of human information processing involving the reception, storage, transformation, and transmission of verbal information." Hence, some of the dominant research issues have included the **processing capacity** of the human information processing system, the possibility of dividing attention over various tasks (**multi-tasking**), and the structure and function of its **memory** component(s). To make the complex task amenable to experimental study, language processing as such is further decomposed in the information processing approach into such subtasks or **component skills** as phoneme and word recognition, lexical disambiguation, syntactic processing ('parsing') and knowledge-based inferencing. Many insights on these issues in 'natural language processing', which constitutes a major field of interdisciplinary research in cognitive science, have been brought to bear on the study of conference interpreting and its component processes (see Moser-Mercer *et al.* 1997). As individual subtasks have increasingly been implemented by cognitive scientists in **neural network** models, or 'connectionist' models, rather than in terms of computer-like **symbol processing**, the connectionist or 'subsymbolic' approach has also been applied to cognitive skills in simultaneous interpreting (e.g. MacWhinney 1997, Paradis 2000, Setton 2003a). Irrespective of the 'cognitive architecture' posited to explain the language processing skills involved in interpreting, the meme of cognitive information processing has proved highly influential, not only for the construction of models of the interpreting process (» 5.4.3) but also for various pedagogical applications (» 9.2.2, » 9.3.3).

3.2.6 *Making sense*

At a time when experimental psychologists were only beginning to explore the intricacies of cognitive processes, pioneers of conference interpreting describing their task started by placing it in its **communicative context**. Herbert (1952), for one, stressed the interpreter's function of enabling mutual understanding in the service of international communication. The interpreter's task within a particular communicative situation was characterized as combining the activities of a **listener** and a **speaker**. Understanding ('making sense of') what had been expressed in a source language, and expressing the **ideas** grasped, i.e. the 'message', in another language so that they would 'make sense' to the target audience, appeared as the main pillars of the interpreter's work. In the words of two pioneer professionals, authors and trainers: "To interpret one must first understand" (Seleskovitch 1978a: 11), and "each part of each idea should be expressed in the way it would normally be expressed by a good public speaker" (Herbert 1952: 23).

Given their special regard for the consecutive mode of interpreting, in which listening and speaking appear as two distinct stages of the interpreter's performance, these early authors naturally foregrounded the communicative skills of listening and speaking rather than problems of Translation. Indeed, the translational element was downplayed to such an extent as to even appear as a counterpart to 'interpreting'. Seleskovitch (1976, 1978a), in particular, pitted the contemporary view of translation as an analytical code-switching operation (« 3.2.4) against interpreting as the spontaneous and synthetic grasping and conveying of **sense**. This apparent antagonism, expressed in phrases like 'interpreting is not translating every word', is still very much in evidence in the professional literature.

In a broader translation-theoretical context, the sense-making vs transcoding distinction, for which Seleskovitch (1978a: 19) also offered the simile of representing an object by a painting (= an interpretation) vs a photograph (= a translation), echoes the age-old dichotomy of literal vs free translation, and the preference for a meaning-based approach. Thus the idea of interpreting as 'making sense' does not capture an aspect unique to the interpreter's task; rather, its innovative force lies in the prominent role attributed to (prior) **knowledge**. Herbert (1952: 19) had pointed to the importance of "a good knowledge of the subject matter"; Seleskovitch, in her sense-based theoretical account known as the interpretive theory of Translation, or *théorie du sens* (» 5.4.1), ventured further into the cognitive dimension of language understanding. At the same time as pioneers in the newly emerging interdiscipline of cognitive science, Seleskovitch (1976, 1978b) argued that interpreting – and understanding in general – involved the activation of previous knowledge which combined with perceptual input to form a conceptual mental representation. In this respect, the meme of making sense, which thrived in the profession- and training-oriented Paris School of interpreting studies (« 2.3.3, » 4.2), has a substantial interface with insights into language comprehension gained by cognitive-science researchers inspired by the information-processing meme. There is now general agreement on the crucial role of prior knowledge of various types in comprehension processes, thus vindicating the sense-making meme for the receptive stage of interpreting.

On the production side, the linkage between knowledge and making sense was given less prominent attention. It is clearly implied, however, when Seleskovitch demands that the interpreter's target-language utterance "must be geared to the recipient" (1978a: 9) and describes the interpreter's job as grasping the speaker's intended sense, or "*vouloir dire*", and "expressing it in the verbal form best suited to understanding by the audience" (1976: 109). Surely, the role of knowledge in making sense of an utterance is no less important in the target audience than in the interpreter. What is more, while the interpreter shares, to a sufficient extent at least, the **socio-cultural background** of the speaker whose message he or she needs to understand, the target audience, by definiton, does not. If the interpreter's mission is to enable understanding, he or she must adapt the message to the audience's prior knowledge or, as Seleskovitch (1978a: 100) puts it, "cultural frames of reference", so as to ensure that it will make sense; that is, that the target text will fulfil its **function** in the target-cultural environment. Hence one can speak of a target-oriented version of the sense-making meme, which found its most comprehensive expression in Hans Vermeer's *skopos* theory of translational action (see Vermeer 1989/2000). This 'functionalist' approach (see Nord 1997) was expressly applied also to simultaneous interpreting (e.g. Kirchhoff 1976/2002) and proved influential especially among German-speaking authors (» 4.5). Its broader significance, however, only came to be revealed when more attention was devoted to interpreting settings beyond international conferences and organizations. In community-based domains, the primary parties are typically of unequal social status and highly discrepant educational backgrounds. In such situations, the injunction to use "the verbal form best suited to understanding by the audience" (Seleskovitch 1976: 109) becomes a critical challenge. If what the interpreter says must make sense against the listener's horizon of socio-cultural knowledge, and if the interpreter is the only person capable of assessing that knowledge, he or she may well have to paraphrase, explain or simplify in order to achieve the **communicative effect** desired by the speaker (» 7.3).

3.2.7 Text/discourse production

Whether it is viewed as a process or a communicative activity, there can be little doubt that interpreting is a production-oriented activity. The question then is how the output produced by the interpreter can best be characterized in analytical terms. Herbert (1952: 23) likened the interpreter to "a good public speaker," which would suggest **rhetoric** as a framework of analysis; psycholinguists would study the interpreter's output as **speech**, with particular attention to temporal features such as pauses; and cognitive psychologists focused on aspects like **information content**. As long as linguists remained preoccupied with lexical meaning and syntactic structure, they had little to say about the interpreter's output beyond these restricted categories. It was only with the reorientation of linguistics in the 1970s towards language use in communication that more holistic conceptualizations of language production came to the fore. The notion of 'text' as a complex web of relations guided by a communicative intention, as developed in particular in the text-linguistic approach of Beaugrande and Dressler (1981), was readily adopted by scholars of Translation. Interpretations, too, have been described as texts in terms of standards of **textuality**, such as cohesion, coherence, and intertextuality (» 7.1.3). Those wishing to foreground the **orality** of the interpreter's output (» 7.1.2) have tended to draw on related theoretical frameworks with a stronger focus on oral language, such as M.A.K. Halliday's (1985) systemic functional linguistics and a range of other approaches centered on the notion of 'discourse'. The conceptual distinction between 'text' and 'discourse' is anything but clear, and is sometimes a matter of geolinguistic tradition and intellectual preference. Whatever the designation and analytical framework, though, the dual text/discourse meme of interpreting has proved a highly significant guiding idea and stands to retain its influence, not least thanks to the increasing application of **corpus-linguistic methods** (» 7.1.2).

The idea of text processing, however, which remains a focal point of cognitively oriented approaches to discourse (» 6.3.2), has been found to reflect a **monologic** bias; that is, a view of discourse in which a text is produced by an active speaker and received by an audience. This view has proved useful as a reflection of the typical constellation at international conferences, but it is less suitable for the analysis of communicative settings where the adoption of speaker and listener roles is much more dynamic and the immediate co-presence of the interlocutor favors an inherently interactive flow of discourse. It is this **dialogic** view of discourse as a joint activity which informs the work of Wadensjö (1998) on dialogue interpreting (» 4.6). And yet, Wadensjö's (1998: 21) distinction between "talk as activity" and "talk as text", which highlights the dual nature of the text/discourse production meme, suggests not a contradictory but a complementary way of conceptualizing the interpreter's activity, since they correspond to different levels of abstraction. Indeed, her description of what else happens, other than text production, at the level of interpreting as an "(inter)activity" closely relates to another idea about interpreting which will be discussed next.

3.2.8 Mediation

Like the meme of making sense, the mediation meme is, in many ways, a 'basic' idea associated with interpreting, and can indeed be traced to its deepest etymological roots (« 1.1). Prototypically, the interpreter, whether professional or not, is "the man (or woman) in the middle" (Knapp-Potthoff and Knapp 1987) – an **intermediary**, not so much between the languages involved as between the communicating individuals and the institutional and socio-cultural positions they represent. The interpreter's two clients, as incumbents of particular roles, have their own intentions and expectations in the communicative interaction. More often than not, these will come into conflict and will force the interpreter to take action as a 'mediator' – not as a broker or conciliator in a negotiation, but as an agent regulating the evolution of understanding. An apparently simple example of speaker conflict is simultaneous or overlapping talk. This requires the interpreter to impose priorities on the primary parties' **turn-taking** behavior and to structure the flow of discourse in a **gatekeeping** capacity. In the more critical case of one party signaling a lack of understanding, the interpreter's mission of enabling communication is at stake and may require some form of mediating **intervention**. Indeed, Knapp-Potthoff and Knapp (1986) found that a lay interpreter performing "linguistic mediation" would often shape the mediated interaction as an active **third party** rather than remain **neutral** and 'invisible'. Such findings have shone the spotlight on the complex issue of the interpreter's **role**; that is, the question of what (else), other than relaying messages, the interpreter is expected and permitted to do in order to facilitate understanding in a communicative event (» 7.4).

The discussion of role issues has been associated in particular with dialogue interpreting in community-based settings, where the constellation of interaction is typically characterized by unequal power relations and widely discrepant socio-cultural backgrounds between which the interpreter is charged to mediate. And yet mediation as part of the interpreter's role and task is no less relevant, in principle, to international conference interpreting (see Kirchhoff 1976/2002: 113, Seleskovitch 1978a: 100). Jones (1998), writing from many years of professional experience, argues that conference interpreters may need to intervene actively, for example "by providing the requisite explanations or even changing the original speaker's references" (1998: 4), in order to overcome "cultural difficulties". Thus, on the assumption that the interpreter's output must be adapted to the communicative needs of the target-cultural audience, the interpreter is, by definition and necessity, a **cultural mediator** (see Kondo and Tebble 1997).

Beyond the interpreter's mediation in concrete situations of interactive discourse and in cross-cultural communication in general, the fact that interpreters ideally represent two cultural systems can be used to view them as points of **cultural interface**. In this sense, interpreters bring together different cultures and represent, as Bowen (1995: 262) notes for Doña Marina, "the culturally hybrid societies of the future". Interpreters, then, can be said to represent those transgressing community boundaries. They are "the mixed" and "the in between"

(Cronin 2002: 392), intermediaries who not only allow for but also embody the meeting, coexistence and mutual reconciliation of cultures. The position accorded in a society to such intermediary agents of culture could thus be taken to reflect that society's attitude towards the cultural Other and intercultural exchange.

3.2.9 A map of memes

As with any discourse on ideas, the level of abstraction at which the memes of interpreting are regarded as separate, or subsumed under a single label, is open to question. Nevertheless, the five memes seem distinctive enough to reflect both the evolution of thinking on interpreting over time and the relative dominance of key conceptual dimensions. This is illustrated in a map of memes (Figure 3.2) which shows how the key ideas informing scholarly and everyday discourse about interpreting are related within a matrix of four basic conceptual dimensions.

All memes relate, more or less closely, to the concepts of **language**, **cognition**, **interaction** and **culture**. These are shown in Figure 3.2 as separate poles but also combine in various ways to form dimensions (e.g. language–culture, language–cognition, cognition–culture) within which the memes take their positions. Within this matrix, the five memes have been plotted in such a way as to suggest their

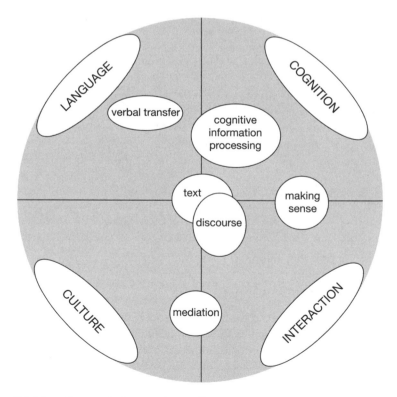

Figure 3.2 Map of memes in interpreting studies

conceptual proximity to the four poles. Though certainly no more than an intuitive visualization, this map of memes should help to give a better picture of the conceptual signposts that have guided the process of theoretical inquiry into interpreting.

3.3 Methodology

While forming ideas about an object of study is essential to the process of inquiry, gaining more detailed knowledge requires some form of engagement with its empirical manifestations. The various options for doing so are the subject-matter of methodology, a key domain in the philosophy of science. Methodology as the study of method is part of epistemology (i.e. the theory of knowledge), which underlies all methodological considerations (» 3.3.1). In a more specific sense, methodology also refers to the body of methods and procedures employed in a particular branch of study (» 3.3.3), or even in a given investigation. Both the former (philosophical) and the latter (practical) aspects of methodology will be briefly reviewed in the sections that follow.

3.3.1 'Ways of knowing'

If the aim of research, or **inquiry**, is to gain knowledge about the 'true' nature of some aspect of the 'real' world, the **scientific** (i.e. knowledge-creating) endeavor fundamentally depends on assumptions regarding such notions as 'truth', 'facts', and 'reality'. Science, understood as an **agreement** on what is known or accepted to be true, has long rested on the belief in ascertainable facts about an objective reality. This epistemological stance, which would have seemed particularly appropriate to the natural sciences, remained largely unshaken even by the modern view that objective aspects of reality are subject to different individual interpretations. The positivist view of reality was ultimately called into question by the **postmodern** (postpositivist, constructivist) view that there is no objective reality, that all experience is subjectively constructed. Adopting this kind of epistemological position in research on interpreting means that there is no such thing as 'natural data'. As Chesterman and Arrojo (2000: 152) point out, **data** are not 'there' as a given, but are ultimately 'taken' by the analyst, with a particular idea and purpose in mind.

Far from precluding the possibility of scientific research, which continues to be associated with notions like 'factual evidence' and 'objectivity', the relativistic view of reality and knowledge enables the researcher to strive for insights which hold up to **intersubjective** examination while continuously reflecting on the inescapable humanness of scientific inquiry. This makes objectivity a **social** endeavor, informed by our individual subjectivity (see Babbie 1999: 36). Hence the need for researchers to make explicit their theoretical perspective and conceptual as well as methodological choices.

3.3.2 'Doing science'

As an essentially social undertaking, engaging in scientific research requires adherence to the rules and standards established for a particular scientific community. Since there are different 'ways of doing science', both across disciplines and within a given field of study, researchers are faced with some fundamental choices regarding their methodological approach. These include the basic mode of inquiry (deduction vs induction), the nature of the data (quantitative vs qualitative), the purpose of inquiry, the overall methodological strategy, and the method(s) of inquiry as such.

The traditional model of science, which largely shapes the notion of **scientific method** and has also provided inspiration for research on interpreting, is based on a **deductive** movement from theory to data: a research problem is defined within a particular theoretical framework and formulated as a **hypothesis**; by defining all relevant variables and specifying measurable (**quantitative**) indicators, the hypothesis is **operationalized**; using an appropriate methodological procedure, the hypothesis is **tested** against the **data** and either upheld or rejected, thus lending empirical support to the underlying theory or necessitating its modification. An alternative route is to construct a theory through the **inductive** method; that is, by observing and seeking to discover patterns which may point to theoretical principles. Pioneered by sociologists in the 1960s, the so-called **grounded theory** approach for generating theory from data has been closely associated with a reliance on **qualitative** data. Fueled by a convergence of social sciences and humanities toward a postmodern, **interpretive approach** to research and theory, **qualitative research** came to drive a methodological revolution which has spread far beyond its disciplinary origins (see Denzin and Lincoln 2000), including the field of Translation studies.

It should be understood that the deductive-vs-inductive distinction does not as such coincide with the use of quantitative vs qualitative data, and that both the operationalization of theoretical assumptions (i.e. deduction) and the process of abstracting and generalizing from empirical data (i.e. induction) can be equally valid ways of doing science. Also, with regard to epistemology, a reliance on quantification does not imply a positivist stance, just as qualitative research need not bespeak a postmodern orientation. Either quantitative or qualitative data (or a combination of the two) may be most appropriate for a given inquiry. The issue underlying the choice between 'aggregates' or 'individuals', between **numerical** or **nonnumerical** data, is whether the people, events or artifacts (e.g. texts) in question have **shared attributes** that are so important to the researcher's concern that their **unique features** can be ignored (see Babbie 1999: 23).

The researcher's concern, or **purpose**, which has a controlling influence on the **design** of a study, can be of various kinds. Leaving aside personal motives and practical purposes, however significant they may be in driving an inquiry, research is carried out, in principle, in order to **explore**, **describe** or **explain**. Depending on a given purpose and object of study, the researcher will adopt an overall methodological **strategy** for dealing with empirical data. Such research strategies can be classified in many different ways, usually tailored to a particular field of study. A broad distinction which has been used frequently in interpreting studies, particularly by Gile (e.g. 1998), is between **observational** and **experimental** approaches. Observational research refers to studying a phenomenon as it occurs, 'naturally', as it were, 'in the field', whereas experimental research makes a phenomenon occur precisely for the purpose of studying it. In the former case, the data are 'there' for the taking, while in the latter – at least in the classic type of experimenting – they are generated for the purpose of the experiment under the control of the researcher, often in a laboratory setting. What is lacking in this bipolar distinction is the research approach which consists of (inter)actively taking data by eliciting them from informants, usually by way of interviews or questionnaires. This **survey** approach, which is particularly prominent in applied social research, typically serves to collect information in standardized form from a larger group of people, often with a view to quantitative analysis.

The observational-vs-experimental dichotomy also leaves an ambiguity regarding observation as an overall research approach and a particular **method of data collection**. In other words, data collection in an experimental situation may include observing what subjects do, and an observational study of interpreting in the field may well involve different data collection techniques, such as participant observation, focus groups, interviewing, cued retrospection, and analysis of recordings. It may therefore be helpful to adopt a threefold distinction of basic **research strategies**, comprising fieldwork, survey and experimental research (see Robson 1993: 40), which can be characterized as follows: **field-work** means collecting data on people or occurrences in their **real-life** context, often conceptualized as studying a unique 'case' (**case study**); **survey research** consists of collecting data in **standardized** form from a larger group of people; and **experimental research** means **measuring** the effects of **manipulating** a particular 'independent' variable on one or more 'dependent' variables.

Though useful for general guidance, this simple categorization does not neatly accommodate every conceivable approach. **Simulation**, for instance, may be regarded as experimental research, particularly when it involves instantiating a computer model, but may also come close to fieldwork, as in the case of role-plays in a quasi-authentic environment. The same holds true for experimentation in authentic settings, or **quasi-experiments**, which can in turn be linked to what is known as **action research**. The latter denotes a form of reflective and collaborative inquiry which involves participants in their real-life context and makes them protagonists, rather than subjects, in a process aimed at enhancing their practices in a given social setting – classroom settings being an obvious case in point (see McDonough and McDonough 1997).

Although the various research strategies tend to be associated with a certain purpose of inquiry – as in exploring through fieldwork, describing through surveys, and explaining through experimental (causal) hypothesis testing – each of the basic approaches may, in principle, serve any purpose (see Robson 1993). A case-study approach, for instance, may also be used for causal explanations, just as experiments can be done for exploration. The same open and variable relationship holds between research strategies and methods for data collection, as has already been illustrated.

With reference to research on interpreting, the basic **techniques** for data collection might be summarized as **watch**, **ask** and **record**. In standard methodological terms, this corresponds to **observational methods**, which range from informal **participant observation** to highly structured observation with the help of **coding** schemes; **interviews and questionnaires**, which can be more or less structured and variously administered; and the collection of **documentary material** (e.g. corpora of authentic discourse or experimental output) for analysis. The latter can be viewed as an indirect and unobtrusive observational technique and is of obvious relevance to the product-oriented study of interpreting.

Whatever the method(s) employed, data will need to be collected with due regard for the complex issue of **sampling**, which also bears on the **validity** of the research findings. Proponents of qualitative research in particular have stressed the value of drawing on multiple sources of data (referred to as 'triangulation') by using more than one data collection technique. Such a **multi-method approach**, which is most typical of case-study research, is widely used also in experimental studies and has been gaining ground also in research on interpreting.

3.3.3 *Methodological approaches in interpreting studies*

Set against this review of methodological options, the field of interpreting studies presents itself as one that has considerable variety of approach as well as wide scope for methodological development. All three of the basic research strategies distinguished – fieldwork, survey, and experiment – have been adopted in research on interpreting, as can be illustrated even with reference to the very first studies on the subject. The pioneering thesis by Paneth (1957) on conference interpreter training, which was based on visits to several training institutions and involved the observation of teaching practices as well as interviews, is a good example of **fieldwork**; the early study by Sanz (1931) also involved observation in the field but was mainly designed as a **survey** among twenty professional interpreters with the help of a questionnaire; and the groundbreaking study of simultaneous interpreting by Oléron and Nanpon (1965/2002) was largely based on data from an **experiment**, after the authors had found their fieldwork data all too 'messy' for their analytical purpose.

Ever since these classic contributions to the literature on interpreting, survey research has been undertaken, particularly for the study of profession-related issues (» 7.5.1, » 8.4.1, » 8.6). Fieldwork, in contrast, played a surprisingly minor role as a strategy for empirical research on interpreting, at least until the late 1980s, when groundbreaking work on court interpreting was carried out (» 7.4.2). Whereas very little large-scale fieldwork has been done on conference interpreting (e.g. Pöchhacker 1994a, Diriker 2001), the focus on dialogue interpreting has given a major boost to case studies based on ethnographic and discourse-analytical techniques (» 4.6). Aside from some work on teaching-related issues, which might be brought under the heading of action research (» 9.3), the methodological option that has taken center stage in research on (conference) interpreting is experimentation. Aligned with the cognitive-processing meme (« 3.2.5) and the experimental research tradition of cognitive psychology (» 4.4.1), hypothesis testing in controlled experiments has commanded overriding attention in interpreting studies. This is reflected both in the large number of experimental studies that have been carried out, often on small samples of student subjects or professionals (» 6.4, » 6.6, » 6.7), and in the centrality of experimentation as a topic of methodological debate among interpreting researchers in various paradigms, as reviewed in the following chapter.

Summary

Approaches to research on interpreting have been reviewed in this chapter with regard to the disciplinary frameworks, the guiding ideas, and the methodological strategies that have proved relevant to interpreting studies. Whereas the sibling discipline of translation studies has provided little impetus beyond basic *theoretical foundations*, the study of interpreting has been sourced by a variety of (inter)-disciplinary frameworks under such broad headings as *psychology, linguistics, sociology,* and *cultural anthropology*. These disciplinary vantage points have shaped the way researchers have sought to conceptualize the phenomenon of interpreting. Underneath the overriding ideas, or *supermemes*, of interpreting as *Translation, processing,* and *communicative activity*, five *memes* have been introduced to characterize the evolution of thinking about interpreting in various periods and disciplinary contexts: *verbal transfer, making sense, cognitive information processing skills, text/discourse production* and *mediation*. All of these have been mapped along basic conceptual dimensions within the coordinates of *language, cognition, interaction* and *culture*. Complementing the theoretical cornerstones of inquiry, a review of fundamental issues in *methodology* has highlighted the *deductive-vs-inductive* and *quantitative-vs-qualitative* distinctions. The *research strategies* of *fieldwork, survey* and *experimental research*, to be implemented by a range of *methods* or *techniques* for data collection and analysis, have been introduced and examined for their role in interpreting studies.

Sources and further reading

On epistemological foundations in Translation studies, see Chesterman and Arrojo (2000) and the subsequent discussion documented in *Target* (especially 13:1, 2001). Comprehensive handbooks surveying disciplines of major import to interpreting studies include: J.R. Anderson (1990), Kintsch (1998) and

Tulving and Craik (2000) on cognitive psychology; Gernsbacher (1994) on psycholinguistics; Hamers and Blanc (2000) on bilingualism studies; and Schiffrin *et al.* (2001) and van Dijk (1997a, 1997b) on discourse studies.

For memes in Translation studies, see Chesterman (1997); for the cognitive-processing meme of interpreting, see Gerver (1975, 1976), Moser-Mercer *et al.* (1997) and *Interpreting* 2:1/2 (1997) as well as the volumes by Danks *et al.* (1997), Englund Dimitrova and Hyltenstam (2000), and Tirkkonen-Condit and Jääskeläinen (2000); for the meme of making sense, see Seleskovitch (1976, 1978a) and Nord (1997: 104–8); for the text/discourse meme of interpreting, see Hatim and Mason (1997), Roy (2000a) and Wadensjö (1998); for the mediation meme, see R.B.W. Anderson (1976/2002) and Wadensjö (1998).

For methodological aspects of (conference) interpreting research, see Gile (1990a, 1994b, 1997, 1998) and the papers in *Interpreting* (2:1/2, 1997); for methodology in dialogue interpreting, see Mason (2000), Wadensjö (1998) and Roy (2000a). For further guidance on methodology, see the references provided in the last section of Chapter 10.

Suggestions for further study

-   What contributions to the literature on interpreting in languages other than English have been made by Translation scholars as well as specialists in cognitive/linguistic and socio/cultural disciplines?
-   What other ideas and assumptions about interpreting could be considered for meme status in interpreting studies, and how have they manifested themselves in the literature?
-   How do textbooks on methodology in other languages and fields categorize various research strategies and methodological approaches?

4 Paradigms

Building on the stocktaking of theoretical and methodological foundations (Chapter 3), this chapter reviews the main research traditions in interpreting studies to date. The notion of 'paradigm' will be used to trace the emergence of particular research models in the interpreting studies community and examine their status and mutual relations.

The **main points** covered in this chapter are:

- the notion of 'paradigm' in the analysis of scientific disciplines
- the emergence of an initial autonomous paradigm
- the role of experimental research in the study of interpreting
- the paradigm status of various research approaches
- the relationship between the main paradigms of interpreting studies

---

4.1 The notion of 'paradigm'

Ever since physicist Thomas Kuhn first analyzed scientific disciplines and change processes in terms of paradigms and paradigm shifts, the notion has become a conceptual cornerstone to the history and theory of science. In Kuhn's (1962/1996) account, scientific thought and research are shaped by 'paradigms', which are made up of the **basic assumptions, models, values and standard methods** shared by all members of a given scientific community. Working within the prevailing paradigm, researchers will design further studies and refine theories so as to account for as many aspects of the phenomenon as possible in a cumulative process. Eventually, though, a paradigm may prove incapable of dealing with 'anomalies' in the data, and new conceptual and methodological approaches come to the fore, pushing the old paradigm into crisis and taking its place. Thus Kuhn conceived of **paradigm shifts** in terms of an overthrow of the old by a new paradigm, a process of revolutionary rather than evolutionary change.

Kuhn's 'radical' account of scientific progress was developed with reference to the natural sciences but has spread far beyond its original context to such diverse fields as political science, sociology, business management, linguistics – and Translation studies. In the humanities and social sciences, however, the object of study is inherently shaped by a multi-dimensional context and can usually be viewed from different perspectives. This suggests a less radical view of paradigm shifts, which would ultimately permit the coexistence of related but distinct paradigms within a single scientific community – as discussed for interpreting studies in the remainder of this chapter.

4.2 Forging a paradigm

In the early years of interpreting research (« 2.2), the community of those studying the phenomenon was small and heterogeneous. It was made up of individual representatives of various scientific disciplines (e.g. Barik, Gerver, Goldman-Eisler) as well as representatives of the conference interpreting profession and training institutions (e.g. Seleskovitch, Longley), with some interpreters (e.g. Kade, Chernov) seeking to approach the subject from within established disciplinary frameworks, especially linguistics and psychology. The increasing academization of interpreter training then prepared the ground for the emergence of an initial paradigm of interpreting studies, championed by Danica **Seleskovitch** at ESIT in Paris (« 2.3.3). Having succeeded in establishing a doctoral studies program in *traductologie* at the Sorbonne Nouvelle in 1974, Seleskovitch supplied her **interpretive theory of Translation**, also known as the "*théorie du sens*" (García-Landa 1981), as the theoretical core of the research model at ESIT.

Built around the interpretive theory of Translation (IT), the paradigm of the so-called **Paris School** may be referred to as the **IT paradigm**. Informing this school of thought was the meme of making sense (« 3.2.6), which Seleskovitch formulated in a triangular model (» 5.4.1), highlighting the conceptual ('deverbalized') result of the interpreter's comprehension process, or **sense**, as the crucial stage in the translational process. The IT approach was first applied to the study of note-taking in consecutive interpreting by Seleskovitch (» 6.4.3) and then to simultaneous interpreting by her disciple, colleague and successor Marianne **Lederer** (» 5.4.2, » 6.7.3). These **paradigm cases** of the ESIT research model reaffirmed the view of interpreting as a knowledge-based process of making sense rather than operating on and between languages. In this and many other respects, the IT paradigm was antithetical; that is, defined by what it was *not*: interpreting was *not* translating words, *not* verbal transfer ('transcoding'); interpreting research was *not* concerned with language as a system (*langue*, in Saussure's terms) or language-pair-specific differences; and it was *not* founded on linguistics, *nor* an object of experimental psychology or psycholinguistics.

While both Seleskovitch (1975) and Lederer (1981) used experimentally generated data, the IT paradigm did *not* envisage scientific experimentation as a necessary or even valid approach to inquiry into interpreting. Rather, it was stressed that professionals had an empirical knowledge derived from **successful practice**, and that the latter was best studied by observation and reflection with the aid of recordings and transcriptions. The IT paradigm focused on the **ideal process**, on interpreting at its best, illustrating on the basis of well-chosen authentic examples how and why conference interpreters were able to perform a highly professional communication service. Not only did the fieldwork approach and the simple formulation of the underlying theory prove attractive and accessible to a number of academically minded professionals; the IT paradigm as a whole appealed strongly to the conference interpreting community at large by addressing issues of professional practice and training, and by providing prescriptive answers, even without recourse to systematic empirical studies. All this ensured the success of the Paris School approach as a '**bootstrap paradigm**' – a first, however limited, effort to lift the study of interpreting (and translation) to scientific status in academia.

Having generated a number of doctoral theses, the IT paradigm came into its own by the late 1970s. As implied by the Kuhnian notion, the paradigm determined the problems considered important, the types of questions asked and the methods used for answering them. Thus at the Venice Symposium (« 2.2.2), which addressed a broad spectrum of research topics, from the measurement of linguistic aptitudes and bilingualism to nonvocal communication and computer-instantiated translation, the Paris School paradigm asserted itself vis-à-vis the interpreting research interests of scientists from other disciplines. Genuine inter-disciplinary exchange appears to have been thwarted by an overly defensive attitude on the part of the interpreters who were staking out their academic claim on the basis of their very own theoretical and methodological approach. One of the most controversial issues in this context was the role of experiments in research on interpreting.

4.3 Experimenting with interpreting

The pioneering experimental studies on (simultaneous) interpreting by psychologists and psycholinguists in the 1960s (« 2.2.2) could be said to have imprinted the field with regard to methodology. Indeed, to psychologists, simultaneous interpreting was attractive not so much as a professional activity but as an experimental task for the study of language processing in general. At the Venice Symposium, Giovanni Flores d'Arcais (1978: 393), a leading researcher in cognitive psychology, observed that

> there are probably very few "real-life" situations which are more similar to a laboratory of psychological experimentation than the situation of the interpreter in a conference booth, both for the control of external variables and for the "artificiality" of the task in comparison to normal linguistic performance.

To professional conference interpreters, on the other hand, what was "artificial" was not so much their task as the psychologists' attempt to dissect it in decontextualized laboratory experiments. **Barik**'s work (» 6.2.2), for instance, which is among the most often cited classics in the literature, drew scathingly critical comments from conference interpreter Eliane Bros-Brann (1975), who rejected Barik's experimental design and findings as "pure unadulterated jabberwocky". While not couched in very constructive terms, Bros-Brann's (1975) criticism was justified on several counts: Barik's **research design** involved four different input conditions and a very heterogeneous group of only six subjects (two subjects had neither training nor experience in SI, another two had training but no professional experience; in each of the three subgroups, the two subjects had different dominant languages). Moreover, Barik's **error classification** scheme (» 7.2.2) for the analysis of experimental output data relied only on his own judgment, and none other than Gerver (1976: 186) characterized the criteria used by his fellow psychologist to classify errors and omissions as "purely subjective".

While **Gerver**'s own experiments (» 6.6) had involved similarly subjective word-based accuracy scores and recorded prose passages from the *UNESCO Courier* as **input material**, he was certainly keenly aware of the complex issues of experimental design which have plagued many experimental studies on interpreting to this day, namely (Gerver 1976: 167):

> defining and isolating both the independent and dependent variables, as well as being able to find experimental designs capable of handling the multiplicity of factors involved and the relatively small numbers of sufficiently skilled interpreters available at any one time in any one place with a particular combination of languages.

Barik, in turn, deserves credit for his awareness that text types and delivery modes might be significant input variables (» 6.6.4). His choice of experimental input material (spontaneous, semi-prepared and prepared speeches as well as one reading of a printed article) was rather felicitous compared to that of **Oléron and Nanpon** (1965), who had their three (professional) subjects interpret extracts from (and written translations of) the *UNESCO Courier* and Saint-Exupéry's *Le Petit Prince*, not only in the form of short paragraphs but also as individual sentences and even words. Explicit criticism of these "errors" in experimental design was voiced by Seleskovitch (1975/2002: 129), who, incidentally, is acknowledged by Oléron and Nanpon (1965) for her assistance in their study.

In describing the methodology of her own (experimental) study on note-taking in consecutive interpreting, Seleskovitch (1975/2002: 128) asserted that her "greatest concern was to ensure that the experiment faithfully reflected reality wherever possible". And yet some of her professional subjects, faced with the task of interpreting taped speeches in a laboratory setting while being recorded, reported that they had adopted an interpreting style that was different from their everyday practice. This experience of the **experimental paradox** – that is, the fact that an experiment may alter significantly the phenomenon it is designed to reproduce under controlled conditions – may explain the rather antagonistic attitude of the Paris School towards experimental research. In fact, Lederer (1978/2002: 131) actually argued that the task of simultaneous interpreting obviated the need for laboratory experiments:

> Interpreting is a human performance in which cognitive activity is first and foremost; it therefore leads us into the field of psychology with no need to resort to special experiments; in this field the connection between thinking and speaking can be observed as it materializes with each segment of speech.

Though apparently sharing a view of simultaneous interpreting as a quasi-experimental task for psychological research on language processing, IT scholars and scientists working in what Colin Robson (1993: 45) calls the "psycho-statistical paradigm" remained at odds over the issue of experimentation. Indeed, centered on the issue of **ecological validity** – that is, the extent to which experimental conditions have a 'denaturing' effect on interpreting as it would happen in 'real life' – the controversy surrounding the experimental approach lingered until well into the 1990s, despite (or perhaps even as a result of) an apparent paradigm shift in (conference) interpreting research in the 1980s.

4.4 Aspiring to science

4.4.1 Scientific standards

In the early 1980s, research-minded conference interpreters such as **Gile**, **Mackintosh**, **Moser-Mercer** and **Stenzl** (« 2.4.2) voiced the need to move beyond the certainties and 'truths' established by the Paris School and to take a more descriptive, empirical approach to research on interpreting. As Mackintosh stated at the 1986 Trieste Symposium, expressing the attitude of the **new breed**: "I believe in the importance of finding a less subjective and individualistic way of analyzing our profession" (Gran and Dodds 1989: 266). Gile in particular had begun to undermine the Paris School's prescriptive idealization of the interpreting process with papers on such supposedly easily 'translatable' items as proper names and technical terms (Gile 1984) and sought to explain processing failures on the basis of interpreters' management of their mental "energy" (» 5.4.2).

The master's theses completed by Mackintosh and Stenzl in London in 1983 similarly reflected this new outlook and proved more influential than their unpublished status would suggest. Mackintosh (1983) addressed the issue of message loss in direct as well as relay interpreting in a highly focused experimental study for which she devised a technique for scoring information content. She explicitly acknowledged the lack of authenticity of her experimental data, stressing that her initial conclusions "would have to be checked against a corpus constituted under 'real life' conditions" (Mackintosh 1983: 5f). Though Mackintosh made do with only seven items in her bibliography, two of her entries related to the theory of discourse processing as advanced by psychologist Walter Kintsch and text linguist Teun van Dijk (1978).

The MA thesis by Stenzl (1983) also drew on advances in text theory, albeit with reference to the literature in German. Apart from her adaptation of a translation-theoretical model to interpreting (» 5.3.3), Stenzl undertook a lucid analysis of **methodological issues** in empirical research which, *inter alia*, led to the following (much-quoted) assessment:

> The literature on simultaneous interpretation offers a limited range of experimental data and theoretical approaches, but practically no system-atic observations and descriptions of interpretation in practice. . . . It is fascinating to speculate about the mental processes involved in interpretation, but speculation can do no more than raise questions. If we want answers to those questions they will have to be based on facts rather than mere assumptions.
>
> (Stenzl 1983: 47)

Stenzl's appeal for systematic **descriptive studies**, reiterated at the Trieste Symposium (see Stenzl 1989: 24), was seconded by Gile (1990a) in his disputation on "speculative theorizing vs empirical research" directed against Seleskovitch and the IT paradigm. While giving credit to Seleskovitch for her eminently practical "ideas (or 'theories')," Gile labeled her work "unscientific", citing a number of flaws in her doctoral dissertation to back up his judgment. At the same time, Gile cautioned against the methodological pitfalls of experimental studies and recommended "giving priority to observational research" (1990a: 37), not least to prepare the ground for experimental hypothesis testing. Indeed, Gile's vision of progress for the field of conference interpreting research rested on a 'division of labor' between practicing interpreters engaging in research, or "practisearchers" (Gile 1994a), and specialists in the **cognitive sciences**. While identifying with the former, Gile acknowledged the superior research skills of scientists in established disciplines, stating that "the best results require the contribution of experts in scientific disciplines such as cognitive psychology, psycholinguistics and applied linguistics" (Gile 1988: 363) and that "cognitive scientists are working with more precision, logic and depth than practisearchers" (Gile 1994a: 156).

Gile's tempered attitude towards the academic capabilities of practisearchers may have been shaped by his exposure to the ESIT approach, where, having completed his training as a conference interpreter, he attended the research seminar offered by Seleskovitch. His charge against the Paris School paradigm was seconded by Barbara Moser-Mercer, who described the conference interpreting research community as divided into two largely incompatible camps:

> The first group prefers explorations which require precision of logical processes, and where members are interested in the natural sciences and quantification; the second group prefers explorations which involve the intellect in a less logically rigorous manner, where members are interested more in a liberal arts approach and general theorizing.
>
> (Moser-Mercer 1994a: 17)

Moser-Mercer's (1994a) account is explicitly based on the Kuhnian notion of paradigm, which she uses in the broader sense of "the specific intellectual preference, rules and research approach of a particular scientific community" (1994a: 18). Seleskovitch and Lederer are cited by Moser-Mercer as best representing the (less logically rigorous) "liberal arts community", whereas names like Barik, Pinter, Gerver, Moser, Stenzl, Lambert, Mackintosh, Gile, Gran and Fabbro "would all qualify under the same natural science paradigm" (Moser-Mercer 1994a: 20).

Though illuminating as a sketch of the fundamental tensions in the field of conference interpreting research, Moser-Mercer's broad-brush account blurs some relevant distinctions, including the combination of liberal-arts translation scholarship and a commitment to empirical research in Stenzl's (1983) work, Gile's high regard for 'naturalistic' observation, and the differentiation between practitioner-researchers and non-interpreter scientists within the interpreting research community. Rather than the research model of natural science, what united those challenging the IT paradigm was an aspiration to more **stringent standards** of scientific research and an openness toward other theoretical and methodological approaches, and indeed other disciplines. While sharing the Paris School's focus on the interpreting process, the new – and considerably more heterogeneous – paradigm was guided not, or not merely by the meme of making sense (« 3.2.6), but by the view of interpreting as a complex 'cognitive information-processing skill' (« 3.2.5) best studied from the perspective of the cognitive sciences.

Based on a concern with cognitive processing (CP), the **CP paradigm** is firmly rooted in the pioneering work of Gerver (« 2.2.2, » 6.6) and shares the broad agenda of cognitive scientists to explain the interplay of **language and cognition**. In fact, Gerver's influential definition of (simultaneous) interpreting as human information processing (« 3.2.5) had also included a crucial admonition to take account of factors beyond the cognitive mechanics as such: "Furthermore, linguistic, motivational, situational, and a host of other factors cannot be ignored" (Gerver 1976: 167). This broadens the agenda of the CP paradigm even further and makes it appear virtually open-ended with regard to the variables to be studied. In fact, the broad scope of CP-oriented research makes it difficult to single out a few **paradigm cases**. Apart from Gerver's PhD research (see Gerver 1976), followed up, among others, by S. Lambert (1989) and Ingram (1992), one might cite Moser's (1978) work on **processing skills** based on her model of SI (» 5.4.3) and Gile's **Effort models** (» 5.4.2). The latter, which reflect the long-standing psychological concern with the issue of divided attention, have become particularly popular in the interpreting studies community and constitute a key theoretical ingredient of the CP paradigm, appearing in a similar role as the sense-based triangular model by Seleskovitch in the IT paradigm.

While research in the CP paradigm has generally been receptive towards methods and findings from the cognitive sciences, interpreting researchers have embraced the principle of **interdisciplinarity** to a variable extent. One could make a distinction within the CP paradigm between those who would like to "have at least one foot firmly planted on the solid soil of Science" (Shlesinger 1995a: 7) and those working with the more modest means available to interpreters without training in the research methods of cognitive science. The latter, including practisearchers and students preparing graduation theses as part of their university-level training, have consistently been encouraged by Gile to pursue small-scale empirical studies within their methodological reach. The former group, championed by Moser-Mercer (e.g. Moser-Mercer *et al.* 1997), is more decidedly interdisciplinary and exhibits a methodological preference for experimental hypothesis testing as practiced by cognitive psychologists. The post-doctoral research by Kurz (1996) and the PhD thesis by Shlesinger (2000a) are but two paradigm cases of this explicitly interdisciplinary orientation within the CP paradigm. An even stronger version of interdisciplinarity was pioneered at the University of Trieste and introduced to the interpreting research community at the 1986 Symposium.

4.4.2 *Interdisciplinarity*

At the Trieste Symposium, Franco Crevatin, then head of the institution hosting the event (« 2.4.2), spoke out in favor of research on interpreting but expressed the conviction that "such research must be controlled from without, as interpreters working scientifically in the field run the risk of deforming their theories through their daily practice" (Gran and Dodds 1989: 266). With reference to Galileo, Crevatin emphasized that "measurability" rather than personal experience and intuition were to be the hallmark of interpreting research as a "true science". The implications of this position, which was palpably antagonistic to the IT paradigm, can be illustrated by the way S. Lambert responded to the unease voiced by professional subjects participating in one of her experiments: "What did not occur to them was that in order for an experiment of this nature to be published in a respectable journal, let alone be taken seriously, stringently controlled experimental conditions had to be adhered to" (S. Lambert 1994: 6). The appeal – and allegiance – here is obviously to the 'higher' scientific standards of other disciplines serving as a platform for **research *on*** interpreters rather than **research *with*** or even **research *by*** interpreters.

In large measure, Crevatin's proposition was vindicated by the neurolinguistic approach to interpreting research that was spearheaded in Trieste by neurophysiologist Franco **Fabbro** in cooperation with Laura **Gran** at the SSLMIT (« 2.4.2). Based on neuropsychological findings on the organization of **language(s) in the brain** and on intricate experimental designs involving tasks such as dichotic listening and verbal-manual interference, the studies by Fabbro and his associates (see Fabbro and Gran 1994) centered on the hypothesis that bilinguals in general, and interpreters in particular, exhibited a characteristic pattern of cerebral lateralization, that is, asymmetric distribution of linguistic functions in the brain (» 6.1.2). Gran (1989) sought to apply the experimental findings for training purposes, and Valeria Darò (e.g. 1994, 1997) extended the neuropsychological approach to a broader range of speech-related topics. Interdisciplinary work along these lines has also been pursued at the universities of Vienna and Turku. In association with neurophysiologist Hellmuth Petsche, **Kurz** (1994, 1996) used EEG mapping to visualize differential patterns of cerebral activation, whereas Jorma **Tommola** teamed up with neuroscientists using positron emission tomography (PET) to study "the translating brain" (Rinne *et al.* 2000). Indeed, Tommola (1999) has presented this '**neuro' approach** as a research model *sui generis*, in contrast to the "cognitive-behavioral approach" here labeled as the CP paradigm. One could therefore speak of a neurophysiological/neurolinguistic or **NL paradigm** in interpreting studies that is closely linked to advanced neuroscientific imaging techniques (see Tommola 1999).

The increasing dissemination of neuroscientific methodologies certainly suggests considerable future potential for the NL paradigm of interpreting research. At the same time, however, the neuro approach is highly dependent on the sustained interest of neuroscientists in the study of interpreting and interpreters. Given its specific focus on the level of brain function and its considerable methodological challenges, it is unlikely that the NL paradigm will become a widely shared research approach of the interpreting studies community in the near future. Indeed, the NL paradigm seems to have lost much of its momentum, not only in Vienna but also at the University of Trieste.

Irrespective of the present, or future, paradigm status of the NL approach, the interdisciplinary outlook which thrived in the wake of the Trieste Symposium has remained a significant feature of interpreting studies and is reflected in many of the key socio-academic initiatives in the field. The 1994 Turku Conference (« 2.5.1), the launching of *Interpreting* as an international refereed journal with an editorial board of psychologists, and a number of explicitly interdisciplinary events and publications, such as the 1995 Kent Psychology Forum on *Cognitive Processes in Translation and Interpreting* (Danks *et al.* 1997), the 1997 and 2001 Ascona Workshops (*Interpreting* 2:1/2, 1997 and 5:2, 2000/01), and the "International Symposium on Language Processing and Interpreting" held in early 1997 in Stockholm (Englund Dimitrova and Hyltenstam 2000), reflect a substantial degree of inter-action between the interpreting community and scientists in other disciplines. At the same time, though, there has been a growing awareness of some serious obstacles to 'true' (i.e. joint and interactive) interdisciplinary research – as opposed to the mere importing of models and methods from other disciplines. Gile, a long-time advocate of interdisciplinary research on conference interpreting, has pointed critically to what he calls "doorstep interdisciplinarity" (1999a: 41); that is, a lack of sustained interdisciplinary cooperation and exchange as a result of socio-academic communication problems and divergences in conceptual and methodological orientation.

Against this background, it is striking to note a comment on interdisciplinarity by Laura Gran, who, after many years of co-representing the NL paradigm at the University of Trieste, reached the following conclusion for the interpreting research community as a whole:

We interpreters have got in closer contact with psychologists, linguists, experts in communication etc. Much as we owe to these scholars however, we shall have to become more and more aware of the specificity of our discipline, identify our own problems, set our own goals and be able to use the tools we need to inquire into the various facets of the interpretation process.

(Fabbro and Gran 1997: 26)

Clearly, what Gran is (re)claiming here for interpreting research is a paradigm of its own, a conceptual and methodological approach shared by the community of interpreting scholars at large, and a research policy determined by those with a professional background and academic responsibility in the field of interpreting. Those who, like Gran, focus on the (mental) process of interpreting, are certainly well served by the CP paradigm, which may either be viewed as a competitor of the original IT paradigm or, in hindsight, as a successor carrying on the former's pioneering work on a broader and more scientific basis. The latter view is illustrated most forcefully by Setton's (1998/2002, 1999) **cognitive-pragmatic analysis** of SI (« 2.6.1, » 5.4.3, » 6.3.2). Setton's decidedly interdisciplinary approach to corpus-based linguistic analysis can be said to reconcile the IT and CP paradigms: it offers a more sophisticated account of "sense" in the light of state-of-the-art research in cognitive science, and it explicitly builds context processing into the analysis of linguistic input. Indeed, Setton's influence may be seen as moving the CP paradigm towards a 'pragmatic turn', so that its abbreviated label might also stand for 'cognitive pragmatics'. There can be little doubt, then, that Setton would fit in well with the list of practitioner-researchers (including Gile, Lederer, Moser, Seleskovitch and Stenzl), whom Mackintosh (1995: 121), in a distinctly conciliatory perspective, gives credit for having developed "a generally accepted description of the interpreting process".

4.5 Broadening the view

Given their focus on the interpreter's mental processing activity, the paradigms described so far have tended to leave a broad range of socio-communicative issues unaccounted for. An approach to remedy this by focusing on a more systematic analysis of the **situational and socio-cultural context** emerged from translation-theoretical frameworks that had come to fore in the 1980s.

In contrast to the French scholars studying the interpreting process to arrive at a general theory of Translation, German scholars at around the same time launched into an analysis of Translation in general which would apply to all and any manifestations of translational activity. Drawing on the work of Kade (« 1.2.1) as well as theories of action, culture and interaction, Hans Vermeer (see 1989/2000) formulated his ***skopos* theory** on the premise that the *skopos* (Greek for 'aim', 'function' or 'purpose') for which a target text was commissioned constitutes the controlling principle of translational activity, over and above such traditional criteria of source–target correspondence as equivalence, invariance, or fidelity (» 7.2.1). The *skopos* does not emanate from the original, nor is it imposed arbitrarily by the translator/interpreter. Rather, it is essentially determined by the communicative needs and expectations of the target audience and its situational context and socio-cultural environment. Hence, the *skopos*-oriented, or **functionalist** approach is strongly inspired by the memes of making sense (« 3.2.6) as well as text production (« 3.2.7) and mediation (« 3.2.8).

The idea of **target orientation**, expressed by Seleskovitch as early as the 1960s (see 1978a: 9), was shared by Hella Kirchhoff, a colleague of Vermeer's at the University of Heidelberg, whose own work was based on the ideas of Kade (« 2.3.1) as well as psycholinguistic studies of bilingualism. Although working on the basic assumption of 'functional equivalence', Kirchhoff explicitly acknowledged the need to adapt the source text to "the communicative needs of receivers with a different sociocultural background" (1976/2002: 113). Both Kirchhoff and Vermeer proved highly influential for **Stenzl**'s work, as evident from her appeal for a 'broader view' at the Trieste Symposium (Stenzl 1989: 24):

> we need a reorientation or perhaps more accurately a widening of our research framework so that rather than the predominantly psychological perspective we adopt a more functional approach that considers interpretation in the context of the entire communication process from speaker through the interpreter to the receiver. We have been paying too little attention to those who have been proposing such an approach for years, Kirchhoff, for example.

Along these lines, though apparently without interaction, the work of Kade was carried on in an action-theoretical functionalist framework by his disciple Heidemarie **Salevsky** (1987). Most comprehensively, **Pöchhacker** (1994a, 1994b, 1995a) used the functionalist theory of translational action as a foundation for conceptual models and empirical analyses of interactional, situational and textual features of simultaneous conference interpreting (» 5.3.1). On the whole, however, relatively little empirical research on interpreting has been carried out within this functionalist school of thought; hardly enough, at any rate, to speak of a paradigm in interpreting studies, were it not for its convergence with another significant current in Translation theory.

By the end of the 1980s, the target-oriented paradigm of **Descriptive Translation Studies**, centered on the notion of **translational norms** (Toury 1995), had become extended beyond its initial concern with literary translation. The role of translational norms in interpreting was first discussed by **Shlesinger** (1989a) and subsequently applied to empirical research on interpreting by **Schjoldager** (1995/2002). A principal implication of this **target-text-oriented translation-theoretical** approach, or **TT paradigm**, is an analytical interest in the textual product, with regard to both its structural ('intratextual') and its pragmatic dimensions. In other words, the interpreter's output would not be viewed as a 'window' on cognitive processes (as suggested e.g. by Lederer) but as a product and instrument in the **macro-process** of mediated communication. This focus on the interpreter's output in terms of text and discourse has allowed scholars working in the TT paradigm to draw on the full range of methodologies in such areas as text linguistics and discourse studies (« 3.1.2). Thus **paradigm cases** include Shlesinger's (1989b) corpus-based analysis of orality and literacy in English–Hebrew SI and Pöchhacker's (1994a) conference-level case study of English–German SI, which describes the interplay of situational and textual variables and analyzes interpreters' target texts from a functionalist perspective.

Another conceptual focus of the TT paradigm, particularly in the German functionalist approach, has been the way in which the communicating parties relate to each other and **interact** from their particular socio-cultural positions. Interest in **culture-specific patterns** of communicative (including nonverbal) behavior had been nurtured by novel approaches to communication and culture in anthropology and sociology (« 3.1.3), promoted in Germany by Heinz Göhring (2002), a conference interpreter teaching at Germersheim in close cooperation with Vermeer. The fact that the TT paradigm was not as strongly linked to the conference interpreting profession as the IT and CP paradigms facilitated its extension to the study of liaison interpreting in various cross-cultural settings. Even though work in this direction by TT scholars remained largely at a conceptual and didactic level, it provided for an interface between the functionalist paradigm and the **interactionist** approaches which were to underpin the emergence of a new paradigm of interpreting research in the 1990s.

4.6 Focusing on interaction

In the course of the 1980s, interpreting research interests and initiatives emerged on a broader scale beyond the highly professionalized domain of international conference interpreting (« 2.4.1). In the wake of impressive progress toward becoming a full-fledged profession, sign language interpreting, particularly in the US, attracted increasing attention as an object of research. Moving beyond some of the groundbreaking work done by linguists, psycholinguists and psychologists in the 1970s (see e.g. Brislin 1976b, Gerver and Sinaiko 1978), Dennis Cokely and Cynthia B. Roy, in PhD research completed in the mid- to late 1980s, embarked on a more comprehensive analysis of the sign language interpreting process. Despite Cokely's (1992a) explicit aspiration to make his process model (» 5.4.3) sensitive to the sociolinguistic dimension, his empirical work, based on an authentic corpus recorded in a conference setting, clearly reflected the tradition of SI research in the CP paradigm (» 6.2.3).

It was the 1989 PhD thesis by **Roy** that was to mark a wholly new conceptual and methodological departure. Inspired by Deborah Tannen (e.g. 1982), one of the leading representatives of sociolinguistic discourse studies, Roy carried out a case study of dialogue interpreting in a 15-minute meeting between a university professor and her deaf graduate student. Roy's **qualitative analysis** of the videotaped corpus focused on the dynamics of **interactive discourse**, with special regard for **turn-taking** processes (e.g. Roy 1996). Drawing on the methods of conversation analysis (ethnomethodology) and discourse analysis (interactional sociolinguistics, ethnography of communication), Roy (2000a: 66) provided evidence that "an interpreter's role is more than to 'just translate' or 'just interpret'," and highlighted the interpreter's active involvement in the interaction (» 7.4).

At the time that Roy carried out her study at Georgetown University in Washington DC, work on spoken-language dialogue interpreting was being launched onto a similar course at the University of Linköping in Sweden. Under the supervision of discourse scholar Per Linell in the Department of Communication Studies, Cecilia **Wadensjö** (« 2.5.2) carried out discourse-based fieldwork on Russian–Swedish immigration and medical interviews mediated by state-certified Swedish dialogue interpreters. Uninspired by what she found in a cursory review of the translation-theoretical literature, she sought to overcome the predominantly 'monologic' view of 'text' and proposed instead an interaction-oriented perspective on discourse (« 3.2.7), with particular emphasis on the role of context and the dynamics of **interactivity** in **face-to-face communication**.

Drawing on Goffman's work for a model of the role constellations in interpreter-mediated encounters (» 5.3.1) and taking a descriptive **discourse-analytical approach** to her data, Wadensjö showed that the interpreters' performance went beyond the 'ideal interpreting' norm of 'just translating' and included the function of 'coordinating' the primary parties' utterances (see 1993/2002). As summarized in the revised version of Wadensjö's pioneering 1992 dissertation: "In dialogue interpreting, the translating and coordinating aspects are *simultaneously present*, and the one does not exclude the other" (Wadensjö 1998: 105).

The highly congenial work of Roy and Wadensjö supplied both a coherent conceptual approach to (dialogue) interpreting and a broad base of discourse-analytical methodology, thus launching a new paradigm for the study of interpreting as **dialogic discourse-based interaction** (DI). The **DI paradigm** gained momentum in the course of the 1990s with further discourse-based empirical studies, including work on the coordination of turn-taking in industrial training sessions (Apfelbaum 1995), on power and face in high-stakes media interpreting (Baker 1997), and on the "myth of neutrality" in sign language interpreting (Metzger 1999). A special issue of *The Translator* (5:2, 1999) as well as a companion volume on *Dialogue Interpreting* (Mason 2001) testify to the status of the DI paradigm and Wadensjö's exemplary work.

The success of the DI paradigm was clearly associated with the increasing recognition of community interpreting as a significant field of professional practice and hence a fruitful area of research (« 2.5.2). Although it takes its inspiration from sociological and sociolinguistic discourse studies rather than Translation theory, the DI paradigm shares with the TT paradigm both the functionalists' concern with (inter)action and mediation, and the interest in translational norms as manifested in actual discourse and extra-textual sources such as professional codes of ethics (» 8.3.1). What is more, the focus on the pragmatics of interactive discourse suggests considerable shared ground between the DI paradigm and the cognitive-pragmatic approach of Setton (1998/2002, 1999). Clearly, then, there are multiple points of interface between the more recent and the more established research traditions in interpreting studies.

4.7 Unity in diversity

In a survey of paradigms from other disciplines ("interdisciplinary paradigms") which seem to hold promise for research on (simultaneous) interpreting, Shlesinger (1995a: 9) captures the paradigm status of interpreting studies in the statement: "We do not have – nor should we necessarily desire – a unifying paradigm." Though Shlesinger uses 'paradigm' in a somewhat narrower sense, her assessment also applies to the review of paradigms offered in this chapter, which has shown (1) that there are several conceptually and methodologically distinct research traditions in interpreting studies to which one may attribute paradigm status, and (2) that the main paradigms of interpreting studies are variously interrelated and largely complement rather than compete with one another.

In an intuitive visualization, one might depict the various paradigms and interrelations described in the course of this review as a **cluster** situated between the underlying field of professional practice and training on the one hand, and the cognitive, linguistic, and social sciences on the other (Figure 4.1). The dominant CP paradigm may be conceived of as a science-oriented extension of the largely profession-based IT paradigm. The CP paradigm reaches well into the domain of cognitive science, where the NL paradigm stands out as the most specialized research model for interpreting. The TT paradigm, in contrast, appears as the cluster's base, overlapping with the domain of profession-oriented theory and training rather than with other sciences. Holding a middle ground, the DI paradigm is shown as offering interfaces all around, with a significant participation in the linguistic sciences.

The image of a cluster as depicted in Figure 4.1 is meant to reflect a high degree of both diversity and overall coherence between the various paradigms which fill the space between the profession and established sciences. Admittedly, it fails to account for the large number of individual research efforts which have been carried out with no particular affiliation, or with insufficient momentum to acquire

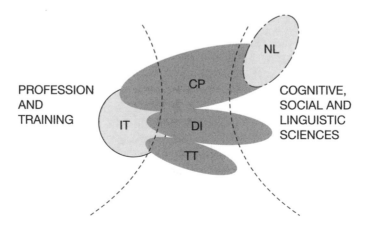

Figure 4.1 Cluster of paradigms in interpreting studies

critical mass. While certainly a matter of opinion and perspective, the account of paradigms presented here should be acceptable as a compromise between viewing interpreting studies as a wide field of scattered, isolated efforts, and idealizing it as a discipline united by a single, generally shared paradigm. This vision of unity in diversity for interpreting studies can be reinforced by citing cases of interpreting researchers who have done substantial work in more than one paradigm: Kurz, for instance, a pioneer of psychological experimenting on interpreters (» 6.2.1), presented her user expectation surveys (» 7.5.1) in terms of the functionalist TT paradigm and also engaged in collaborative research in the NL paradigm (» 6.1.2); similarly, S. Lambert worked directly in Gerver's tradition of the CP paradigm (» 6.4.1) while also engaging in and promoting neurolinguistic/ neuropsychological studies; Shlesinger made pioneering contributions to the TT paradigm (1989a, 1989b) and also carried out sophisticated experimental research in the CP paradigm (» 6.4.2); Pöchhacker used the TT paradigm as a foundation for fieldwork on conference interpreting and also contributed to the DI paradigm; and Tommola was involved in experimental work within the CP paradigm (» 6.6.1, » 6.6.4) while also cooperating with neuroscientists to advance the NL paradigm.

In contrast to Kuhn's (1962/1996: 150) assumption, then, that paradigms would function like a "gestalt switch" which allows for the perception of only one or the other version of an ambiguous image, there is evidence in interpreting studies that individual researchers and subcommunities may adopt variable perspectives on their multi-faceted object of study – as highlighted by the variety of models of interpreting reviewed in the following chapter.

Summary

This chapter has reviewed the *research traditions*, or paradigms, that have emerged in interpreting studies since the mid-1970s, when interpreting research first became established as a field of academic study in its own right. The initial '*bootstrap paradigm*' championed by Seleskovitch and Lederer at ESIT in Paris sought to explain the *ideal process* of (conference) interpreting on the basis of observing and reflecting on *successful professional practice*. Resting on the conceptual core of the *interpretive theory* of Translation, the *IT paradigm* came to be challenged and superseded by research-minded conference interpreters, such as Daniel Gile, Jennifer Mackintosh, Barbara Moser-Mercer, and Catherine Stenzl, who aspired to *more stringent standards* of scientific research in investigating the cognitive process of interpreting, and professed an openness to the concepts and methods of other disciplines, particularly in the *cognitive sciences*. More than the broad and heterogeneous *cognitive processing* or *CP paradigm*, which is fundamentally inspired by the work of David Gerver, the *neurolinguistic* or *NL paradigm* pioneered by neurophysiologist Franco Fabbro at Trieste was firmly based on theories and methods beyond the realm of translational activity. The latter was foregrounded by interpreting researchers like Pöchhacker and Shlesinger, who drew on such *translation-theoretical* notions as the *skopos* (target function) and *translational norms* to investigate interpreting as *target-oriented text production* (*TT paradigm*). Against the background of the increasing recognition of community-based dialogue interpreting as a field of professional practice and research, Cynthia B. Roy in the US and Cecilia Wadensjö in Sweden investigated interpreter-mediated encounters as *dialogic discourse-based interaction*. This *DI paradigm*, which draws on concepts from sociolinguistics and sociology and applies *discourse-analytical methods*, established itself in the course of the 1990s as yet another research tradition alongside and in conjunction with the other paradigms – as summarized in matrix form in Figure 4.2.

Sources and further reading

On paradigms in interpreting studies, see Moser-Mercer (1994a), Shlesinger (1995a), and Setton (1999, ch. 2).

On the IT paradigm, see García-Landa (1981), Lederer (1978/2002, 1981, 1990), Seleskovitch (1976, 1978a, 1978b, 1991), Seleskovitch and Lederer (1984); on the CP paradigm, see Englund Dimitrova and Hyltenstam (2000), Gerver (1975, 1976), Gile (1994b, 1995a, 1997/2002), *Interpreting* 2:1/2 (1997), *Interpreting* 5:2 (2000/01), S. Lambert (1989), Moser-Mercer (1997, 1997/2002), Moser-Mercer *et al.* (1997), Shreve and Diamond (1997), Tirkkonen-Condit and Jääskeläinen (2000); on the NL paradigm, see Fabbro and Gran (1994, 1997), Fabbro *et al.* (1990), Kurz (1994), Petsche *et al.* (1993), Rinne *et al.* (2000), Tommola (1999); on the TT paradigm, see Nord (1997: 104–8), Pöchhacker (1992, 1994a, 1994b, 1995a), Schjoldager (1995/2002), Shlesinger (1989a, 1989b, 1999); on the DI paradigm, see Mason (2000, 2001), Roy (1996, 2000a), Wadensjö (1993/2002, 1998), and the special issue on *Dialogue Interpreting* of *The Translator* (5:2, 1999).

Suggestions for further study

–   How have geopolitical, linguistic and institutional factors influenced the development of different paradigms in interpreting studies?
–   Viewing the various paradigms as points of reference in a much wider and diverse disciplinary landscape, what other influential approaches can be identified, and how do they relate to the research traditions accorded paradigm status in this chapter?

	IT	NL	CP	TT	DI
SUPERMEME	communicative activity + process(ing)	process(ing)	process(ing)	Translation	communicative activity
MEME	making sense	cognitive information processing	cognitive information processing	making sense + text production + mediation	discourse production + mediation
INFLUENTIAL MODEL/THEORY (THEORIST)	interpretive theory (Seleskovitch)	hemispheric specialization (Fabbro)	skills models (Gerver, Moser-Mercer), Effort models (Gile)	translational norms (Toury), *skopos* theory (Vermeer)	participation framework (Goffman)
LEADING MEMBERS	Seleskovitch, Lederer	Fabbro, Tommola	Moser-Mercer, Gile, Setton	Shlesinger, Pöchhacker	Wadensjö, Roy
PARADIGM CASES	Seleskovitch 1975, Lederer 1981	Fabbro et al. 1990, Fabbro and Gran 1994	Gerver 1976, Moser 1978, Gile 1985, 1999a	Shlesinger 1989b, Pöchhacker 1994a	Wadensjö 1998, Roy 2000a
INTERDISCIPLINARY ORIENTATION	(psychology)	neurophysiology, neuropsychology	cognitive psychology	Translation and discourse studies	sociology, sociolinguistics
METHODOLOGICAL STRATEGY	fieldwork	experiment	experiment, survey, fieldwork	fieldwork, survey	fieldwork
INTERPRETING TYPE (MODE)	conference (consec. + SI)	SI	conference (SI + consec.)	conference (SI) + dialogue	dialogue

Figure 4.2 Summary table of paradigms in interpreting studies

5 Models

Various conceptions of interpreting with different focal points on the map of memes (« 3.2.9) have been elaborated in the form of models. Proceeding from the broader levels of social context to the intricacies of cognitive processes, this chapter reviews a number of modeling approaches and discusses a range of selected examples.

The **main points** covered in this chapter are

- the nature and purpose of modeling in the process of inquiry
- the conceptual dimensions in which the phenomenon of interpreting can be modeled
- interaction-oriented models of interpreting
- process-oriented models of interpreting
- tests and applications of models

5.1 On modeling

5.1.1 Nature, form and purpose

A model can be described as some form of representation of an object or phenomenon. Models usually indicate the type and number of components which are assumed to form part of the object or phenomenon under study, and reflect the way in which the components fit together and relate to one another. In essence, then, a model is an assumption about what something is like and how it functions, so that modeling can be regarded as a particular form of theoretical endeavor. Such theoretical models can take various forms of representation, from verbal description to imagery and mathematical formulas. More often than not, the desire to 'reflect' and 'represent' a phenomenon suggests recourse to graphic forms of expression, and indeed most of the models presented in this chapter are visualized as diagrams.

Models can be used for various purposes of inquiry. As a basic form of **theorizing** they can express intuitive assumptions and ideas (memes) about a phenomenon. Models constructed on the basis of more immediate observations and empirical data are used for the purpose of **describing** some aspect of 'reality', bearing in mind that a model, by definition, is an incomplete representation, one which singles out features and relationships that are of particular concern to the analyst. Where models seek to capture a dynamic relationship, such as a sequence over time or a relation of cause and effect, they can be used for **explaining** how or why a phenomenon occurs. On the assumption that a model includes, at a sufficient level of detail, all factors and relationships which may have an impact on the phenomenon under study, it can be used for **predicting** the occurrence of future phenomena, as in a controlled experimental setting. The latter is one way of **testing** the model and its underlying assumptions, others being continued observation and computer simulation, always with a view to further theoretical elaboration and refinement.

In principle, models of interpreting can be envisaged for any of these purposes. As evident from the evolution of ideas about interpreting, however, the phenomenon is of such complexity as to elude attempts at constructing a comprehensive predictive model. Most models of interpreting are therefore of the descriptive kind and are pegged to a particular level of analysis.

5.1.2 Levels of modeling

With the conceptual space for theorizing about interpreting extending from the more micro-process-oriented cognitive sphere all the way to the socio-cultural dimension of the macro-process of communication, modeling implies a choice of one or more conceptual levels to be foregrounded in the representation. Which, then, are the levels of analysis that one can distinguish as potential conceptual reference points for models of interpreting?

In light of the discussion on memes of interpreting, which ended with references to the role of interpreters in the history of intercultural relations, one could conceive of a broadly **anthropological** model of interpreting and its role in the history of human civilization. With less abstraction and historical depth, and a more specific focus on societal structures, one would arrive at a **socio-professional** conception of interpreting; that is, a model of interpreting as a profession in society. Narrowing the focus to particular social institutions, such as international organizations, parliaments or courts, would highlight the **institutional** function of interpreting, while setting one's sights on a particular type of communicative event, like a conference or interview, would foreground the **interactional** aspects of interpreting as an activity taking place in and, at the same time, shaping a particular situation. Concentrating on the text as the material instrument in the communicative process, the analyst would view interpreting primarily as a **textual** or **discursive** process, whereas an interest in the mental processes underlying language use would give rise to **cognitive** models of interpreting. Finally, the material substrate of mental processes can be targeted with models of cerebral organization and brain activity at the most fundamental, **neural** level of inquiry.

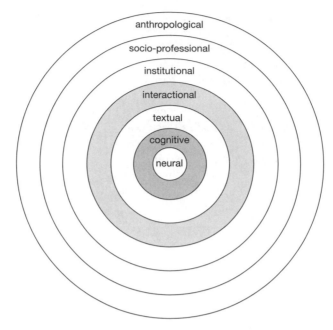

Figure 5.1 Levels of modeling

Bearing in mind that these seven levels of analysis are meant as variable focal points rather than rigidly separable categories, they can be visualized as a set of concentric circles, extending from the 'outer' spheres of social context to a neuro-cognitive core, or, more pointedly, from **socio-cultures** to **synapses** (Figure 5.1).

Not all the dimensions suggested in the multi-level model have attracted a similar degree of analytical interest in interpreting studies. Indeed, as indicated in the diagram by variably shaded rings, modeling efforts to date have focused mainly on the level of cognitive processes, with some consideration also given to the level of interaction. These preferential focal points, which once again reflect the two supermemes of interpreting, process(ing) and communicative activity, also shape the presentation of selected models that follows.

5.2 Socio-professional and institutional models

While a model of interpreting in the **anthropological** dimension, with reference to intersocietal relations and cultural identities in the course of history, has not been put forward as such, the model of interpreting in various societal contexts depicted in Figure 1.1 (« 1.3.1) could be cited as an illustration of the kind of issues which models at this level might address. Another example can be found in Cronin's (2002) account of "heteronomous" and "autonomous" systems of interpreting in the context of colonial empires and travel (see 2002: 393f).

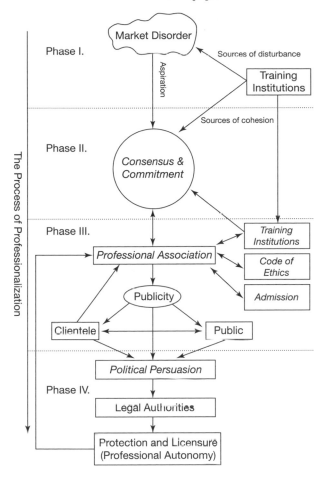

Figure 5.2 Tseng's model of the professionalization process (from Tseng 1992: 43)

A **socio-professional** model which focuses on interpreting as a recognized occupation in society was developed by Joseph **Tseng** (1992) with reference to conference interpreting in the social context of Taiwan. The model describes four phases in the process of **professionalization**, from "market disorder" to "professional autonomy" (Figure 5.2).

Tseng's model has been applied to the field of (spoken-language) community interpreting in various countries (e.g. Fenton 1993, Mikkelson 1999) as well as to the profession of sign language interpreting in Great Britain (Pollitt 1997). In more general terms, Uldis **Ozolins** (2000) has modeled different stages of interpreting service provision with reference to key determinants of professionalization.

More specifically still than at the level of a given society or socio-culture, the development, function and economics of interpreting can also be modeled at the **institutional** level. A pertinent example is the Grounded Theory study by

Niels **Agger-Gupta** (2001) on interpreting-related changes in fourteen health organizations in Canada and the US. Based on a wealth of qualitative data, Agger-Gupta's account features a number of models to represent the emergence of interpreting services in various institutional contexts from the stage of "making do" to an established feature of culturally appropriate care.

While these examples highlight the importance and potential of modeling the phenomenon of interpreting in a broader socio-institutional dimension, interpreting scholars to date have expended relatively little effort on models of interpreting in history, society or in specific institutions. Rather, interpreting models tend to relate to the domain of **interaction** (» 5.3) or, much more so, focus on the complexities of cognitive **processing** (» 5.4).

5.3 Interaction models

Interaction models represent the social, situational and communicative relations obtaining between the various parties involved in the process of interaction. They can be broadly subdivided into those which model the **constellation** of interacting parties as such (» 5.3.1) and those which focus on the process of **communication** (» 5.3.2) or, more specifically, the role of **text** or **discourse** in communicative interaction (» 5.3.3).

5.3.1 Constellation

The basic constellation, or **type case**, of interpreter-mediated interaction was modeled by R.B.W. **Anderson** (1976/2002) as a monolingual speaker of language A communicating with a monolingual speaker of language B via an interpreter commanding both languages (Figure 5.3).

Anderson's linear constellation model is one way of highlighting the pivotal position of the bilingual interpreter in the mediated exchange. Other authors have sought to express this by using a triangular representation in which the interpreter is depicted at the apex. Such models have become the default representation in the domain of community interpreting (e.g. Gentile *et al.* 1996, Erasmus 1999), which is, after all, also referred to sometimes as 'three-cornered interpreting'. They take account of the communicative interaction between the primary parties and foreground the **role of the interpreter** as a more or less active participant in the interaction rather than a mere 'switching station' (» 7.4).

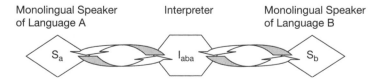

Monolingual Speaker   Interpreter   Monolingual Speaker
of Language A   of Language B

S_a I_{aba} S_b

Figure 5.3 Anderson's 'type-case' model of three-party interaction (from R.B.W. Anderson 1976: 211)

The basic three-party interaction model can be and has been extended in various ways to account for more complex constellations. Anderson (1976: 211) himself modeled variant forms including a negotiation with two interpreters, one for each side, and an interpreted lecture, with a larger number of speakers of language B adopting a listener role in an essentially one-directional process of communication. Similarly, **Wong** Fook Khoon (1990: 112) depicts several complex constellations of interpreting in Malaysian courtrooms, with one or two bilingual interpreters or a trilingual interpreter mediating between a judge, a defendant and a witness speaking different languages or dialects.

A simple model of the interactional constellation in **conference settings**, where a monolingual speaker addresses a more or less numerous audience, part of which cannot comprehend the language of the original speech, was suggested by **Gile** (1995b: 24) and is shown in Figure 5.4.

Though not necessarily involved directly in the interaction process, the "client" in Gile's model plays a significant role at the conference level. This dimension could be specified further by accounting for a range of human agents who may have an impact on the interpreter's working conditions, such as conference organizing staff, document services, and technicians. Similar considerations apply to colleagues in the interpreting team, especially in the case of relay interpreting.

An illustrative case of institution-specific complexity is the models discussed by Delia **Chiaro** (2002) for various constellations in TV interpreting, where mediated face-to-face communication combines with 'one-to-many' communication as typical of the mass media. Clearly, then, such models of the interaction constellation in an interpreted communication event also go some way toward addressing the institutional level of modeling which has hitherto received little attention.

Models of interpreted interaction, whether reflecting a 'one-to-one' or a 'one-to-many' constellation, can thus be extended and specified by adding further participant positions. At the same time, they can also be refined to reflect relevant features of the interacting parties. This is the aim of **Pöchhacker**'s (1992) model of the interpreting situation, which hinges on the "perspective" of the individual **interactant** on the communicative event (Figure 5.5).

The interactant model of the situation foregrounds the "role(s)" of the communicating "person" in the interaction. It suggests that the interactant's "perspective" on the situation, constituted by a continuous "assessment" of and intentional "orientation" toward the other interactants and their behavior,

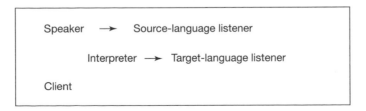

Figure 5.4 Gile's interaction model of conference interpreting (from Gile 1995b: 24)

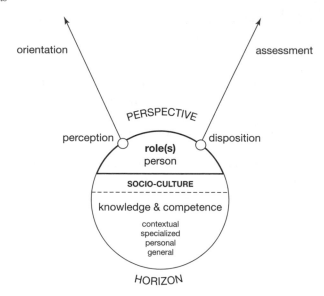

Figure 5.5 Pöchhacker's interactant model of the interpreting situation (adapted from Pöchhacker 1992: 216)

is essentially shaped by the individual's socio-cultural 'background', or "horizon," made up of various types of cognitive competence and experience. In other words, the situation, in the more cognitive sense, exists only 'in the eyes of' (i.e. as seen from the perspective of) the interactant. Modulated by psycho-physical factors relating to "perception" and "disposition," the individual's orientation and assessment (including factors like motivation, emotional attitude, expectations and, not least, intentions) thus determine 'what the situation is like' and how it should be acted upon.

While the individualized interaction model applies both to the 'one-to-many' constellations typical of conference settings (see Pöchhacker 1994a: 144) and to triadic interaction in mediated face-to-face communication, it addresses positions and roles at the level of the speech event as such rather than the utterance-level dynamics of the communicative exchange. In the terminology of Goffman as applied to interpreting by Wadensjö (1998), the interactant model highlights "activity roles" within a "situated activity system" in which individuals interact to perform a single joint activity (see Wadensjö 1998: 84).

Further analytical distinctions for the macro-level of mediated encounters have been proposed by Bistra **Alexieva** (1997/2002). In her multi-parameter model of interpreting constellations, she outlines a proto-**typology of** interpreter-mediated **events** on the basis of seven scales, most of which relate to the socio-situational constellation of the interacting parties. The parameters which bear directly on the constellation of interactants are:

- "distance" vs. "proximity" (between speaker, addressee and interpreter);

- "equality/solidarity" vs. "non-equality/power" (related to status, role and gender of speaker and addressee, as well as the interpreter in some cases);
- "formal setting" vs. "informal setting" (related to number of participants, degree of privacy, and distance from home country);
- "cooperativeness/directness" vs. "non-cooperativeness/indirectness" (relevant to negotiation strategies);
- "shared goals" vs. "conflicting goals".

(Alexieva 1997/2002: 230)

Alexieva applies her multi-parameter model to an assessment of interpreter-mediated events in terms of their degree of "culture-specificity," thus reaffirming the role of "culture" in the conception of interpreting as interaction.

In contrast to such constellations at the level of the communicative event, modeling the dynamic constellation(s) of interaction at the micro-level of individual utterances requires finer analytical distinctions – as made in **Wadensjö**'s (1998) theoretical framework for interpreter-mediated encounters. Wadensjö's model for the analysis of dialogue interpreting is based on Goffman's influential conception of the **participation framework**, which serves to describe an individual's involvement, or "status of participation," in communicative interaction. A "hearer", in Goffman's terms, may be "ratified" (as an addressed or unaddressed recipient or as a 'bystander') or "unratified" (as in the case of an 'overhearer' or eavesdropper). A "speaker," in contrast, may take up three different positions (or combinations thereof) toward his or her utterance, which Goffman discusses under the heading of **production format** (see Wadensjö 1998: 88):

- the speaker as "animator" – or "vocalizer" (Clark 1996: 20) – is responsible only for the production of speech sounds;
- the speaker as "author" is responsible for formulating the utterance (hence Clark's suggestion of "formulator");
- the speaker as "principal" bears ultimate responsibility for the meaning expressed.

Wadensjö complements Goffman's triple production format by an analogous breakdown of 'listenership'. With a view to multiple listener roles of the interpreter, Wadensjö (1998: 91f) proposes a threefold distinction under the heading of **"reception format"**:

- listening as a "reporter" (expected only to repeat what has been uttered);
- listening as a "recapitulator" (expected to give an authorized voice to a prior speaker);
- listening as a "responder" (addressed so as to make his or her own contribution to discourse).

Wadensjö puts special emphasis on the simultaneity of speakership and listenership, arguing that talk in face-to-face communication is always carried out simultaneously with listening, and that listening may include overt verbal activity (e.g. back-channeling). Hence she defines Goffman's (1981) key notion of "footing" in the participation framework as "a person's alignment (as speaker *and* hearer) to a particular utterance" (1998: 87). Wadensjö's model, then, serves to account for dynamic changes in the constellation of "speaker–hearer roles" at an utterance-to-utterance level, and thus to reconstruct the organization of communicative interaction "through potentially changing alignments in the ongoing flow of discourse" (1998: 86).

5.3.2 Communication

Rather than conceptualizing interaction between human beings, early communication models of interpreting were largely shaped by the mathematical theory of communication as 'signal processing' (Shannon and Weaver 1949). The classic information-theoretical model of communication (« 3.2.4), in which a 'message' originating from a 'source' is 'encoded' and 'transmitted' through a 'channel' for 'decoding' by a 'receiver', has been variously applied also to interpreting.

An early model of interpreting based on the standard communication model was developed in the 1970s by **Ingram** (see 1985). Originally conceived for sign language interpreting, Ingram's model goes beyond a verbal-linguistic conception of 'message transfer' and represents "messages in a multiplicity of interwoven codes" (1978: 111). The idea of **multiple codes** is the distinctive feature of Ingram's semiotic model of interpreting as depicted in Figure 5.6.

Ingram's model is clearly reminiscent of the classic linear model of sender–receiver communication and, despite explicit reference to "context," essentially depicts the interpreter as a 'code-switching' station in the 'channel'. A more elaborate representation, though still founded on the assumption of language as a code and hence language processing as 'encoding' and 'decoding', was drawn up by **Kirchhoff** (1976), as represented in an English adaptation in Figure 5.7.

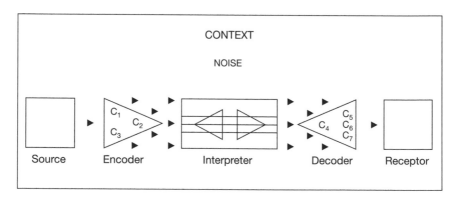

Figure 5.6 Ingram's semiotic communication model of interpreting (from Ingram 1985: 98)

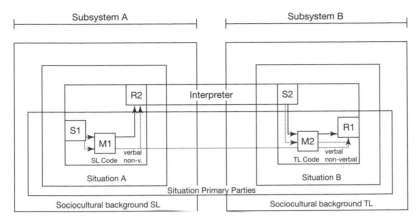

Figure 5.7 Kirchhoff's three-party bilingual communication system model (from Kirchhoff 1976: 21)

Kirchhoff posits a **dual system of communication** in which a message (M1), composed of both "verbal" and "nonverbal" signals, is encoded by a primary sender (S1) in a given situation and socio-cultural background for reception by a primary receiver (R1) in a target-language context. The two parts of the communication system are linked together by the interpreter, who is depicted as a 'side participant' outside the situation of the primary parties and serves as both a secondary receiver (R2) of M1 and a secondary sender (S2) of M2 in the target-language code.

An elaboration of Kirchhoff's model which adds feedback mechanisms between the three interactants and foregrounds the ideational or concept level of communication has been described by **Kondo** (1990: 61, 2003: 81). Comparable, albeit less detailed, models were developed independently by other authors. With special reference to communication studies, Erich **Feldweg** (1996) drew up several variants of a basic communication model to account for increasingly complex constellations of communicating parties and information flows in consecutive and simultaneous conference interpreting (e.g. 1996: 223).

While both Kirchhoff and Feldweg conceive of interpreted communication as a 'multi-channel phenomenon', their account of the sign systems involved in the interpreting process is sparse compared to the ambitious semiotic model developed by Fernando **Poyatos** (1987/2002). Poyatos represents the verbal and nonverbal systems involved in (spoken-language) simultaneous and consecutive interpreting in the form of a matrix cross-tabulating acoustic and visual sign-conveying systems with various constellations of auditory and/or visual co-presence (see 1987/2002: 237). The matrix model by Poyatos does not cover whispered interpreting or simultaneous sign language interpreting, but nevertheless remains the most sophisticated such analysis to date.

5.3.3 *Text / discourse*

Ever since the 'pragmatic turn' in linguistics in the late 1970s, a number of authors have focused on the notions of text and discourse in their efforts to model mediated interaction. One of the earliest attempts in interpreting studies to use insights from text theory and translation theory for a model of interpreting as an interaction process was made by **Stenzl** (1983). Elaborating on a **text-theoretical model** of the translation process, Stenzl gives an account of the **communicative information flow** in (simultaneous) interpreting which centers on text processing by the speaker, interpreter and target text receiver. The key features of her model, as shown in Figure 5.8, are communicative "intention" (and, on the receiver side, "function"), "situation", "socio-cultural context", "knowledge" and "text".

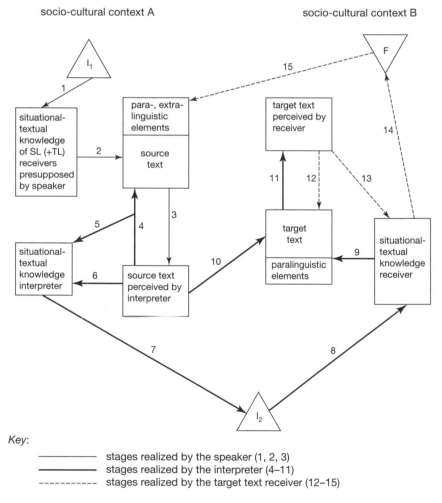

Figure 5.8 Stenzl's communicative information flow model (from Stenzl 1983: 45)

According to Stenzl's (1983: 46f) description of the fifteen stages, or "steps," in the flow of communication, a speaker from socio-cultural context A defines the communicative intention I_1, assesses the receiver's situational and textual knowledge (step 1), and constructs and utters (steps 2 and 3) the source message. The latter consists of linguistic as well as para- and extra-linguistic elements (e.g. intonation, gestures, visual means, etc.) and is linked to the receiver's presupposed knowledge. The acoustic and visual signals of the source message are perceived by the interpreter (step 4) and processed together with situational and textual information (step 6) to yield I_2 (step 7), the interpreter's communicative intention as a reflection of I_1. Assessing the receiver's situational and textual knowledge (step 8), the interpreter constructs and emits the target message (steps 9 and 11), which consists of linguistic and paralinguistic elements and may also include elements transferred from the source text with minimal processing (step 10). The receiver processes the target text – as well as some information perceived directly from the speaker (step 15) – by drawing on situational and textual knowledge (step 13) and performs the communicative function F (step 14).

Although designed for simultaneous interpreting, Stenzl's model covers considerable ground as a general account of the communicative flow in interpreting. The model depicts processing stages as a number of discrete "steps," but Stenzl (1983: 47) points out that these are characterized by "considerable interaction and simultaneity". Indeed, her dynamic flow model is as much an interaction model as it is a processing model, representing not only the 'interactants' and what is going on *between* them, but also (some of) the processes going on *within* the interpreter.

A related conception of knowledge-based text production and comprehension in interpreting was proposed by Sylvia **Kalina** (1998). Inspired by discourse models of monolingual communication, Kalina's model focuses not so much on the dynamic but on the **cognitive** dimension of **text processing**. It represents "communicative mediation" as a text/discourse-based process which begins with a speaker's mental discourse model and leads to a mental discourse model constructed by a target-language addressee on the basis of linguistic knowledge and world/situation knowledge (Figure 5.9).

Concepts of text and discourse processing have been applied to interpreting also by Basil **Hatim** and Ian **Mason** (1997). As part of their general discourse framework for the analysis of Translation, Hatim and Mason use three key concepts of discourse theory for a tripartite model to distinguish different types of interpreting: the dimensions of "texture", "structure" and "context" are seen, respectively, as most significant to input processing in simultaneous, consecutive, and liaison interpreting (1997/2002: 256f).

5.4 Processing models

While many models at the interactional and textual levels are not necessarily geared to a particular type of interpreting, processing models have mostly been designed for the simultaneous mode. Whether addressing the issue of **multiple task**

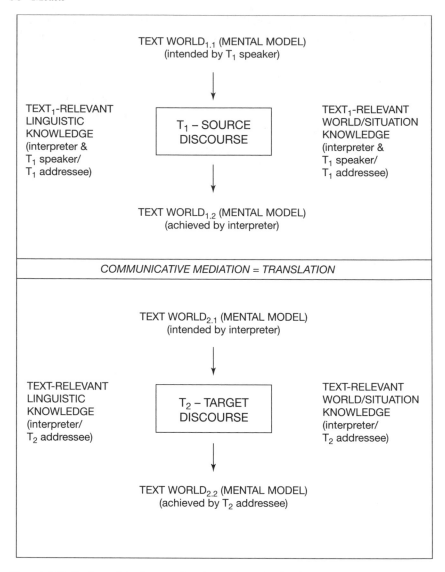

TEXT WORLD$_{1.1}$ (MENTAL MODEL)
(intended by T$_1$ speaker)

TEXT$_1$-RELEVANT
LINGUISTIC
KNOWLEDGE
(interpreter &
T$_1$ speaker/
T$_1$ addressee)

T$_1$ – SOURCE
DISCOURSE

TEXT$_1$-RELEVANT
WORLD/SITUATION
KNOWLEDGE
(interpreter &
T$_1$ speaker/
T$_1$ addressee)

TEXT WORLD$_{1.2}$ (MENTAL MODEL)
(achieved by interpreter)

COMMUNICATIVE MEDIATION = TRANSLATION

TEXT WORLD$_{2.1}$ (MENTAL MODEL)
(intended by interpreter)

TEXT-RELEVANT
LINGUISTIC
KNOWLEDGE
(interpreter/
T$_2$ addressee)

T$_2$ – TARGET
DISCOURSE

TEXT-RELEVANT
WORLD/SITUATION
KNOWLEDGE
(interpreter/
T$_2$ addressee)

TEXT WORLD$_{2.2}$ (MENTAL MODEL)
(achieved by T$_2$ addressee)

Figure 5.9 Kalina's model of comprehension and production in interpreting (from Kalina
1998: 109)

performance in general (» 5.4.2) or the specific **processing stages** and **mental
structures** involved (» 5.4.3), reference is made mainly to the process of
simultaneous interpreting. An exception is early models of the interpreting process
whose focus is on the nature of the **translational process** (» 5.4.1).

5.4.1 *Translational process*

The earliest and most general description of the processes assumed to take place in interpreting goes back to **Herbert** (1952: 9), who asserted that "interpretation really consists of three distinct parts: (*a*) understanding; (*b*) conversion; (*c*) delivery". However, Herbert's discussion of the central translational component was limited to language-related issues and questions of interpreting technique, with little reference to the underlying mental processes.

The interpreter who most famously ventured into a more cognitive analysis of the task was **Seleskovitch** (« 2.2.1). In an essay published ten years after Herbert's *Handbook*, Seleskovitch (1962: 16) posited that the 'mechanism' of (consecutive as well as simultaneous) interpreting was "a triangular process", at the pinnacle of which was the construct of **sense** (Figure 5.10).

According to this model, the essential process at work in Translation is not linguistic "transcoding" (which is limited to items with fixed correspondences like proper names, numbers and specialized terms) but the interpreter's understanding and expression of "sense" (« 3.2.6). "Sense," according to Seleskovitch (1978b: 336), is (1) "conscious", (2) "made up of the linguistic meaning aroused by speech sounds and of a cognitive addition to it" and (3) "nonverbal", that is, dissociated from any linguistic form in cognitive memory. The idea that translational processes are essentially based on language-free ("deverbalized") utterance meaning rather than linguistic conversion procedures ("transcoding") is the cornerstone of the interpretive theory of Translation championed by the Paris School (« 2.3.3, « 4.2).

Given its high level of abstraction as a general model of Translation, the triangular process model by Seleskovitch left ample room for further elaboration (see e.g. Laplace 1994: 230). With reference to psycholinguistic research, **García-Landa** (1981) fleshed out the triangular model as two **acts of discourse** linked together by the principle of "equivalence of sense", that is, the speaker's intention for the original act of discourse equals the interpreter's perception of the intended sense, which in turn becomes the interpreter's intention for the target discourse, which equals the client's perception of the intended sense. (For a more elaborate

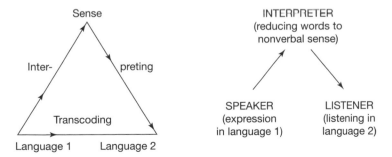

Figure 5.10 Seleskovitch's triangular model (two versions) (from Seleskovitch and Lederer 1984: 185, 168)

pseudo-mathematical formulation of this equation, see García-Landa 1998.) García-Landa (1981) offers an enriched conceptualization which involves attention thresholds, memory structures (working memory, long-term memory activation), discourse components and situational variables to reflect the processes of discourse comprehension and production. In a similar vein, Betty **Colonomos** (see Ingram 1985: 99) drew up a model centered on the **formless** conceptual **message** and featuring various (short-term and long-term) memory, monitoring and feedback operations. The model by Colonomos, which was complemented by a variant representing the process of transliteration, proved influential particularly in the American sign language interpreting community and its training initiatives (see Baker-Shenk 1990).

5.4.2 *Multiple tasks*

Departing, as did García-Landa (1981), from the triangular process model of the *théorie du sens*, **Lederer** (1981) developed a more detailed model of simultaneous interpreting involving **eight mental operations**, with two or more running concurrently at any time. Lederer (1981: 50) distinguishes three types of operations depending on their manifestation over time:

- Continuous successive and concurrent operations

  - listening
  - language comprehension
  - conceptualization (i.e. constructing a cognitive memory by integrating linguistic input with prior knowledge)
  - expression from cognitive memory

- Continuous 'underlying' operations with intermittent manifestation

  - awareness of situation
  - self-monitoring

- Intermittent operations

  - transcoding
  - retrieval of specific lexical expressions

While Lederer also relates the main processing stages – perception of linguistic input, conceptualization, expression – to the function of working memory and long-term memory, her model of the interpreting process and its main components is rather holistic. The same can be said about the model of simultaneous interpreting proposed by **Kirchhoff** (see p. 112 in the *Reader*). Couched in the terminology of information theory, the basic process model includes "decoding", "recoding", "production", and "monitoring". In addition, Kirchhoff posits a more complex variant involving short-term storage of input segments in memory, particularly to account for syntactic divergence between the source and target languages. In this respect, and on the whole, Kirchhoff's **multi-phase model** reflects a concern with linguistic surface structure, in stark contrast to the focus on conceptual processing in the *théorie du sens*. What is more, Kirchhoff's aim is not to model the process of 'interpreting at its best' but to account for psycholinguistic **processing difficulties**. Relating her multi-tasking model to the psychological processing constraints of the interpreter, Kirchhoff's analysis focuses on such notions as "cognitive load" and "processing capacity". On the assumption that individual task components require a certain (and variable) amount of processing capacity, Kirchhoff discusses instances in which the interpreting process yields less than perfect results, involving linguistic infelicities, distortions and loss of information: "Multiple-task performance becomes a problem if task completion requires cognitive decisions which, in sum, reach or even exceed the individual's processing capacity limit" (1976/2002: 118).

This issue is also at the heart of the **Effort models** of interpreting formulated by **Gile** (1985, 1997/2002). Assuming three basic efforts, labeled "listening and analysis" (L), "production" (P), and "memory" (M), Gile (1985) originally used his effort model of simultaneous interpreting to express the basic tenet that there is only a limited amount of mental "energy" (or processing capacity) available for the interpreter's processing effort, and that the sum of the three efforts must not exceed the interpreter's processing capacity:

$$(L + P + M) < C_{apacity}$$

In subsequent refinements of the model, a "coordination effort" (C) was added, and the relationships between the model components were expressed in a set of formulas and relationships as follows (see Gile 1997/2002: 165):

(1) $SI = L + P + M + C$ 'Simultaneous interpreting modeled as a process consisting of the three main efforts plus a coordination effort.'

(2) $TR = LR + MR + PR + CR$ 'Total processing capacity requirements are a (not necessarily arithmetic) sum of individual processing capacity requirements.'

(3) $LA \geq LR$,
(4) $MA \geq MR$,
(5) $PA \geq PR$, and
(6) $CA \geq CR$ 'The capacity available for each effort must be equal to or larger than its requirements for the task at hand.'

(7) $TA \geq TR$	'Total available capacity must be at least equal to total requirements.'

Gile uses his effort model of simultaneous interpreting as well as the variants formulated for consecutive interpreting and simultaneous interpreting with text (see Gile 1997/2002: 167ff) to account for a number of processing difficulties and failures. On the assumption, also known as the "tightrope hypothesis" (Gile 1999b), that interpreters, particularly in the simultaneous mode, usually work at the limit of their processing capacity, Gile uses his model to explain the effect of "problem triggers" such as proper names, numbers and compound technical terms, which may result in "failure sequences" and require special "coping tactics" (see Gile 1995b, 1997/2002 for an extensive discussion).

The models reviewed here, all of them developed by interpreters rather than cognitive scientists, are at an intermediate level of specificity, between models of the basic translational process and more detailed representations of psycholinguistic operations. They focus on the simultaneity of task components and do not make specific claims regarding the ontology and 'architecture' of their components, that is, the existence and interplay in the brain of particular mental structures and procedures. The latter are the mainstay of language processing research in the cognitive sciences, which has provided foundations for various detailed models of the complex psycholinguistic processing operations in (simultaneous) interpreting.

5.4.3 Complex operations

The very first psychological processing model for simultaneous interpreting was developed by **Gerver** (1971). On the basis of his experimental findings regarding interpreters' time lag, memory use and output monitoring, Gerver drew up a **flow-chart model** of the **mental structures and procedures** involved in input processing and output generation. (For a graphic representation, see p. 151 in the *Reader* or Gerver 1975, 1976.) The model features memory structures (short-term buffer store, long-term memory system, output buffer) and procedures at the control of the interpreter, such as discarding of input, pre-testing of output, output monitoring and 'back-tracking' (reprocessing) to improve previous output. Source-language input is received in buffer storage and subjected to "input routines" depending on the state of the buffer store and on the interpreter's segmentation strategy. Through a process of "active reinstatement", linguistic knowledge in the interpreter's long-term memory becomes available in a short-term "operational memory" or "working memory" which serves the processing operations involved in source-language "decoding" and target-language "encoding". Maintenance in operational memory is also a prerequisite for monitoring and self-correction procedures which Gerver views as integral parts of the process and as particularly vulnerable to temporary shortages of processing capacity.

Gerver's model, which aims at a psychological rather than a linguistic description of the interpreting process, is not very explicit about translational processes as such. Even so, Gerver clearly distinguishes linguistic surface elements (sounds, words, sentences) from the "deep" level of meaning as understood by the interpreter, and suggests that grasping the relational meaning structure (subject, predicate, object) may be crucial to the translational task. While not incorporating it as an explicit feature in his model, Gerver also acknowledges the potential role of expectation-based processing, which is central to the model by Chernov (1978) discussed below.

Another model of **memory structures and processing operations** in simultaneous interpreting was devised by Barbara **Moser** in the mid-1970s. (For a graphic representation, see pp. 152f in the *Reader*; see also Moser-Mercer 1997.) Moser's (1978) model, which is based on a psycholinguistic model of speech comprehension, devotes considerable attention to input processing stages up to the level of meaningful phrases and sentences, but also reflects the assumption of a close interaction between the input-driven sequential process and knowledge in long-term memory. Pivotal features of Moser's model are the search for the "conceptual base" and the construction of a prelinguistic meaning structure with the help of various types of knowledge (conceptual network, contextual knowledge, general knowledge). The conceptual meaning base then serves to activate target-language elements for syntactic and semantic word and phrase processing on the way to output articulation. The model posits a number of decision points at which processing is either moved on or looped back to an earlier stage. One of these decision points concerns "prediction", which allows for the elimination of all processing stages except feature detection up to the activation of target-language elements. Moser (1978) assumes a high degree of interaction between bottom-up and top-down processes (» 6.3) and also discusses trade-offs between the operations or stages competing for available processing capacity.

More than any other author, **Chernov** (1978, 1979/2002) viewed expectation based processing, or prediction, as fundamental to the (simultaneous) interpreting process. Using the redundancy of natural languages as his point of departure, Chernov emphasizes the distinction between message elements that are new ("rhematic") versus those that are already known ("thematic"), and argues that the interpreter's attention is focused on components that carry new information. Such "information density peaks" are processed by marshaling available knowledge in a mechanism of **probability prediction** which operates concurrently on different levels of processing – from the syllable, word, phrase and utterance to the levels of the text and situational context. In Chernov's model, redundancy-based anticipation of sound patterns, grammatical structures, semantic structures and message sense is the essential mechanism underlying the comprehension process. On the production side, Chernov posits an analogous mechanism of **anticipatory synthesis**, which dovetails with the knowledge-based processes of comprehension. This focus on message sense construed with the help of knowledge-based expectation patterns suggests a basic compatibility of Chernov's model with both the *théorie du sens* and models such as Moser's which incorporate insights on knowledge structures from cognitive science.

The fundamental importance of knowledge-driven ('top-down') processing is also reflected in the sequential model by **Cokely** (1992a), which gives explicit consideration to the modality of input and output (spoken or signed) as well as to various **sociolinguistic** and **cultural** as well as **psychological factors** involved in the interpreting process. Cokely posits a total of seven major processing stages leading from message reception to production (Figure 5.11).

Aside from the main process sequence ("message reception" – "preliminary processing" – "short-term message retention" – "semantic intent realization" – "semantic equivalence determination" – "syntactic message formulation" – "message production"), Cokely devotes considerable space in his model to the many types of knowledge in long-term memory which are brought to bear on the various processing stages. Thus the stages of semantic and syntactic output generation involve such factors as "cross-linguistic awareness", "cross-cultural awareness", "linguistic markers" and "social markers", which Cokely (1992a: 125f) admits have yet to be subjected to more detailed analysis and validation.

Validation and testing (» 5.5), which constitute a fundamental challenge for theoretical models, come naturally, as it were, to models designed for a **computer**-based **implementation** of interpreting operations. The simultaneous interpreting system designed by Artificial Intelligence researcher Deryle **Lonsdale** (1997) comprises a limited-capacity working memory, comprehension and production modules for generating "semantic trees" and "parse trees" and an inter-lingual mapping system. Though focusing on low-level processing operations such as parsing and ambiguity resolution, Lonsdale also envisages a "dialogue processing system" in the form of a database of pragmatic factors (knowledge about the speaker and the situation, cooperative maxims, etc.) which provides context for the processing of individual utterances.

A full-scale implementation of dialogue interpreting was described by Hiroaki **Kitano** (1993), whose speech-to-speech automatic translation system DMDIALOG is designed to handle simple telephone conversations. The model assumes a high degree of interaction between a central knowledge base and the various processing stages (discourse processing – analysis – generation – voice synthesis), and foregrounds the role of hypothesis-building in speech processing. Kitano's is a hybrid system comprising both a symbolic (information-processing) component (for rule-based operations like sentence parsing) and a connectionist network for top-down processing in the form of pattern matching against previously encountered phrases and sentences stored in a database. Kitano (1993) characterizes his model as a "massively parallel" system, thus highlighting the connectionist aspect of its architecture (see also Moser-Mercer 1997, Setton 2003b).

Connectionism (« 3.2.5) also underlies the theoretical model described by **González** *et al.* (1991) in their comprehensive textbook on court interpreting. Taking note of the models by Gerver, Moser and Cokely, the authors propose an updated human information-processing model which seeks to account for

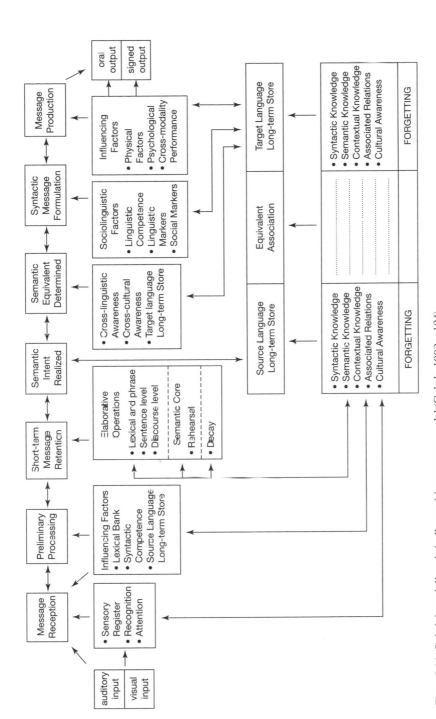

Figure 5.11 Cokely's sociolinguistically sensitive process model (Cokely 1992a: 124)

unconscious processing operations and multiple simultaneity. Their highly complex "non-linear" conceptualization of **Simultaneous Human Information Processing** is an attempt to reconcile connectionist neural models of cognitive functions with the specific translational norms of court interpreting (» 7.4.1). In view of these rather broad aspirations for their model, González *et al.* (1991: 358) acknowledge the lack of research verifying their "seemingly untestable theories".

A connectionist model backed by findings from neurolinguistic research, particularly on bilingual aphasia, was proposed by Michel **Paradis** (1994). His model of simultaneous interpreting (Figure 5.12) features memory buffers (circles), processing mechanisms (squares) and non-linguistic mental representations (diamonds), and highlights the **multiple simultaneity** of **segment-by-segment processing operations** at any given point in time.

The flow-chart representation of phrase processing in simultaneous interpreting shows each chunk (i.e. syntactic phrase and/or semantic unit) passing through eight steps: echoic memory, linguistic decoding, meaning representation, target-language encoding, target-language output, own output in echoic memory, linguistic decoding of own output, and meaning representation of own output (for comparison with the meaning constructed from source-language input). What is not evident from Paradis's parallel sequential flow-chart representation are the connectionist neurolinguistic assumptions underlying his model – the so-called "subset hypothesis" and the "activation threshold hypothesis" as well as the distinction between implicit linguistic competence and metalinguistic knowledge (» 6.1.3).

A process model which is largely compatible with both connectionist and rule-based computational approaches but essentially focuses on the level of **inter-mediate** cognitive **representation** of meaning was proposed by **Setton** (1999) in his relevance-theoretical ("cognitive-pragmatic") analysis of SI. Characterized by its author as "a hybrid of best available theories" (1999: 63), Setton's processing model incorporates a range of cognitive-scientific research to address all relevant aspects of comprehension, memory and production in simultaneous interpreting (Figure 5.13).

Though depicted as a sequential structure, from the sensorimotor level of audiovisual input processing (bottom-left) via concurrent meaning assembly and formulation controlled by a (working-memory-based) "Executive" (top center) on to output parsing and articulation (bottom-right), Setton conceptualizes all the processes as variably superimposed. Most importantly, "context" (i.e. all accessible knowledge) is assumed to play an integral part at all stages of cognitive processing, hence the pivotal role of the "task-oriented mental model" in adaptive memory. The mental model, which is sourced by both situational and world knowledge, shares with the "Assembler" a "language of representation" which encodes meaning in terms of propositions and attitudes. It is this operationalization of intermediate representations that permits Setton (1998/2002, 1999) to carry out a "blow-by-blow micro-analysis" of various discourse phenomena which had been left unaccounted for in previous cognitive (rather than cognitive-linguistic) processing models of SI.

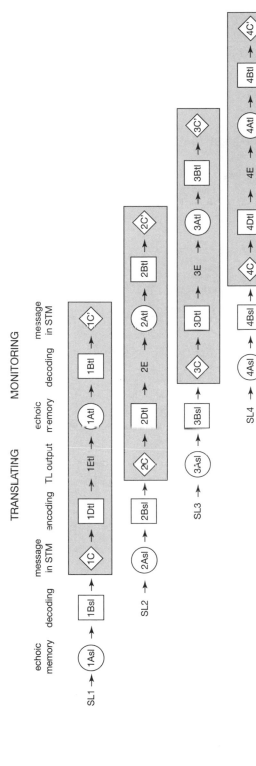

Figure 5.12 Paradis's flow-chart model of simultaneous interpreting (Paradis 2000: 24)

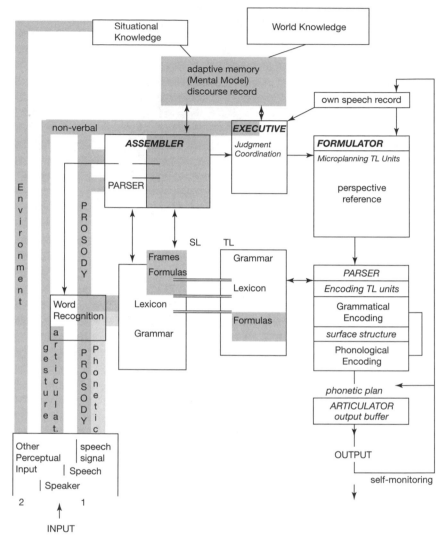

Figure 5.13 Setton's processing model for simultaneous interpreting (Setton 1999: 65)

5.5 Models, tests and applications

The models reviewed here, although representing only a selection of the modeling efforts in various conceptual dimensions, testify to the complex and multi-faceted nature of interpreting. Aspects of society and culture, social institutions, settings and situations, purposes of interaction, features of text and discourse, mental structures and neurophysiological processes are shown to be involved in inter-preting as a communicative activity and process. Therefore, no single model, however complex and elaborate, could hope to be validated as an account for the phenomenon as a whole, that is, for 'interpreting as such'. This holds true for descriptive as well as explanatory models, and all the more so for predictive models which, as stated at the outset, need to account for all relevant variables at a sufficient level of detail.

Depending on the type of model and on the scholar's, or researcher's, epistemological position, a model can be 'tested' conceptually or in relation to specific empirical data. For predictive models, in particular, experimental testing is often viewed as the method of choice, even though it confronts the researcher with a paradoxical difficulty: given the complexity of the phenomenon, models should be as 'complete' as possible; the more complete the model, though, the more difficult its experimental validation. Cokely, for instance, whose model of seven main processing stages is complemented by a long list of highly abstract "subprocesses" (see Figure 5.11), points out that "it is not clear that the procedure used to validate the major stages in the process would be the appropriate one to use in validating sub-processes" (1992a: 125f). This problem is also acknowledged by Setton (1999: 64):

> It is fair to say that in the current state of knowledge, our assumptions about the workings of peripheral systems, like word recognition and articulation, are more secure than those concerning central processes, which are less accessible to experimentation.

Rather than experimentation in the classic sense of hypothesis testing in a controlled laboratory environment, the methodological option for models chosen by authors such as Cokely and Setton is therefore close observation and analysis of a textual corpus generated in authentic or simulated interpreting sessions. Considering the numerous variables involved in real-life data, however, such analyses cannot strictly 'test' the model. Rather, they will serve to demonstrate the usefulness of the model in guiding the researcher's description and explanation of the empirical data.

A more stringent approach to the testing of models is to instantiate them as computer programs. The simulation by Lonsdale (1997) highlights the potential of computer modeling as well as its limitations, particularly regarding the role of knowledge-based processes and the multi-medial nature of discourse. More holistic models, such as the Seleskovitch triangle or Gile's Effort models, have been applied successfully to experimentally generated empirical data. Clearly, though, such studies (e.g. Seleskovitch 1975, Gile 1999b) can validate only the principle underlying the model, which after all is not detailed enough to reflect real-time processing events.

Generally speaking, experimental hypothesis testing, which is the method of choice in disciplines like cognitive psychology and psycholinguistics that have provided the foundations for most processing models of interpreting, does not seem to be a viable option for testing 'full-process' models of interpreting as a whole. Hence the importance of 'partial models' which single out particular aspects and components for specific analysis. Since there are likely to be as many of these submodels of interpreting as attempts to tackle particular research problems, it would be impossible to offer even a selective overview. Some of the prime examples are models of comprehension processes (e.g. Mackintosh 1985) and working memory (e.g. Darò 1994, Padilla *et al.* 1995, Shlesinger 2000a, Liu 2001), which will come up in the review of selected research in Chapter 6.

Apart from their application to experimental research and corpus-based fieldwork, models have also played a prominent role with regard to training. Indeed, several models, most notably Gile's, were originally conceived for didactic purposes and applied to research only later. Conversely, models such as Moser's were initially developed in the context of 'basic research' and subsequently came to be applied to pedagogical issues such as aptitude testing (» 9.2.2) and skill acquisition. Regardless of their nature and orientation, however, models clearly play a crucial role in the process of systematic inquiry. The present review of selected models and modeling approaches, which concludes Part I of this book, should therefore serve as an ideal point of departure for the more detailed exploration of research in Part II.

Summary

Models, as representations of a phenomenon made up of components and relations holding between them, can be devised for interpreting in various conceptual dimensions, ranging from the broader *anthropological, socio-professional* and *institutional* levels to the *interactional* and *textual* levels and the 'internal' levels of *cognitive* and *neural* processes. Efforts to model interpreting date back to the 1970s and reflect a primary concern with aspects of communicative *interaction* and cognitive *processing*. In the former dimension, *constellation* models (e.g. by R.B.W. Anderson, Gile, Wadensjö, Alexieva) seek to represent the interactants and the relations holding between them in the communicative event, whereas models such as those by Kirchhoff, Ingram and Poyatos focus on the nature and flow of *communication* signals, and Stenzl's and Kalina's foreground the role of knowledge and *text* in communicative interaction. Models focusing on cognitive processes, on the other hand, are aimed either at a more or less holistic representation of processing phases or *tasks* (e.g. Seleskovitch, Lederer, Kirchhoff, Gile) or at a detailed breakdown of psycholinguistic operations in terms of hypothesized *mental structures and procedures* (e.g. Gerver, Moser, Cokely, Paradis, Setton). Given the complexity of the phenomenon, models of interpreting can hardly be comprehensive and are thus difficult to 'verify' by their predictive power. Rather, most models of interpreting primarily aim to describe and explain, and are thus 'validated' by their usefulness in guiding teaching and further inquiry.

Sources and further reading

For a review of (processing) models in conference interpreting, see Part 3 of the *Reader* and Setton (2003b). For further details on the models reviewed in this chapter, see the respective references in the text.

Suggestions for further study

– To what extent can models foregrounding a given conceptual dimension (e.g. interactional, textual) be said to be compatible with conceptualizations at other levels of modeling?
– Which features of different interpreting models, in the sphere of interaction as well as cognitive processing, can be identified as shared conceptual ground?
– How does the meaning of key concepts such as 'speaker', 'situation', 'role', 'context' or 'knowledge' differ from one model to another?

Part II

Selected topics and research

6 Process

The mental processing operations performed by the interpreter, which have been of prime concern in efforts to model the phenomenon (Chapter 5), also constitute the dominant theme of empirical research. Centered on the cognitive processing of language, the topics and findings reviewed in this chapter are of a distinctly inter-disciplinary nature. Most process-oriented research draws on insights and methods from the cognitive sciences and focuses on spoken-language conference interpreting in the simultaneous mode.

6.1 Bilingualism

The use of two (or more) languages (bilingualism, polyglossia) is a phenomenon which is open to a range of linguistic, psychological and sociological research perspectives. A distinction is usually made between the use of two or more languages in a society ('societal bilingualism') and bilinguality in the individual. The latter, which involves such aspects as second-language acquisition, bilingual processing and language switching, was explored early on with reference to translation and interpreting.

6.1.1 Linguistic dominance

As early as the 1950s, psychologists in North America, chief among them Canadian psychologist Wallace E. Lambert, measured the reaction time of bilinguals on word-translation tasks to establish the degree of automaticity of **verbal behavior** in either language (usually French and English) and thus distinguish between **balanced vs dominant** bilinguals. Unlike other experimental tasks, facility of translation yielded a contradictory pattern of results, with some subjects translating faster into their acquired (non-dominant) language. Lambert *et al.* (1959: 81) speculated that this effect might be due to an individual's **active** vs **passive** approach to second language acquisition (as reflected also in the AIIC classification of conference interpreters' working languages), and pointed to the significance of motivational, attitudinal and cultural factors shaping a person's bilinguality. In more recent psycholinguistic experiments with word translation to address the issue of 'translation asymmetry' (e.g. de Bot 2000), reaction times were found to be consistently longer for translation from the dominant into the weaker language, and the effect of the direction of translation diminished with increasing proficiency in the acquired language.

An influential acquisition-related hypothesis which has been applied to bilinguality and translation is the distinction of **compound vs coordinate** bilinguals introduced in the 1950s. This theory holds that compound bilinguals, who learned both their languages in a single context of acquisition, have two sets of linguistic signs for a single set of representational meanings, whereas coordinate bilinguals have separate sets of linguistic signs as well as somewhat different sets of representational meanings as a result of different socio-cultural contexts of acquisition. According to some psychologists, the latter is typical of "true bilinguals" and a prerequisite for "true cross-cultural translation" (Ervin and Osgood 1965: 143). In one of the few empirical contributions on the subject, Christopher Thiéry, in his 1975 doctoral dissertation, surveyed four dozen fellow AIIC members with a double-A language classification and analyzed the acquisition histories and language-use patterns of thirty-four respondents. Thiéry (1978) concluded that **true bilinguals** have two 'mother tongues', acquired before or at puberty, and need to make a conscious effort to retain their true bilingualism in adult life.

6.1.2 Cerebral lateralization

Another approach to bilinguality which bears on the issue of linguistic dominance concerns the **neurophysiological foundations** of linguistic functions in bilinguals as studied by neuropsychologists in general and researchers in the NL paradigm of interpreting studies in particular (« 4.4.2). Departing from the fact that the left cerebral hemisphere is specialized for language (in right-handed individuals), research since the late 1970s has sought to establish whether individuals with a command of more than one language, including interpreters, exhibit a characteristic pattern of cerebral **lateralization**. Neuropsychological studies have yielded some, albeit contradictory, evidence of a more balanced neurolinguistic representation (i.e. of greater right-hemisphere involvement in bilinguals and polyglots) associated with factors like the age of acquisition (i.e. early vs late bilinguals), relative language proficiency, sex, and spoken vs signed language (e.g. Corina and Vaid 1994). For interpreters, in particular, Franco Fabbro and associates (see Fabbro and Gran 1994) found more bilateral cerebral involvement during verbal processing in the simultaneous mode. The overall picture, however, is clouded by statistical limitations and uncertainties regarding experimental tasks and designs. Results achieved for certain subject groups with experimental techniques such as dichotic listening or 'finger-tapping' (see Fabbro and Gran 1994) are difficult to compare with findings from electroencephalographic analyses (e.g. Petsche *et al.* 1993) or brain imaging studies (e.g. Rinne *et al.* 2000). In one of the most methodologically rigorous studies in this paradigm, Green *et al.* (1994) found no evidence to support the hypothesis, fielded by Fabbro and associates, that simultaneous interpreters may develop a different, less asymmetrical pattern of cerebral lateralization. Rather, evidence of more right-hemisphere involvement has been explained by attentional strategies and recourse to nonverbal (pragmatic) knowledge, particularly when using an acquired language.

6.1.3 Neurolinguistic mechanisms

Apart from neuropsychological experimentation, neurolinguists have used clinical data on **aphasia** (i.e. linguistic impairment caused by cerebral lesions) in bilingual and polyglot individuals to develop explanatory hypotheses for translational behavior (see Fabbro and Gran 1994). Paradis (2000: 20), speaking out against the "fruitless search for a differential cerebral asymmetry", has advanced the so-called **subset hypothesis**, according to which a bilingual's two languages are subserved by two subsystems of the larger cognitive system known as "implicit linguistic competence". Each of the two separate networks of connections can be independently activated and inhibited, and the **activation threshold** of a given trace in linguistic memory is assumed to be a function of the frequency and recency of activation (see also the "gravitational model" by Gile 1995b). Paradis cites neurolinguistic evidence to suggest that interpreting involves at least four neuro-functionally independent systems – one for each language involved and one for each direction of translation – and that the process may be either conceptually mediated or based on direct linguistic correspondence. In the neural-network account proposed by Paradis (2000), simultaneous interpreters thus have to acquire a peculiar state of inhibition/activation for each of the linguistic component systems involved so as to permit concurrent use with a minimum of interference.

6.2 Simultaneity

Ever since the introduction and spread of simultaneous conference interpreting sparked off scientific interest, the issue of simultaneity has been a key topic in processing-oriented research. While simultaneity in the form of 'overlapping talk' and the interpreter's multiple involvement in the interactivity of discourse also plays a significant role in dialogue interpreting research (« 4.6), the focus here is on the 'classic' view of the problem in terms of divided attention and the synchrony of psycholinguistic operations.

6.2.1 Divided attention

Early cognitive psychologists in the 1950s and 1960s, such as Donald Broadbent and Alan Welford, worked on the long-standing assumption that **attention-sharing** is possible only for habitual, largely automatic tasks. In an experiment requiring subjects simultaneously to listen and respond to simple questions, Broadbent (1952) found that "the saying of even a simple series of words interferes with the understanding of a fresh message" and concluded that "we cannot attend perfectly to both the speech of others and to our own" (1952: 271ff). This was questioned in the 1969 PhD thesis by Ingrid Pinter (« 2.2.2), whose experiment with beginning and advanced students of interpreting as well as experienced conference interpreters clearly demonstrated the effect of practice on proficiency in the skill of simultaneous listening and speaking (see Kurz 1996). Welford's suggestion, in turn, that interpreters learned to ignore the sound of their own voices so as to avoid interference, was refuted by Gerver (1971), who pointed to self-corrections in interpreted output as evidence that simultaneous interpreters were indeed monitoring their own voices.

Gerver endorsed proposals by contemporary psychologists to replace the notion of a fixed (single) channel of limited capacity by that of a "fixed-capacity central processor", whose activity could be distributed over several tasks within the limits of the total **processing capacity** available (see 1971: 15f). This capacity-sharing approach has proved fundamental to processing models of interpreting (« 5.3) and is at the heart of recent studies on working memory in SI (» 6.4.2). While the principle of attention-sharing in the interpreting process is now beyond doubt, the details of interpreters' selective allocation, if not switching, of their attentional resources remain unclear. Gran (1989: 97), for one, hypothesized a process of alternate switching of attention between listening and target-language output, which would become more coordinated and automatic with exercise and experience.

6.2.2 Pauses and synchrony

Both interpreters and psycholinguists have suggested that the simultaneous interpreter might take advantage of pauses in the source speech to avoid the simultaneity of listening and speaking. The idea that interpreters would try to crowd as much of their output as possible into the speaker's pauses (see Paneth 1957/2002: 33, Goldman-Eisler 1967: 128) was tested in the 1969 PhD thesis by Barik (« 2.2.2). Although he found support for the hypothesis in his experimental data, Barik (1973: 263) conceded that interpreters' speech activity during source-speech pauses might also be an epiphenomenon of the task as such rather than a **strategy** to aid performance. These doubts were confirmed by Gerver (1975, 1976) on the basis of pause-time analyses of authentic conference speeches. Employing a pause criterion of 250 milliseconds, he found that most pauses in his sample (71% of 804 pauses) lasted no more than 750 milliseconds and only 17% were longer than one second. As for the interpreter's strategic behavior, Gerver (1975: 123) concluded that "there is obviously not much he can fit into most pauses, but then neither can he avoid filling them if he is already speaking." Further evidence of the essential simultaneity of speaking and listening in SI, which had also been studied by Soviet authors (e.g. Chernov 1978, Shiryayev 1979), was supplied by Ivana Čeňková in her 1985 PhD research. Based on an oscillographic analysis of 29 minutes of fieldwork data involving Russian and Czech, Čeňková (1988) reported a ratio of concurrent activity of roughly 90% for source speeches delivered at a speed of over 200 syllables per minute.

Apart from the comparative study of pause times, which has recently seen a revival thanks to the availability of computer-assisted speech data analysis (e.g. Lee 1999, Yagi 1999, Tissi 2000), the synchrony of source and target speeches in simultaneous interpreting has also been studied by comparing speech and articulation rates, the number and duration of 'speech bursts' or 'chunks' of speech between pauses, and the number of source–target 'overlap events'. The findings from such analyses are rather varied, however, given the differences in measurement techniques, pause criteria, language pairs, discourse types, and skill levels.

6.2.3 *Time lag and segmentation*

The crucial feature of synchrony in SI is the 'time lag', also known as ***décalage***, between the original speech and the interpreter's output. Paneth (« 2.2.1), stressing that "the interpreter says not what he hears, but what he has heard" (1957/2002: 32), measured lag times in fieldwork data and found average values between 2 and 4 seconds. These stopwatch measurements were confirmed by Oléron and Nanpon (1965/2002), who employed special equipment to analyze time delays on parallel visual tracings. They found mean values of 2 to 3 seconds for various language combinations in a range between 0.5 and as much as 11 seconds. The average of 2–3 seconds, or 4–5 words at average presentation rates (see Gerver 1969/ 2002), has proved highly robust (see also Lederer 1981: 290). Cokely (1992a) reported average onset lag times of 2.8 seconds (min. 1 second, max. 8 seconds) for English–ASL interpretation while pointing to a considerable spread of average lag times (min. 1.7 seconds, max. 4.8 seconds) among the six interpreters in his sample. Dörte Andres (2002) used time-coded video-recordings to study lag times in note-taking for consecutive interpreting, and found that average lag times for professional subjects working from French into German are between 3 and 6 seconds and may reach as much as 10 seconds.

Interest in simultaneous interpreters' time lag, variously referred to also as 'phase shift' or **ear–voice span** (EVS), extended beyond temporal measurements to the cognitive activity underlying the delay. In an early experiment involving constructed 100-word passages of English and French and an essentially word-based analytical approach, Anne Treisman (1965) measured the EVS of (untrained) bilingual subjects during **shadowing** (i.e. immediate verbatim repetition of the input in the same language) and simultaneous interpreting. She found the EVS to be greater for the interpreting task (4–5 words vs 3 words in shadowing) and attributed this to "the increased decision load between input and output" (1965: 369). This differential performance on a shadowing and an interpreting task was demonstrated for professional subjects by Gerver (1969/2002) and subsequently confirmed in a more ecologically valid experiment by Linda Anderson (1994), who found an average ear–voice span of 1.4 seconds for shadowing compared to nearly three seconds for SI.

A crucial aspect of decision-making in SI relates to the segmentation of the input speech into 'chunks' serving as **units of translation**. From an experiment involving six professionals interpreting short (3–6 min) speeches in three language combinations, Goldman-Eisler (1972/2002) concluded that EVS units were not of a lexical but of a syntactic nature. EVS units mostly consisted of at least a complete predicative expression (noun phrase + verb phrase), with the verb phrase (predicate) playing a crucial part. Having identified propositional meaning units as the main psycholinguistic correlate of EVS, Goldman-Eisler nevertheless observed that interpreters' **chunking** behavior in output production did not follow the sequence of the input segments. Rather than "identity" between input and output chunks, Goldman-Eisler (1972/2002) found the onset of the interpreter's output to lie either before the end of the (pause-delimited) input segment ("fission") or after two or more chunks of input ("fusion"). Apart from her detailed consideration of the **language factor**, Goldman-Eisler (1972/2002: 73) briefly made reference also to factors like the "nature of the message" and the interpreter's capacity or **preference** for storing or **anticipating** input information (» 6.7.3). The fact that simultaneous interpreters might opt for various patterns of timing as a matter of personal preference, technique or strategy had been suggested early on by Paneth (1957/2002) and was found also in studies with sign language interpreters (Llewellyn-Jones 1981, Cokely 1992a). In a recent study by Benedetta Tissi (2000), the output of ten recently graduated subjects who simultaneously interpreted two German source texts into Italian was found to reflect highly individual pausing patterns, thus pointing to the role of subject-specific determinants of temporal target-text characteristics.

6.3 Comprehension

As a crucial topic at the interface of language and cognition, language comprehension is a primary object of study in the cognitive sciences. A basic distinction is made in research on language understanding between 'bottom-up' (i.e. input-driven) and 'top-down' (i.e. knowledge-based) operations, both of which are required for a full account of comprehension, defined here as 'the act of building a mental representation of language-mediated meaning.

6.3.1 Language understanding

Psycholinguistic research on spoken language understanding has long reflected a particular concern with the initial stages of the comprehension process. Component operations like phoneme identification, word recognition, lexical disambiguation and sentence parsing, which have been modeled in the serial information-processing as well as the connectionist paradigm of cognitive science, are naturally relevant, though hardly unique, to interpreting. Indeed, with the significant exception of speech recognition research in the context of automatic interpreting (» 8.5.3), very little interpreting-specific work has been done on the so-called **low-level processes** in language comprehension. An interesting approach was taken from the perspective of second-language acquisition research by Robert McAllister (2000), who studied (inferior) comprehension performance in an acquired language; another is psychological research on interpreters' specialized **lexical skills** in tasks like word identification and categorization, for which Bajo *et al.* (2000) found a presumably training-related superiority among interpreters in contrast to bilingual controls. In general, however, interpreting scholars, particularly in the IT paradigm, have shown little interest in the lower-level stages of language understanding as studied in the psycholinguist's laboratory. Their main interest has rather been in the way interpreters comprehend utterance meaning ('sense') in situated discourse by drawing on their contextual, situational and encyclopedic knowledge.

6.3.2 *Knowledge-based processing*

It is now an established fact that comprehension is not a passive, receptive process but depends crucially on what is already known. Processing new information thus requires the active construction of some form of mental representation by integrating the input with various kinds of pre-existing knowledge – lexical, syntactic, pragmatic, encyclopedic, etc. The so-called cloze technique, developed in the early 1950s, is based on such a knowledge-based conception of comprehension: confronted with gaps in verbal structures, subjects will use their lexical and grammatical knowledge to fill in what is missing by a process of anticipatory reconstruction or pattern-based 'closure'. The fact that prior knowledge serves to generate **expectations** which guide the comprehension process was demonstrated early on for SI. Chernov (« 2.3.2) had eleven professional interpreters work on realistic 20-minute speeches (United Nations speeches, lectures) that had been manipulated to include meaningless (i.e. semantically anomalous) sentences and unpredictable turns of phrase (i.e. utterances which defied the phrasal expectations generated by their preceding context). Most subjects omitted or mistranslated the anomalous sentences and rendered the unpredictable utterances according to the contextually prompted expectation (see Chernov 1979/2002: 100). Chernov thus identified the principle of subjective redundancy and, hence, **predictability** of contextualized utterances as crucial to the comprehension process, and made "probability prediction" the core of his processing model of SI (« 5.4.3).

Using the linguistic notions of theme and rheme to refer to 'given vs new' information, Chernov modeled the semantic level of comprehension as a process of "cumulative dynamic analysis" resulting in "sense structures". On the whole, he described the dynamic process of **understanding** as covering (1) the gradual addition of rhematic components to those already foregrounded; (2) the bridging of sense gaps; (3) the combination of rhematic and thematic components to form more complex configurations, and (4) the moulding of the resulting sense structure to fit the situational context and the hearer's knowledge (see Chernov 1979/2002: 104f). Chernov's approach is largely compatible with state-of-the-art models of discourse comprehension. With reference to the influential model by van Dijk and Kintsch (1983), for instance, Chernov's account can be related to (1) building a **propositional textbase**, (2) **inferencing**, (3) building **macro-structures** (macro-processing) and (4) building a **situation model**. Some of these notions have been taken up in research on comprehension in interpreting.

In one of the most extensive experimental studies on the topic to date, Mike Dillinger (1994) used a proposition score to compare comprehension processes in untrained bilinguals and professional interpreters. His study, which addressed a number of relevant input variables such as text type and information density (» 6.6.4), yielded little evidence of interpreting-specific comprehension skills, possibly for reasons of experimental design. Beyond a quantitative propositional approach, Mackintosh (1985) pointed to the relevance of macro-processing operations such as 'deletion', 'generalization' and 'construction' in both simultaneous and consecutive interpreting, and Pöchhacker (1993) discussed interpreters' use of **knowledge structures** like 'frames', 'scripts' and 'MOPs' to make inferences and build **mental models** of message content. Isham and Lane (1994), who investigated comprehension in signed language interpreting by using a cloze task requiring inferences, found that subjects who had interpreted (rather than transliterated) the English input passages and thus processed them at a more conceptual level were better able to draw the necessary inferences.

Just what level or **conceptual depth** of comprehension is required for interpreting remains a moot point, not least because of the methodological difficulty of measuring the level of "operational comprehension" (Gile 1993: 67) during interpreting. One of the few attempts to address the contentious dichotomy between language-based 'transcoding' and 'deverbalization'-based interpreting on the basis of experimental research was made by William Isham (1994), who replicated the so-called Jarvella effect (i.e. the impact of syntactic boundaries on verbatim recall of the most recent clause) in a study involving nine English/French professional interpreters and twelve bilingual controls. Isham found that some of the interpreters displayed a similar recall pattern to listeners, whereas others showed inferior verbatim recall and appeared to be oblivious to syntactic boundaries. He concluded that both a more **form-based** approach and a **meaning-based** strategy (» 6.7.4) may be viable in particular language pairs.

Most work on the psychology of discourse comprehension has been concerned with monologic texts (as prevalent in SI) rather than interactive discourse in social situations. Here again, Chernov (1994: 144f) pointed to promising avenues of research by emphasizing the role of situational and **pragmatic inferences** and the need for sociolinguistic studies, which have indeed come to the fore in the study of dialogue interpreting (« 4.6). In conference interpreting, Setton's (1998/2002, 1999) *cognitive-pragmatic analysis* of interpreted discourse data has gone farthest in merging the cognitive-psycholinguistic and pragmatic-sociolinguistic dimensions of comprehension.

6.4 Memory

The modern conception of memory for the mental representation of sensory input emerged in the mid-twentieth century, when psychologists developed the hypothesis of a temporary storage system distinct from a more durable form of 'storage' based on networks of neurochemical traces or activation patterns. Various models of memory allowing for 'short-term' and 'long-term' storage have since been proposed, and short-term memory resources, generally referred to as 'working memory', have emerged as a central concern in research on cognitive processing.

6.4.1 Storage and process

Early studies of cognitive operations in language processing by interpreters tested subjects for recall after interpreting and related tasks. Gerver (1974a), in an experiment with nine trainees and scripted texts, found that recall (as measured by content questions) was better after listening than after simultaneous interpreting or shadowing, and identified simultaneous listening and speaking as the cause of impaired memorization. This was confirmed in subsequent work by Isham (1994), who concluded from the differential performance of signed- and spoken-language interpreters that post-task recall was not only a function of the interpreting process itself but reflected the impact of modality-related processing interference (see also Ingram 1992: 114).

Gerver's (1974a) conclusion that superior recall after interpreting compared to shadowing was evidence of more complex, deeper processing operations in interpreting was followed up in the 1983 PhD thesis by Sylvie Lambert (1989). In the theoretical framework of the **depth-of-processing** hypothesis, put forward as a unitary model of memory in the early 1970s, Lambert compared the recall and recognition scores of sixteen subjects (eight professionals, eight trainees) following simultaneous interpreting, consecutive interpreting, shadowing and listening. While she found a less clear-cut pattern of results than Gerver (1974a), with recall scores yielding no significant differences between listening and the two interpreting conditions, shadowing resulted in significantly lower recall than listening and consecutive interpreting. Lambert found that a similar relationship held for recognition scores, particularly with regard to the post-task recognition of semantic (rather than lexical or syntactic) source-text information. In a comparable study with eleven professional sign language interpreters, Ingram (1992) found significantly lower semantic recognition scores for listening than for English–ASL simultaneous interpreting as well as for transliterating, even though the latter had been hypothesized to be a 'shallow', form-based processing task analogous to shadowing (see Isham 1994). Ingram (1992: 115) therefore concluded that "transliteration is not simply a programmed sensorimotor task but a task like interpretation that involves complex and deep cognitive processing". A similar view is also held for 'oral interpreting', or 'lipspeaking', for the benefit of hearing-impaired persons who rely on lipreading rather than sign language (Frishberg 1990: 162).

The depth-of-processing hypothesis was also used by Maurizio Viezzi (1990) to compare information retention after two forms of interpreting in the simultaneous mode – sight translation and SI. In an experiment involving eighteen professional and twenty-four student interpreters working from English or French into Italian, Viezzi found that recall scores were lower after sight translation than after SI only for the morphosyntactically dissimilar language pair (English–Italian). For structurally similar languages like French and Italian, recall after the simultaneous processing tasks was as good as after listening. Viezzi (1990) explained this deviation from previous findings (Gerver 1974a, Lambert 1989) as being due to the impact of morphosyntactic transformations on processing resources, but left unclear why this effect should obtain only for the simultaneous rendition of visual input.

The original depth-of-processing hypothesis has largely been superseded by a multiple-systems approach. In particular, the online interaction between fresh input and knowledge stored in long-term memory is seen as crucially mediated by short-term storage and processing resources, which British psychologist Alan Baddeley has conceptualized as a tripartite system of **working memory** (e.g. Baddeley 2000). This model, which underlies several recent studies of memory in interpreting, posits a limited-capacity attentional system, the "central executive," which controls two "slave systems," one for holding and dealing with speech-based information ("phonological loop") and another for visual or spatial information ("visuo-spatial sketchpad"). Another approach to working memory, which is in part compatible with Baddeley's model, is the theory of 'skilled memory,' including "long-term working memory," by Ericsson and Kintsch (1995).

6.4.2 Working memory and attention

In keeping with Baddeley's model of working memory as both a storage and an attentional control system, experimental research on memory capacity in interpreters has addressed either of these dimensions. Darò (1994), reporting results from a complex auditory shadowing experiment with three beginning and five advanced student interpreters, suggested that experience in simultaneous interpreting was associated with enhanced verbal short-term memory. Padilla *et al.* (1995) applied standard tasks for measuring memory capacity to four groups of ten subjects (trained interpreters, beginning and advanced interpreting students, and bilingual controls) and found that the professional interpreters clearly outperformed the other groups on the digit span task (i.e. memorizing auditorily presented series of up to nine digits) and on the more complex phrase span task. In order to assess whether interpreters perform differently not only in terms of **memory capacity** but also in terms of attentional coordination, the authors tested their subjects on free recall after memorizing (visually presented) word lists with and without concurrent articulation of the syllable "bla". Only the trained interpreters remained unaffected by the concurrent vocalization task and achieved significantly higher recall scores than the rest of the subjects, thus demonstrating more efficient control of **attentional resource allocation**.

The allocation of attentional resources in SI has been investigated in recent PhD research involving experimental designs with particular regard for ecological validity. With the aim of establishing to what extent expertise in SI was a function of general cognitive qualities (such as working memory capacity) rather than task-specific skills acquired through experience and training in SI, Minhua Liu (2001) conducted an experiment involving a total of thirty-six native Chinese subjects (roughly one third each of professional interpreters, advanced students, and beginning students of interpreting). Apart from taking a comprehension and a listening span test, subjects were asked to simultaneously interpret three (11–17-minute) English texts, each of which contained twenty 'critical sentences' followed by a continuation sentence, the first words of which were essential for a full and correct understanding. Cognitive load in the critical sentences was manipulated in terms of readability and presentation rate. Unlike Padilla *et al.* (1995), Liu (2001) found that working memory span scores did not differentiate between the three groups of subjects. Rather, professional interpreters outperformed students only on the interpreting task as such, in which they demonstrated superior (selective) semantic processing skills in the critical sentences and more efficient management of attentional (working memory) resources as reflected in significantly higher correctness scores for continuation sentences and markedly better quality ratings for meaningfulness, smoothness and naturalness of output.

In the even more specific investigation of working memory in SI by Shlesinger (2000a), the point of departure was Baddeley's finding that the capacity of phonological working memory has a temporal limit of roughly 2 seconds; that is, that the memory traces of the acoustic input will decay after this time unless they are refreshed by a process known as 'subvocal articulatory rehearsal'. Since the latter clashes with the concurrent articulation task required in SI (an effect referred to as 'articulatory suppression'), linguistic input which demands longer storage and structural transformations must be expected to overload the capacity of the short-term store. Shlesinger thus investigated the behavior of (sixteen) professionals who were asked to interpret simultaneously, from English into Hebrew, texts containing high load-inducing input strings (each made up of four adjectives preceding a noun, e.g. "clumsy, stylized, heavy, stilted language"). Since Hebrew is a head-initial language requiring post-modification, subjects were forced to carry out storage and restructuring operations that severely taxed their working memory capacity. Memory load was varied in terms of word length and presentation rate. The main hypothesis that slow delivery rates would result in poorer performance as a result of greater decay of unrehearsed memory traces in the short-term store was largely borne out by the experimental findings. However, Shlesinger's professional subjects generally retained only few modifiers, or none at all, in their target-language renditions, presumably as a result of performance norms licensing the omission of 'minor' linguistic items. Thus, aside from supplying highly relevant evidence of the temporal limitation of working memory capacity in SI and highlighting the methodological complexities of using strictly controlled input materials for an 'authentic' experimental task, Shlesinger's (2000a) study points to strategic aspects of interpreting which seem to play a no lesser role than cognitive constraints (» 6.7.1).

6.4.3 Long-term memory and note-taking

In contrast to working memory and attention, the role of long-term memory in interpreting has attracted little research interest. Long-term memory (LTM) is defined by Kintsch (1998: 217) as "everything a person knows and remembers: episodic memory, semantic memory, as well as declarative and procedural knowledge." Apart from the general role of knowledge use in comprehension (« 6.3.2), there is no evidence to date of specific long-term memory skills in simultaneous interpreters. While Bajo *et al.* (2000) found interpreters to be faster in accessing lexical and semantic information in long-term memory, this again is crucially mediated by working memory. Ericsson and Kintsch (1995) explain such expert comprehension by what they call "long-term working memory"; that is, "retrieval structures" which make available a subset of LTM that is linked to a cue in short-term memory. In contrast to the limited capacity of (short-term) working memory, long-term working memory is constrained only by the extent and nature of the retrieval structures, which depend on efficient 'chunking' strategies for storing input in LTM.

Much more so than in SI, of course, semantic chunking of input for storage in LTM and the use of efficient retrieval cues are essential skills in the 'classic' form of consecutive interpreting. Indeed, interpreting practice in the formative decades of the profession in the early twentieth century highlighted interpreters' long-term memory and note-taking skills as the most salient aspects of the interpreting process. Interpreters' notes, which serve to support memory both as **external storage** devices (e.g. for numbers and names) and as **retrieval cues** for memorized conceptual structures or patterns of sense, have since been the subject of some empirical studies and of numerous writings with a strongly didactic orientation (» 9.3.2).

In the pioneering experimental study of note-taking by Seleskovitch (1975), a dozen professional interpreters produced a consecutive rendition of two speeches and subsequently commented on their notes. Although Seleskovitch aimed at demonstrating the nature of interpreting as a 'sense-based' process (« 3.2.6, « 5.4.1) rather than testing specific memory-oriented hypotheses, she appears to have anticipated current conceptions of long-term working memory by stressing the nature of notes as minimal cues, in whatever form, for retrieving a maximum of conceptual content (see 1975: 84). In addition, she pointed out that interpreters need to divide their attention between the conceptual processing of input and the taking of notes, and that the latter must not detract from the attention needed for comprehension processes (see 1975: 120f).

Thus note-taking for consecutive interpreting is as much a matter of attentional resource management ('short-term processing') as of long-term storage, and relatively little is known to date about the complex cognitive mechanisms involved. Various experimental studies on the extent to which note-taking competes with comprehension processes for scarce attentional capacity have yielded a mixed picture of findings. In her PhD study involving fourteen professionals and fourteen student subjects, Andres (2002) found abundant evidence of processing overload in the receptive phase of consecutive interpreting, even at a low presentation rate. As reflected in her time-coded video recordings, the note-taking behavior of student interpreters in particular was often insufficiently automatic and made substantial demands on attention. Students tended to fall behind in their note-taking by more than 6 seconds and to catch up by leaving gaps in their notes which showed up directly as omissions in their target-language renditions.

6.5 Production

Compared to the substantial body of language-processing research focusing on comprehension (« 6.3), production processes have received rather less attention, both in cognitive science in general and in the CP paradigm of interpreting studies in particular. In the DI paradigm, in contrast, where the emphasis is on language use in interaction, researchers have shown a keen interest in 'speaking' as a situated activity. This is reflected in different lines of research relevant to interpreting as 'text/discourse production' (« 3.2.7): one which studies 'speaking' as the production of linguistic utterances as such, and another which studies utterances as tools in the interactive creation of discourse.

6.5.1 From intention to articulation

Ever since Herbert (1952: 59) demanded that "A good interpreter must be a trained public speaker," conference interpreters, particularly when working in the consecutive mode, have foregrounded their professional skills of expression (e.g. Déjean le Féal 1990: 155). On the assumption, however, that the interpreter's speech process would be the same as that of any (native) speaker (see Seleskovitch 1978a: 97), the explanation of production processes was left to psycholinguists, who have indeed managed to elucidate the process over the course of decades of experimental research. One of the most widely accepted and influential models of production is the **three-stage model** of *Speaking* by Willem Levelt (1989), in which a "conceptualizer" generates 'preverbal messages', a "formulator" encodes them as 'internal speech', and an "articulator" produces 'overt speech'. This model has been adopted, among others, by Setton (« 5.4.3) and by Kees de Bot (2000), whose account of bilingual language use and SI includes a critical discussion of production in early process models (« 5.4.3). One of these is the model by Gerver (1971), who was the first to stress that **monitoring** and correction are an integral part of the process of SI (see 1976: 202). Indeed, with the ideational component largely inaccessible to research, components of the production process such as output planning and monitoring, as manifested in self-corrections and false starts, have been of particular interest to psycholinguists and interpreting researchers alike.

6.5.2 Hesitation and correction

Psycholinguistic research on spontaneous speech as undertaken by Goldman-Eisler since the late 1950s (« 6.2.2) focused on hesitation, in particular pausing, as a 'window' on the cognitive planning activity intrinsic to speech production. Ever since Goldman-Eisler's (1967) 'pausological' approach to SI, **silent** and **filled pauses** ('ums and ahs') have been acknowledged as significant features both of the process of output generation and of the interpreter's output as a textual product

(» 7.1.2). Lederer (1978/2002, 1981) and Setton (1999), for instance, discuss the simultaneous renditions in their corpora with reference to the interpreters' pauses as reflected in their transcriptions, and Setton (1999: 246) suggests that various types of hesitancy phenomena correspond to different levels of attention.

Applying the study of pauses and hesitations to consecutive interpreting, Peter Mead, in a PhD thesis completed in 2002, analyzed a large corpus of consecutive interpretations (English/Italian) with regard to both the quantitative incidence of **disfluencies** and his (forty-five) subjects' retrospective explanations of their pausing behavior. On the basis of precise software-assisted measurements, Mead (2000) found an average proportion of pause time of 11 seconds for professionals working into their A language, compared to more than 20 seconds for student interpreters working into their B. In a similar vein, Tissi (2000) described student interpreters' experimental output in terms of **stalls** and **repairs**, that is, silent and filled pauses, lengthened syllables and other disfluencies such as repetitions, corrections and false starts. In a process-oriented perspective, such phenomena have been conceptualized not so much as faults and imperfections, but as typical features of **impromptu speech** (Enkvist 1982) and thus of the 'spontaneous' production required of the interpreter (see Lederer 1981: 41, Pöchhacker 1995b).

6.5.3 *From utterance to interactive discourse*

While the process leading from ideation to utterance is the focus of psycholinguistic studies of production in and by a speaking individual, research on speaking from a sociolinguistic perspective essentially investigates how two or more speakers use utterances in the process of conversational interaction. This approach to interactive discourse implies a fundamental concern with **contextual factors**, as listed early on in the mnemonic SPEAKING model (Situation – Participants – Ends – Act sequences – Key – Instrumentalities – Norms – Genres) by Hymes (« 3.1.3), which has come to be adopted in various domains of interpreting research. Within the 'dialogic' conception of discourse underlying the DI paradigm, production is viewed as a joint activity, or **inter-activity**, involving all participants as speakers and hearers in the interaction (« 5.3.1). Central to the discourse-analytical view of production is the notion of **turn-taking** as foregrounded in the paradigm of conversation analysis (e.g. Apfelbaum 1995, Roy 2000a). The study of turn-taking behavior in particular highlights the role of **nonverbal features** in discourse production by the interpreter and the primary participants (see Poyatos 1987/2002).

6.6 Input variables

The complex interplay of attention, memory and comprehension in the interpreting process is variously affected by a number of 'external' factors. These relate primarily to the nature of the source message which serves as the immediate 'input' to the interpreter's mental processing operations. Prior to source-text processing as such is the issue of acoustic and/or visual access and perception.

6.6.1 *Sound and vision*

In interpreting from a spoken language, an essential condition for the viability of the process is the **acoustic quality** and perceptibility of the input. In face-to-face consecutive interpreting without technical equipment, various background noises and unsuitable positioning, for instance, can impair the interpreter's perception and thus comprehension of the original speech, but the interactive setting usually offers ways of resolving such problems. Not so in simultaneous interpreting, whether in the whispering mode, from spoken to signed languages, or in spoken-language SI with electro-acoustic transmission systems. Since simultaneous interpreters are assumed to be working at the limit of their processing capacity (see Gile 1995b, 1999b), the issue of sound quality is particularly acute. As early as the 1950s and 1960s, psychologists such as Broadbent (1958) had assumed that the effort involved in recognizing degraded input would impair the performance of concurrent tasks. This was also emphasized by Seleskovitch (1978a: 128ff) and investigated with reference to SI by Gerver (1971, 1974b), who asked twelve experienced professionals to interpret and shadow short passages of scripted French prose into English at three different noise levels. Although Gerver's analytical techniques for assessing source–target correspondence are open to question, his findings clearly point to the detrimental effect of noise on the performance of simultaneous verbal tasks. More errors and omissions were recorded for both shadowing and SI in noisy vs no-noise conditions, and the quality of the renditions deteriorated more sharply in the interpreting task. Gerver (1974b: 165) concluded that difficulty in perceiving source language input had resulted in less channel capacity being available for translation and output monitoring by the interpreter (see 1974b: 165). Tommola and Lindholm (1995) obtained similar results in a study with eight professionals who were asked to interpret simultaneously realistic conference presentations from English into Finnish with or without the addition of white noise at −5dB. Interpretations were scored by two judges for propositional accuracy and reflected a significant impact of poorer sound quality on accurate performance.

While technical standards for adequate transmission quality in conference interpreting were set in the early 1980s (» 8.6.1), the issue of noise, or signal quality, has re-emerged with a vengeance in connection with teleconferencing and remote interpreting (» 8.5.1). More so than sound quality, these developments impinge on the interpreter's **visual access** to the speaker and proceedings. Although conference interpreters have long insisted on the need for a direct view of the conference room, research on the role of visual information in SI has yielded an ambiguous pattern of findings. Survey research has documented conference interpreters' demands to see the speaker as well as the rest of the participants so as to have access to the full range of nonverbal visual cues, including speaker **kinesics** (gestures, facial expressions), turn-taking signals and audience reactions (see Altman 1990, Bühler 1985, Cooper *et al.* 1982). However, several attempts at experimentally validating the need for visual access to ensure adequate performance have failed to produce clear-cut results. Maurizio Balzani (1990) conducted

an experiment with twelve final-year students who interpreted short extemporaneous or read speeches from either audio- or videotape. Performance was
assessed by two judges for aspects of "fidelity", "target-language correctness" and
"presentation". Balzani found significantly better performance in the video
condition for extemporaneous texts but not for read speeches. In an earlier study
by L. Anderson (1994), which involved twelve professional subjects who interpreted
short authentic spontaneous speeches presented either with or without the video
image, no such effect had been found. Similarly, Tommola and Lindholm (1995)
reported no significant difference in propositional accuracy between SI with or
without the video image.

The impact and helpfulness of speaker kinesics like hand movements and facial
expressions was investigated by Luis Alonso Bacigalupe (1999) in a live experiment with eight final-year interpreting students. Subjects were asked to interpret
simultaneously a short speech presented either without distinct kinesics or with
eighty kinesically reinforced expressions. The findings revealed no differential
impact of kinesic reinforcements in the oral presentation, and a comparative
analysis of subjects' output for general information content even yielded poorer
results for the group receiving the speech with kinesics. While similar experiments
in the context of MA research have failed to produce conclusive evidence, fieldwork
carried out in conference settings (e.g. Pöchhacker 1994a) has documented –
though not measured in terms of output 'quality' – the communicative impact of
visual cues on the proceedings and on simultaneous interpreters' renditions.

6.6.2 Accent and intonation

In interpreting from spoken languages, the aspect of message delivery, apart
from voice quality, that relates most closely to perception is the speaker's
pronunciation and the resulting phonetic quality of the source-language input.
Like any perceptual process, the recognition of speech sounds depends on prior
knowledge, and any deviation from familiar acoustic-phonetic patterns is likely to
make perception more difficult for the interpreter. In surveys on job stress among
conference interpreters, 'unfamiliar accent' is cited by a majority of respondents
as a frequent and serious problem (Cooper *et al.* 1982: 104, AIIC 2002: 25). The
detrimental effect of a particularly strong accent on simultaneous interpreting
performance has been demonstrated in several small-scale experiments for MA
theses. A study with a somewhat broader scope was reported by Andrea Mazzetti
(1999), who had fifteen final-year students interpret a German speech read either
with native German accent and intonation or with a large number of **phonemic**
('segmental') and **prosodic** ('suprasegmental') **deviations**. Five subjects with
German as their A-language as well as five native Italian students interpreted the
degraded version of the (1075-word) speech while another five Italian students
interpreted the control version. Though the lower reading speed of the non-native
version appears to have leveled the quantitative pattern of semantically incorrect
renditions by native Italian subjects, the author found evidence in the data to
conclude that the degraded version impaired the performance of native Italian

subjects more than that of the native German subjects. This is in line with findings from second-language acquisition studies on "perceptual foreign accent" (McAllister 2000), which predict greater perceptual difficulties for users of an acquired language, particularly when the speech signal is masked by noise or an unfamiliar accent. Such research points to the possible advantage of working from one's A- into one's B-language, at least in difficult perceptual conditions, and there is even some evidence suggesting that a speech delivered with a non-native accent may be less difficult to interpret if the speaker's native language (i.e. the source of interference) is among the interpreter's working languages.

As highlighted by Mazzetti (1999), what interpreters loosely refer to as 'foreign accent' goes far beyond the non-standard pronunciation of individual phonemes and extends to deviations at suprasegmental as well as lexical and syntactic levels. The input language that is most often subject to such multiple deviations is English, the world's dominant *lingua franca* and conference language, and most studies have therefore focused on the non-native features of English used by speakers of other languages. In native and non-native speech alike, however, **intonation** and other components of **prosody**, such as tempo and rhythm, are particularly relevant to perception and understanding in the interpreting process. In an early experiment testing the impact of prosodically degraded input on the performance of simultaneous interpreters, Gerver (1971) had six professional interpreters render ten short texts from French into English. Half of the source texts had been read on tape (at 100 words per minute) with standard prosody, whereas the other half had been recorded with minimal intonation and stress and any pauses of 250 milliseconds or more eliminated. Based on the percentage of "words correctly translated", Gerver (1971) found that the monotonous (i.e. flat and inexpressive) passages had significantly lower scores and were also associated with significantly more "errors of substitution" (» 7.2.2). Notwithstanding the weaknesses in its analytical approach, Gerver's study strongly suggests that prosodic cues like pauses, stress and intonation assist interpreters in segmenting and processing the source-language message. This was brought out clearly also by Karla Déjean le Féal (1982), who demonstrated the link between intonation patterns and the perception of input speed (» 6.6.3).

6.6.3 *Speed and mode of delivery*

Though closely interrelated with prosodic cues like intonation and rhythm, the speed of message delivery, also referred to as 'input rate', 'presentation rate' or 'delivery rate', stands out as a key input variable in its own right. Special attention to the input rate has been linked almost exclusively to the simultaneous mode of interpreting, for which participants in the 1968 Alpbach meeting on "Interpreters and Interpreting" (« 2.2.1) had stated: "The Input rate is all-important. Slow input can disrupt processing as much as fast input" (Alpbach 1968: 2). A few years earlier, at an AIIC symposium on interpreter training in 1965, a rate of 100 to 120 words per minute had been suggested as comfortable for SI, and this was confirmed in an experimental study by Gerver (1969/2002). At speeds above the range of 95 to 120 words per minute, subjects showed a decrease in the proportion of text correctly interpreted and an increase in ear–voice span and pausing. With reference to short-term-memory limitations, Gerver concluded that simultaneous interpreters can increase their output rate to cope with faster input only up to a point, at which they reach "a steady state of throughput at the expense of an increase in errors and omissions" (1969/2002: 66). As regards low-speed input, an explanation for its detrimental effect in SI was supplied by Shlesinger's (2000a) work on the decay of unrehearsed traces in working memory (« 6.4.2).

Notwithstanding the rather clear findings on the effect of input speed, measuring this variable is in fact a complex problem. Apart from the choice of unit (words vs syllables), delivery rates depend on the frequency and duration of pauses, and thus on the **pause criterion** used to net out the **articulation rate** from the composite of speech bursts and pauses. Given the use of word counts for morphologically dissimilar languages, and the use of pause criteria varying between 70 and 600 milliseconds, it is hard make comparisons across different studies. But even assuming that this issue has been resolved, the analyst is faced with the discrepancy between the input speed measured and the input speed actually perceived. Déjean le Féal (1982), in particular, showed that intonation patterns influence interpreters' perception of the delivery rate: at the same objective rate, a source speech with **monotonous intonation** and short pauses was perceived as faster, and more difficult to interpret, than a speech with marked intonation contours. Contrasting impromptu speech with the reading of scripted material, Déjean le Féal suggested that the former was easier to understand because of a greater number of pauses (i.e. shorter speech segments), a distinct "acoustic relief" (i.e. hesitation pauses followed by stressed content words), and a higher degree of (accidental or deliberate) redundancy. What Déjean le Féal had established in her 1978 dissertation based on a corpus of six authentic speeches was put to the test by Christopher Taylor (1989) in an experiment with twenty student interpreters. Judging by the smaller number of omissions in his subjects' renditions of the ad-libbed version of the input text, Taylor (1989: 96) concluded that "an 'impromptu' delivery, full of non-relevant remarks and frippery is more conducive to 'getting the message' (not 'getting everything') than a straightforward, careful reading of a prepared written speech." Balzani (1990), too, found that the student interpreters in his experiment performed significantly better on improvised rather than 'oralized' (read) input material. Nevertheless, 'mode of delivery' must not be construed simply as a binary concept. As proposed by Kopczyński (1982) and developed in Pöchhacker's (1994c) "text delivery profile," there is a broad middle ground between improvised speech and reading, not to mention the combination of oral presentation and visual media. Clearly, much further corpus-based research is needed on the extent to which input variables such as speed, delivery mode, and prosody are correlated with one another before specific hypotheses about their individual and joint effects on the interpreting process can be tested.

6.6.4 Source-text complexity

One of the most difficult parameters of input load is the information content of the source message. Apart from Treisman's (1965) early attempt to calibrate her experimental input passages in terms of information per word (based on cloze testing 100 subjects on samples of ten words from each passage), few authors have systematically addressed this issue. At the **lexical** level, research might begin by considering such aspects as word frequency and lexical variability (for which corpus-linguistic tools are increasingly available), move on to non-redundant items such as proper names and numbers (e.g. Gile 1984), and pay special attention to semantic phenomena like false cognates in a given language pair (e.g. Shlesinger 2000a), non-standard and culture-bound usage (e.g. Sabatini 2000/01), and 'creative' or humorous language use (e.g. Viaggio 1996). Notwithstanding the significance of such research, the informational complexity of a text clearly could not be pegged to difficulties at the lexical level.

In the study by Liu (2001), the complexity of the experimental input material was gauged with the help of a simple readability index – the Flesch–Kincaid formula based on sentence length (lexical density) and word length. Questioning the adequacy of Flesch's formula, Alexieva (1999) proposed a "listenability coefficient" based on the ratio of implicit (i.e. condensed, participial) to explicit **predications**. Similarly, Dillinger (1994), studying the effect of text structure on interpreters' comprehension, focused on propositions and related them to their syntactic environment in terms of clause density and embedding as well as textual macro-structures ("frames"). Dillinger's experiment, though criticized for some questionable choices of design, showed a clear negative effect of **propositional density** on accuracy of interpreting, with lower accuracy for propositions in embedded clauses. In contrast, syntactic variables as such (clause density and clause embedding) had only a weak overall effect on performance in Dillinger's English–French study. This would seem to agree with the conclusion drawn by Setton (1999) from his corpus-based analysis of professional Chinese–English and German–English SI that "syntactic structure . . . does not of itself constitute an obstacle to SI" (1999: 270). In contrast, Tommola and Helevä (1998), in an experimental study with student interpreters working from English into Finnish, found a significant effect of syntactic complexity on output accuracy as measured by propositional analysis.

Finally, at the level of **text type**, the professional as well as untrained subjects in Dillinger's (1994) study performed significantly better on the narrative passage than on the text describing a procedure. Since the two texts were closely matched for the number of words, clauses, cohesive elements and propositions, Dillinger attributed his findings to the effect of the informational structure and concluded that the sequence of episodes making up the narrative text was more amenable to comprehension than the hierarchical structure of procedures and subprocedures.

6.7 Strategies

As a goal-directed activity, interpreting has been conceptualized as an essentially 'strategic' process, particularly by researchers viewing it as a complex cognitive information-processing task or text-processing skill (e.g. Flores d'Arcais 1978: 398f). Of particular influence in this regard has been the strategic model of discourse comprehension and production by van Dijk and Kintsch (1983), which has been adopted by a number of authors in interpreting studies. More generally, a wide array of psycholinguistic processing steps has been discussed under the heading of 'strategy', defined as a 'goal-oriented process under intentional control' (see Kalina 1998: 99). With strategies thus appearing rather ubiquitous, the focus here is on strategies specific to interpreting and their role in the broader context of the interpreter's goal-oriented behavior.

6.7.1 Norms, strategies, constraints

The topic of processing strategies in interpreting has been closely linked with difficulties arising from the interpreter's input. In particular, high delivery speed (« 6.6.3) and structural complexity (« 6.6.4) have been cited as factors inducing high processing loads and thus requiring coping strategies, especially under the temporal and cognitive constraints of SI. Indeed, the corresponding strategies of 'compression' (» 6.7.4) and 'anticipation' (» 6.7.3) are among the most widely discussed topics in the processing-oriented literature on interpreting. And yet, as demonstrated by the crucial work of Shlesinger (1999, 2000a, 2000b), strategies cannot be accounted for purely in terms of input load. Rather, the interpreter's awareness of – and attempt to meet – certain expectations regarding his or her product and performance, which Chesterman (1993) refers to as translational "expectancy norms", may be as powerful as cognitive constraints in shaping the interpreter's strategic response. A performance standard such as fluent and smooth output, for instance, internalized in the course of an interpreter's training and professional experience, could be taken to license certain kinds of omissions or additions (see Schjoldager 1995/2002, Shlesinger 1999). This suggests a distinction between **process-oriented** strategies for **coping** with high-load-inducing input (» 6.7.3) and **product-oriented** strategies for **communicating** effectively with the target-language audience (» 6.7.4). Nevertheless, the line between the two would be hard to draw. Gile (1995b), for example, addressing the interplay between strategic and norm-guided behavior, suggests that an interpreter's choice of "coping tactics" may be guided by various "rules," such as "maximizing the communication impact of the speech" or "self-protection" (1995b: 201ff).

6.7.2 Task-related strategies

The many strategies, variously referred to also as 'techniques' or 'tactics', that have been described as specific to interpreting, can be classified in different ways. With reference to the overall task, one may distinguish between **on-line** strategies (as considered here) and **off-line** strategies preceding or following translational cognitive processing as such (e.g. preparing glossaries or marking up documents). On-line strategies, in turn, may be specific to or typical of a given **mode** of interpreting. This applies for instance to note-taking in consecutive interpreting and lag adjustment in the simultaneous mode, even though notes may also be used in the booth and time lag may be significant in note-taking behavior (« 6.2.3). In face-to-face communication, interpreting involves a broad range of strategies for interactive discourse management, in particular with regard to face-protection (see Mason and Stewart 2001) as well as verbal or nonverbal turn-taking cues and communicative feedback (see Englund Dimitrova 1997). Notwithstanding this breadth of application, most work on the subject of strategies to date, including a growing body of MA and doctoral theses in a variety of countries and languages, has focused on simultaneous conference interpreting, particularly in relation to the 'classic' issue of structural dissimilarity between the source and target languages.

6.7.3 Coping with structure: timing, restructuring and anticipation

Ever since Glémet (1958: 120f) described output production in SI as involving "mortgaging your grammatical future", researchers have studied ways of coping with the challenge of dissimilar grammatical structures. Kade (1967), Kirchhoff (1976/2002) and others giving special consideration to German as a source language mentioned the strategy of **waiting**, if not 'for the verb', as anecdotes would have it, at least for further disambiguating input. In line with Herbert's (1952: 65) injunction against any pauses in the interpreter's speech, waiting for further input can take the form of **stalling**, that is, slowing down delivery or using 'neutral padding expressions' or 'fillers' (e.g. Glémet 1958: 121, Kirchhoff 1976/2002: 116). However, the higher storage load resulting from such **lagging** strategies limits their application and suggests the need for more pre-emptive action such as **chunking**, also referred to as "salami technique" (Jones 1998: 101). As described by, among others, Kirchhoff (1976/2002), this involves the extraction and rendition of independent input segments at phrase or clause level before the end of a complex input structure. This widely taught strategy, which Seleskovitch and Lederer (1995: 125) refer to as "working with subunits of sense", is reflected even in Goldman-Eisler's experimental findings on the prevalence of "fission" as a segmentation strategy (« 6.2.3). Chunking and the concomitant reformulation strategies have been studied on the basis of experimental as well as fieldwork data, and discussed in particular for SI from Asian languages (e.g. Setton 1999, Ishikawa 1999a).

The most widely discussed strategy of SI, however, is **anticipation**. Aside from its fundamental role in comprehension in the broader sense of expectation-based ('top-down') processing (« 6.3.2), anticipation is defined specifically as the simultaneous interpreter's production of a sentence constituent before the corresponding constituent has appeared in the source-language input (see Setton 1999: 52). Authors such as Wilss (1978) and Lederer (1978/2002, 1981) have described and exemplified various subtypes of syntactic anticipation and made a basic distinction between 'linguistic anticipation' (i.e. 'word prediction' based on familiar lexico-grammatical patterns) and 'extra-linguistic anticipation' on the basis of 'sense expectation'. Linguistic anticipation and the search for structural transfer regularities constituted a focal interest of interpreting scholars working in the tradition of the Leipzig School (« 2.3.1). This is best reflected in the large-scale experimental study of syntactic strategies in Russian–German SI carried out in the PhD research by Salevsky (1987). While most German authors, and not they alone, seem to have shared the belief that "any SI process is language-pair-specific" (Wilss 1978: 350), scholars in the IT tradition have played down the role of syntactic asymmetries. Aside from theoretical argument, the question has been addressed in various empirical studies, including Gile's (1992a) corpus analysis of the length and function of predictable sentence endings in Japanese, Alessandra Riccardi's (1996) experiment on German–Italian SI with students and professional subjects, and the MA research on verb anticipation in German–English SI reported by Udo Jörg (1997). Jörg's experiment, which involved both student subjects and professionals with either English or German as their A-language, addressed the issues of expertise and directionality which were also raised by Van Besien (1999) in his re-analysis of anticipation in Lederer's (1981) corpus. Setton (1999) used the findings from his German–English and Chinese–English corpus analysis to express skepticism about a "strategies-for-structure" approach, pointing out that "marked syntactic structure alone does not obstruct SI" (1999: 282), and fore-grounding instead the cognitive-pragmatic processing of linguistic and contextual cues.

6.7.4 Communicating content: condensation and adaptation

Strategies relating to various forms of adaptive processing of content evidently bear on the fundamental topic of performance standards and 'quality' (» 7.2, » 7.4). Nevertheless, some content-processing strategies, particularly of the 'reductive' kind, have been analyzed primarily as forms of coping with process-ing constraints. This applies especially to the strategy of **compression**, or 'abstracting', in response to high input speed and/or information density in the simultaneous mode. As early as the late 1960s, Chernov (see 1978, 1994) discussed lexical and syntactic compression and omission in response to excessive input speed, and the issue was taken up by several interpreting researchers in Eastern Europe (e.g. Alexieva 1983). In a similar vein, Kirchhoff (1976/2002: 116) envisaged strategic "information reduction . . . through selection (omission of irrelevant information)".

The fact that compression can be viewed not only as a 'rescue technique' but also as a strategic orientation underlying the translational process is best illustrated with reference to consecutive interpreting. Herbert (1952: 67) stipulated that full consecutive interpretation should only take up 75% of the time taken by the speaker. Such a reduction was to be achieved by speaking at a faster pace and avoiding repetition, hesitation, and redundancy. From an experimental corpus of Spanish–Danish consecutive interpretations produced by ten students and two professional interpreters, Helle Dam (1993) concluded that "text condensing," achieved by various types of substitutions and omissions, was a necessary and usually good interpreting strategy. In a similar vein, Sergio Viaggio (1991: 51) argued that "saying it all" – that is, reproducing the sense of the message with all stylistic and semantic nuances – was not always necessary for the interpreter to "convey all of the sense". The latter explicitly relates to the sense-based vs verbal-transfer view of the interpreting process and to the basic distinction between a **form-based** and a **meaning-based** interpreting approach (« 6.3.2), formulated by authors such as Gran (1989) and Isham (1994), and tested empirically by Dam (1998/2002, 2001).

The case for a 'synthetic' rather than a 'saying it all' approach (see Sunnari 1995) thus rests on the basic strategy of 'condensation', or **implication**. The latter term in particular points to the link between various techniques of compression and the language pair involved: what needs to be said or may remain unstated depends on the language and culture in question. Conversely, and quite apart from its postulated status as a universal feature of Translation, **explicitation** (see Blum-Kulka 1986/2000) may be needed as a strategy to circumvent linguistic and socio-cultural differences, as studied for English–ASL educational interpreting by Livingston *et al.* (1994) and for Japanese–English SI by Luli Ishikawa (1999b). More generally, Kohn and Kalina (1996: 127) posit the need for **adaptation** strategies with regard to target-discourse conventions, including "appropriate cultural adaptations" – an issue which has been touched on by many authors but has received very little systematic attention as a topic of empirical research.

Further reading

Bilingualism

de Bot (2000), de Groot (1997), Fabbro and Gran (1997), Fabbro *et al.* (1990), Grosjean (1997), Kurz (1994, 1996), W.E. Lambert (1978), Paradis (1994, 2000), Petsche *et al.* (1993), Rinne *et al.* (2000), Shreve and Diamond (1997), Thiéry (1978), Tommola (1999), and the papers in Lambert and Moser-Mercer (1994).

Simultaneity

Barik (1972, 1973), Cokely (1992a), Gerver (1975, 1976), Gile (1997/2002), Goldman-Eisler (1967, 1972/2002), Kurz (1996), Lee 1999, Oléron and Nanpon (1965/2002), Paneth (1957/2002), Tissi (2000), Yagi (1999).

Comprehension

Bajo *et al.* (2000), Chernov (1979/2002, 1994), Dillinger (1994), Gile (1993), Isham (1994), Lederer (1990), MacWhinney (1997), Pöchhacker (1993),

Setton (1998/2002, 1999), Shreve and Diamond (1997), Tijus (1997); for comprehensive reference, see Kintsch (1998).

Memory

Andres (2002), Baddeley (2000), Bajo *et al.* (2000), Darò (1994, 1997), Gerver (1971, 1974a), S. Lambert (1989), Liu (2001), Padilla *et al.* (1995), Seleskovitch (1975), Shlesinger (2000a), Shreve and Diamond (1997), Taylor (1989); for comprehensive reference, see Tulving and Craik (2000).

Production

de Bot (2000), Gerver (1975, 1976), Goldman-Eisler (1967, 1972/2002), Mead (2000, 2002), Moser-Mercer (1997/2002), Pöchhacker (1995b), Poyatos (1987/2002), Roy (2000a), Setton (1999), Wadensjö (1993/2002, 1998, 2001); for general reference, see Levelt (1989).

Input variables

Alonso Bacigalupe (1999), L. Anderson (1994), Balzani (1990), Barik (1973), Déjean le Féal (1982), Dillinger (1994), Gerver (1969/2002, 1974b, 1976), Kopczyński (1982), Mazzetti (1999), Pöchhacker (1994c), Taylor (1989), Tommola and Helevä (1998), Tommola and Lindholm (1995).

Strategies

Chernov (1978, 1994), Dam (1998/2002, 2001), Gile (1992a, 1995b), Ishikawa (1999a, 1999b), U. Jörg (1997), Kade and Cartellieri (1971), Kalina (1998), Kirchhoff (1976/2002), Kohn and Kalina (1996), Riccardi (1996), Setton (1999), Shlesinger (1999, 2000b), Sunnari (1995), Van Besien (1999), Wilss (1978).

7 Product and performance

Research on the outcome of the interpreter's cognitive processing operations and on communicative aspects of translational behavior investigates interpreting as a process in the wider sense – as language use in social interaction. As has emerged from the evolution of linguistic theory toward the end of the twentieth century (e.g. Beaugrande 1997), the examination of the textual product ('language as structure') is closely intertwined with the analysis of communicative performance ('language as social action'). Research on the interpreter's product and performance therefore draws on the social as well as the linguistic and cognitive sciences to study the translational and interactional features of mediated communication.

7.1 Discourse

The notions of 'text' and 'discourse' shared much conceptual ground in the formative decades of text linguistics and discourse analysis. In current usage though, 'discourse' serves as the more comprehensive – and less easily defined   term to refer to 'language use in social interaction' (see van Dijk 1997a) whereas 'text' is taken by many authors to foreground the linguistic concern with formal and semantic structures, often with a bias toward written language. The label 'discourse' has an overwhelmingly broad range of application – from the philosophy of communicative processes in society at large to the empirical analysis of 'talk' in conversational interaction, in both spoken and signed languages (see Roy 2000a). All of these orientations in the study of text and discourse are relevant to interpreting research, and many have supplied conceptual tools for the analysis of the interpreter's product.

7.1.1 Texts in context

The fact that interpreting is part of a process of communicative interaction in a given context was long taken for granted, and analytical work on the social and situational constellation of interaction in interpreting emerged relatively late. Beyond various constellation models (« 5.3.1), few authors have examined the utterances, or 'texts', that constitute the interpreter's source material as parts of more complex **discourse events**, even though this would seem particularly evident in the case of conference interpreting. Lederer (1981) pointed to the contextual knowledge built up in prior parts of conference proceedings, and Alexieva (1985: 196) spoke of "macro-text" to refer to "the whole aggregate of texts delivered at a conference". Taking up the definition of text as a "communicative event" (Beaugrande and Dressler 1981), Pöchhacker (1992) conceptualized the 'conference' as a communicative event with its own **textuality** (» 7.1.3), with a particular communicative purpose, internal structure, and target audience, and labeled the communicative event as a **hypertext** to foreground the multiple links between its constituent parts. The significance of **intertextuality** at the conference level was explored further in particular by Alexieva (1994), who also suggested an event-level typology of **genres** of interpreter-mediated interaction (« 5.3.1).

Genres of discourse and the internal structure of speech events have also been a focus in research on dialogue interpreting. In the work of Wadensjö (1998), for instance, the basic unit of analysis is the "interpreter-mediated encounter" as an interaction event rather than the activity of 'interpreting' per se. Helen Tebble (1999), working within the systemic functional approach to discourse as championed by Halliday (e.g. 1985), proposes a typical **event structure** for medical consultations. Based on an authentic corpus of thirteen interpreted consultations, Tebble distinguishes eleven "genre elements", such as "Introductions", "Stating/Eliciting Problem" or "Stating Resolution/Exposition," which represent the basic stages of the communicative event and can be broken down further into constituents such as "exchanges" and "moves" (see 1999: 184f). Similar analyses of the event structure of interpreted medical consultations have been carried out in the framework of Functional Pragmatics at the Hamburg Research Centre on Multilingualism (e.g. Meyer 2002). Similarly, the identification of "dialogue acts" which make up a particular discourse genre was also part of the German *Verbmobil* project for the development of an automatic dialogue interpreting system (» 8.5.3).

7.1.2 Orality

The concept of 'orality' refers to a significant distinction in the study of text and discourse. In a fundamental sense, orality points to the primordial form of language use in immediate ('face-to-face') interpersonal contact, prior to what Walter Ong (1982) called "the technologizing of the word" by the invention of secondary representations of language, that is, writing systems (see also Clark 1996: 8ff). Despite the apparent incongruity, 'orality' in the sense of primary or **natural language use** also includes communication in sign languages, as long as these are natural language systems rather than contrived manual codes or other secondary sign systems (see Ingram 1985: 92). Interpreting therefore implies 'orality' in the sense of natural language use for immediate communication – that is, 'talk' realized by speech sounds or signs in combination with a range of **nonverbal** signaling systems (see Clark 1996). And yet Ong (1982) and others have shown that written language has become so pervasive in modern societies as to make speech (e.g. the 'scripted speech' used in conferences or broadcasting) secondary to writing. This ambivalent nature of linguistic expression is captured in the analytical distinction of **orality vs literacy**, which is based not on the distinction between spoken/signed and written language use but on dimensions of discourse such as 'involvement vs detachment' and 'fragmentation vs integration' (see Tannen 1982).

For dialogue interpreting in face-to-face communication, orality is generally assumed by default, and the issue of orality vs literacy has attracted little attention. Conference interpreting scholars in the IT paradigm have also foregrounded the notion of 'orality', using it in the common sense of extemporaneous speaking activity (e.g. Déjean le Féal 1982). Indeed, the evanescent, impromptu, and context-bound nature of discourse was a cornerstone in the sense-based approach of the Paris School, which posited 'orality' as the prerequisite for 'true interpreting' and showed little interest in descriptive studies of the complex mix of spoken-like and written-like features in conference discourse.

A pioneering research effort in this regard was undertaken by Shlesinger (1989b), who examined an authentic English/Hebrew corpus of source texts and simultaneous interpretations for **shifts** in orality or literacy associated with the interpreting process. Based on a range of features indicative of factors such as degree of planning, contextual co-presence, and degree of involvement, Shlesinger found that SI reduced the range of the **oral–literate continuum** and consistently rendered a literate text more oral in either language direction. Similarly, SI tended to increase the literateness of oral-type Hebrew source texts and was thus found to have an "equalizing effect" on the position of source texts on the oral–literate continuum. More recently, inquiry into the relative orality of texts in interpreting has received a fresh impetus from the application of corpus-linguistic procedures in the form of text statistical analysis of verbal features in large quantities of machine-readable text. In an MA thesis analyzing Pöchhacker's (1994a) 100,000-word ICSB Corpus with reference to fourteen parameters of orality, Petra Jörg (2001) found a shift towards greater orality in English–German SI, reduced sentence length in the German target-text corpus, and evidence of the 'leveling-out effect' suggested by Shlesinger's (1989b) findings.

A dimension of orality which is most immediately linked with the production process in interpreting is the limited scope of planning and its reflection in the interpreter's product in the form of **hesitation** phenomena, or 'disfluencies'. The most general index of (dis)fluency is filled and unfilled **pauses**, as studied comprehensively by Mead (2000, 2002) with regard to production skills at different levels of expertise (« 6.5.2). In his quantitative analysis of the ICSB Corpus for voiced hesitations ('ums and ahs'), Pöchhacker (1994a, 1995b) found these phenomena to be significantly less frequent in the German interpretations than in the English source speeches – a finding which was subsequently corroborated by P. Jörg (2001) in a corpus-linguistic analysis of a sample of ICSB texts.

Notwithstanding the benefits of corpus-linguistic methods, their application to the study of interpreted discourse is hampered considerably by the very orality of the interpreter's output (see Shlesinger 1998). Aside from the problem of segmenting the flow of speech into punctuation-delimited clauses and sentences, paralinguistic and nonverbal discourse features can be incorporated in machine-readable transcriptions only with great difficulty. Thus, until advances in speech signal detection and electronic text encoding (see Cencini and Aston 2002) make it easier to overcome the written-language bias of corpus linguistics, studies of the paralinguistic features of orality in interpreting will have to rely on the intensive 'manual' analysis of limited-scale corpora, albeit with ever more advanced technological support. A particularly innovative example of such work is the study by Shlesinger (1994), who examined ten random 90-second excerpts of authentic interpreted discourse (English/Hebrew) for **intonational features** and identified non-standard pausing (i.e. within grammatical constituents), anomalous stress, low-rise nonfinal pitch movement and momentary alterations in tempo as the main features of what she called "interpretational intonation".

7.1.3 *Textuality*

Research focusing on the interpreter's textual product has been strongly inspired by the process-oriented approach to text linguistics pioneered by Robert de Beaugrande (1980) and broadly introduced by Beaugrande and Dressler (1981). All seven standards of textuality – cohesion, coherence, intentionality, acceptability, informativity, situationality and intertextuality – have been discussed by a number of authors as relevant to interpreting (e.g. Taylor Torsello 1997), and they serve as the foundation for the integrative text-linguistic approach to Translation by Hatim and Mason (1997). What the latter subsume under the broader label of "texture" (comprising features such as cohesion, coherence and theme–rheme organization) has been the focus of several empirical analyses: Shlesinger (1995b) examined various types of **cohesive ties** (reference, substitution, conjunction, lexical cohesion) in an experimental English–Hebrew corpus produced by thirteen student interpreters and found ample evidence of SI-related shifts, mainly in the form of omissions of seemingly less important cohesive devices; Mizuno (1999) replicated Shlesinger's study with ten student interpreters working into Japanese and interpreted his findings with reference to language-pair-specific differences (e.g. regarding the use of pronouns and ellipsis); Monika Kusztor (2000) applied a proposition-based method of semantic network mapping to represent the **coherence** of an advanced student's consecutive interpretation from English into German and demonstrated a shift in the set of thematically central concepts as a result of explicitation (i.e. less pronominal reference) and increased lexical cohesion (by repetition) in the interpretation; finally, in a dynamic perspective on thematic structure, Carol Taylor Torsello (1997) and Cesira Consorte (1999) have used experimental data to highlight the role of **thematic progression** (theme–rheme structure) in English–Italian SI. While all these studies involve a comparative source–target perspective, their focus is on textual features as such – in contrast to the concern with the translational source–target relation that has traditionally been the center of attention.

7.2 Source–target correspondence

The central – and most theory-laden – issue in the examination of the interpreter's product is the nature of the relationship between the source text and its target-language rendition. Scholars of written translation have traditionally discussed this 'translational relation' in terms of 'equivalence' (see Munday 2001, ch. 3). Interpreting scholars, in contrast, have sought to capture the 'ideal standard' for the interpreter's translational product with notions like accuracy, completeness, and fidelity.

7.2.1 Fidelity and accuracy

The most widely acknowledged demand on an interpretation is that it should be **faithful** to the original. Aside from Glémet's (1958: 106) dictum that interpreters transfer speeches "with the same faithfulness as sound-amplification," most authors have echoed Herbert's (1952: 4) basic tenet that an interpretation "fully and faithfully" conveys the original speaker's ideas. Scholars in the IT paradigm have identified the object of fidelity as 'sense' (see Donovan-Cagigos 1990); with a more concrete focus on information processing, Gile (1992b: 189) demands fidelity to the "message and style" of the original, with priority given to the "informational content" rather than the linguistic "package" of the text (see Gile 1995b: 26); most generally, at the level of translational norms, Harris (1990: 118) refers to the norm of the "honest spokesperson," meaning that interpreters should "re-express the original speaker's ideas and the manner of expressing them as accurately as possible and without significant omissions". The conceptual linkage between **fidelity** and **accuracy** is also evident in Seleskovitch (1968), whose original call for "fidelité absolue" (1968: 166) was translated into English as the demand for "total accuracy" (Seleskovitch (1978a: 102).

Fidelity and accuracy, with the implication of completeness, appear in the literature on interpreting as a widely accepted yardstick, and many researchers have indeed sought to apply this yardstick to measure and quantify interpreters' performance, even at the word level (see Gerver 1969/2002). Given the obvious problems with word-for-word correspondence, attempts have been made to determine accuracy at a deeper, semantic level. For her experiment on message loss in relay interpreting, Mackintosh (1983) devised a scoring system based on the principle of "semantic equivalence", which involved an intuitive segmentation of the source text into (phrase or clause-level) units of meaning, each worth a predefined number of points depending on its informational constituents. Three judges were then asked to score the target texts for the number of correctly reproduced items in each unit and thus to arrive at an overall number of points achieved out of the total score possible. (Average semantic accuracy scores were between 70% and 90% for both the direct and the relay interpreting condition.) Another approach to assessing the **informational correspondence** of source and target texts, proposed by linguist John Carroll for the evaluation of machine translation in the 1960s (see Carroll 1978: 120), was applied by interpreting researchers in the 1970s (e.g. Gerver 1974b, L. Anderson 1994). Judges were asked to rate each sentence of the original on a nine-point scale for its informativeness compared to the target text, thus focusing the analysis on information not conveyed by the interpretation. More recently, Gile (1999c) demonstrated a high degree of variability in fidelity ratings by different groups of assessors and questioned the suitability of transcripts as tools for fidelity assessment.

Efforts to develop stringent scoring systems have been made on the basis of **propositional analysis** as developed in cognitive science for the study of text comprehension and recall. In essence, this calls for a decomposition of the 'natural-language' text into a set of structures ('propositions') made up of a head concept, or 'predicate', and a number of related concepts, or 'arguments'. Lambert (1989), for one, used propositional analysis as proposed by Kintsch and van Dijk (1978) to score her experimental results, and Strong and Rudser (1985) developed a proposition-based assessment system for the output of sign language interpreters. In the 1990s, authors such as Dillinger (1994) and Tommola and Lindholm (1995) adopted variants of the cognitive-scientific approach to propositionalization, whereas Kusztor (2000) adopted a method developed by translation scholars in Germany. Notwithstanding the promise of methodological rigor, propositional analysis is not an all-purpose tool for measuring accuracy in interpreting (see Tommola and Lindhom 1995: 130f). Whatever the formalism used, the propositional decomposition of meaning remains language-bound and cannot resolve the fundamental issue of semantic comparability in Translation. Moreover, concept-based propositionalization usually sidelines expressions of attitude, modality and intentionality. Such 'procedural' elements of discourse call for a pragmatic approach to discourse (» 7.2.3), as implemented for SI by Setton (1998/2002, 1999).

7.2.2 *Omissions, additions and (other) errors*

Ever since the first experimental studies of interpreting, researchers have sought to examine the interpreter's output for various types of lexico-semantic 'deviations' from the source text. Oléron and Nanpon (1965), though largely shying away from the issue of fidelity in their pioneering study, quantified the number of words omitted, added or rendered inaccurately in the target text. Gerver (1969/2002, 1974b) quantified what he called **errors** and **discontinuities** in the interpreters' output in terms of 'omissions', 'substitutions' (or 'errors of commission') and 'corrections', and distinguished various subforms according to the amount of linguistic material involved. Working at the same time, Barik (1972, 1975/2002) devised a comprehensive categorization of "translation departures" for the analysis of his experimentally generated corpus of interpretations. Under the three broad headings of **omissions**, **additions** and **substitutions** (or "errors of translation"), Barik distinguished a number of subtypes with reference to the extent or severity (e.g. "skipping omission", "mild" vs "gross semantic error") or the presumable cause of the departure (e.g. "comprehension omission"). Barik's elaborate analytical scheme has been challenged by various authors (e.g. Gerver

1976, Stenzl 1983) as too subjective and impossible to replicate. Nevertheless, error analyses along the lines of Barik's typology have been vital to the treatment of results in a large number of experimental studies, not least in MA-level research. Since authors have usually devised their own variant of the scheme and its terminology, there are nearly as many error classification systems as there are empirical studies requiring an overall assessment of source–target correspondence. Some of the more innovative approaches include: Kopczyński's (1980) breakdown of the error category with regard to linguistic competence, linguistic performance, and communicative appropriateness; Balzani's (1990) criteria for message fidelity, or lack thereof, including such categories as omissions, meaning errors, unwarranted additions, and errors in rendering figures and proper names; Cokely's (1992a) typology of "miscues" in sign langage interpreting, comprising omissions, additions, substitutions, intrusions (i.e. source-language interference) and anomalies; Wadensjö's (1993/2002) distinction between expanded, reduced and substituting renditions in dialogue interpreting; Schjoldager's (1995/2002) "translational relationships or transformation categories", including permutation, addition, deletion, and substitution, with the latter subdivided into half a dozen subtypes; and Jemina Napier's (2002) classification of omission types in relation to sign language interpreters' linguistic coping strategies.

For all its usefulness to researchers faced with the need to analyze and quantify the (lack of) fidelity in an experimental or authentic corpus, the contrastive lexico-semantic approach to error analysis suffers fundamentally from its disregard for functional and pragmatic considerations. Indeed, notions of 'linguistic equivalence' have been rejected as a yardstick of source–target correspondence by interpreting scholars across the various paradigms: Gile (1992b: 188f) points out that producing an acceptable target-language text "requires at least some 'deviation' from 'linguistic equivalence'", and that some "filtering" to enhance the communicative impact of the text will not necessarily detract from its "fidelity"; Sandra Hale (1997a: 211) concludes that "linguistic omissions and additions are often required to ensure accuracy"; Clare Donovan-Cagigos (1990: 400) stresses that fidelity is not a fixed quantity but relative to a concrete communicative situation; and scholars working in the TT paradigm, by definition, regard source–target correspondence as secondary to the communicative function of the target text.

7.2.3 Textural and pragmatic shifts

Mindful of the problems associated with a prescriptive assessment of 'deviations' from an ideal standard of accuracy, equivalence, or fidelity, some authors investigating the interpreter's product have adopted a more **descriptive** approach to source–target correspondence. Central to this line of research is the identification of shifts resulting from the interpreting process as such and/or the interpreter's behavior in a given context of interaction. The notion of 'shifts' as used by Toury (1978/2000: 201) has been discussed by translation scholars and interpreting researchers with an emphasis on the domain of **texture**; that is, cohesion and coherence (« 7.1.3). Pending larger corpus-based studies, however, it is difficult to ascertain whether textural shifts in interpreting have more to do with idio-syncratic choices, constraint-induced strategies (« 6.7.3), task-related translational norms, or 'universals' of Translation such as the tendency toward **explicitation** (see Blum-Kulka 1986/2000).

A form of translational shifts in interpreting which has proved rather amenable to contrastive discourse-based study is changes in the **pragmatic force** of the interpreted text. Features of 'communicative style' such as **register, politeness** and **hedging** – and their translational fate – have been analyzed by drawing on linguistic pragmatics, in particular speech act theory and Grice's conversational maxims. Most work on pragmatic shifts in interpreting has concentrated on constellations of face-to-face communication, and the institutional setting which has attracted most research interest in this regard is the (adversarial) courtroom. Berk-Seligson (1990), in her seminal ethnography of *The Bilingual Courtroom*, studied such issues as politeness and register in a corpus of 114 hours of judicial proceedings involving interpreting between English and Spanish. Similarly, Hale (1997a, 1997b, 1999) reported findings on English–Spanish interpreters' handling of register and politeness forms in a fieldwork corpus of thirteen Australian court cases. Both researchers found evidence of a number of shifts in the pragmatic force of interpretations compared to the original utterances. Consequential shifts have also been demonstrated in the related domain of police interpreting (e.g. Krouglov 1999), with particular reference to hedges, polite forms and the implications of **footing**. Focusing their analysis on the issue of **face**, Mason and Stewart (2001) discussed court and police interpreters' failure to render devices like hedging, modality and register in such a way as to recreate their face-threatening or face-protecting illocutionary force. In studies such as these, the effect of feature shifts in the interpreter's rendition is gauged by a pragma-linguistic analysis of transcribed discourse, with due regard for the interlocutor's discursive response. An alternative approach involves the use of psychological methods to measure the cognitive and pragmatic effect of the interpreter's product on the addressees.

7.3 Effect

The translational principle of 'equivalent effect' has been invoked since the 1960s for translation and interpreting alike, both with regard to the cognitive end-result of the process – that is, comprehension by the target audience – and with regard to the emotive and pragmatic impact of the target text at the interpersonal level. In either dimension, though, the empirical research base is rather tenuous, except for the field of sign language interpreting, where experimental studies on the effect(ivenes) of interpreting date back to the 1970s.

7.3.1 Comprehension

The postulate of "faithfulness" as measured by "the extent to which people really comprehend the meaning" (Nida and Taber 1969: 173) is a crucial translational norm underlying the interpreter's production. In the words of Seleskovitch (1978a: 102), transmitting the message "with total accuracy" requires the interpreter "to have his listeners understand it as well as it was understood by those who heard it directly from the speaker himself" (see also Déjean le Féal 1990: 155). And yet few authors have attempted to measure comprehension in the interpreter's audience. Pioneering efforts were reported by Gerver (1976), who used post-task content questions to assess comprehension in experimental subjects who were listening to simultaneous vs consecutive interpreting. Gerver did not compare comprehension in interpreting vs direct listening; rather, he tried (and failed) to find differences in the **cognitive end-result** of interpreting under good vs noisy listening conditions, depending on the working mode.

Experimental work on the comparative reception and **recall** of lectures interpreted into American Sign Language (ASL) dates back to the 1970s (see Frishberg 1990: 41f). In a study measuring comprehension by deaf subjects with reference also to hearing listeners, Peter Llewellyn-Jones (1981) focused more specifically on the effect of different types of interpreting performance. Using videotaped experimental interpretations into British Sign Language (BSL), Llewellyn-Jones found that deaf subjects' scores on multiple-choice questions administered in sign language were higher for passages interpreted by native signers, whose output reflected considerable restructuring and simplification. This finding also relates to the contrast between interpreting and transliterating, a uniquely significant issue in the field of signed language interpreting. A number of studies on the **comparative effectiveness** of interpretations into ASL vs Signed English were carried out, but experimental designs did not always control for confounding variables such as a preference for one or the other mode of transmission (e.g. ASL interpreting, 'manual coding', or 'sim-com,' i.e. simultaneous lipspeaking and signing).

Apart from Cokely (1990), the most thorough and comprehensive study on the cognitive effectiveness of sign language interpreting vs transliterating to date was done by Livingston *et al.* (1994), who carefully controlled for variables such as text type (narrative vs lecture) as well as subjects' educational background, sign preference, communicative competence, and knowledge of the subject matter. Their study involved a stratified sample of forty-three deaf students mainstreamed in US colleges who were asked to answer literal and inference-based comprehension questions after live renditions of two videotaped English presentations. The authors found significantly higher comprehension scores for interpretation into ASL than for transliteration, even in students who expressly preferred the latter kind of signing but had been randomized into a group receiving ASL.

No less consequential than in educational interpreting is the effectiveness of language transfer for deaf television audiences. Ben Steiner (1998) investigated the differential cognitive effect of various forms of signed output on TV (interpreting into BSL, sight translation into BSL from autocue, reporting, and spontaneous talk in BSL) in a sample of thirty (BSL-dominant vs English-informed) deaf subjects and a hearing control group. Using twelve authentic sample passages and signed content questions, Steiner found a superior effect for BSL-dominant signing, consistently lower comprehension scores for interpreting compared to other modes of signed presentation, and lower overall scores for the BSL-dominant vs the English-informed group, both of which scored far below the control group of hearing subjects responding to the sample passages as broadcast in English (directly or as voice-over).

While no comprehensive comparative studies of audience comprehension have been undertaken for spoken-language interpreting in conference or media settings, the study by Shlesinger (1994) on intonation patterns in SI also included an audience comprehension test. A total of fifteen subjects listened to three passages either as interpretations recorded in authentic conditions or as transcriptions of the interpreted output read on tape by the interpreter. Comprehension scores based on three content questions on each passage were twice as high for the group receiving the read versions than for the group listening to authentic output with "interpretational intonation". Similar research questions are raised also in Shlesinger's (1995b) study on shifts of cohesion, but little further work on the impact of various textual parameters on cognitive effectiveness has been reported to date.

7.3.2 *Pragmatic impact*

Features of the interpreter's verbal as well as nonverbal production are relevant not only for their cognitive effect but also for their impact on text receivers' evaluative and interpersonal response. In the domain of simultaneous conference interpreting, the experimental work of Collados Aís (1998/2002), who confronted a sample of forty-two expert users of SI with intonationally manipulated Spanish renditions of a German presentation, highlighted that **nonverbal features** of the interpreter's product, in particular monotonous vs lively intonation, affect not only users' assessment of the target text as such but also the confidence they place in the interpreter's professionalism. Similar **attitudinal effects** surfaced in the study by Steiner (1998), whose deaf subjects reacted favorably to signers who gave an impression of "authority" in their demeanor and language production.

A setting in which the pragmatic impact of the interpreter's product on interpretation users is of critical importance is the (adversarial) courtroom. In an experiment using the so-called 'matched guise' technique, Berk-Seligson (1988/2002, 1990) presented a sample of over 500 subjects with two simulated audio recordings of a witness testifying in Spanish through an interpreter. The two versions were identical except for a single feature – the interpreter's consistent rendition or non-rendition of the **politeness** markers. Asked to rate the convincingness, competence, intelligence, and trustworthiness of the witness on a seven-point scale, the mock jurors gave significantly more favorable assessment of the Spanish witness when they had listened to the polite version of the English interpretation. A similar effect was observed with the same experimental design for interpretation in "hyperformal style", that is, an upward shift in **register** by the non-use of contracted forms in English. Using the experiment also to ascertain the effect of **hedging** ('well', 'sort of') and the use of **passive vs active** voice in the English interpretation, Berk-Seligson (1990) found such discourse features to be associated with more negative evaluations of the witness. Moreover, lawyers who were interrupted by the interpreter (e.g. when asking for clarification) were given lower ratings for competence by the mock jurors in the experiment.

7.4 Role

In performing their communication-enabling task, interpreters are subject to certain expectations held by participants in the interaction and in society at large. The notion of 'role', a relational concept defined by sociologists as a set of more or less normative behavioral expectations associated with a 'social position', is therefore pivotal to the analysis of interpreters' performance. Indeed, it has become one of the most prominent topics in interpreting studies, linked particularly to the emergence of interpreting in community-based settings.

7.4.1 Role descriptions and expectations

The role of interpreter, which bilinguals have assumed in various contexts throughout history, has been closely linked with such **intermediary** functions as messenger, guide, and negotiator. It was only with the professionalization of interpreting in the course of the twentieth century that the interpreter's role became codified in more specific terms, making the issue of role an integral part of professional codes of ethics and practice (» 8.3.1). The more narrowly construed professional role generally prescribes accurate, complete, and faithful rendition (« 7.2.1) and proscribes any discourse initiative on the part of the interpreter, who is conceptualized as a 'non-person' in a **neutral** position between the interlocutors. Hence the widespread assumption that in professional and institutional settings, "the interpreter's function in general is comparable to that of a machine, giving a more or less literal translation of what is said in language A in language B" (Knapp-Potthoff and Knapp 1986: 152). This **mechanistic** conception has engendered metaphors such as 'faithful echo', 'channel', 'conduit', 'switching device', 'transmission belt', 'modem' or 'input–output robot' to describe the nature of the interpreter's role (see Roy 1993/2002). This view of the interpreter as an **invisible** translating machine would appear to be inspired by the technology-based mode of simultaneous conference interpreting. In fact, however, it is deeply rooted particularly in the field of court interpreting, where the legal profession has traditionally denied court interpreters any latitude in dealing with meaning (i.e. 'interpreting') and limited their role to "verbatim translation" (see Morris 1995). As described by Laster and Taylor (1994: 112f), the standard of "literalism" associated with the **conduit model** of interpreting is a legal fiction necessitated by the inadmissibility of hearsay evidence (i.e. information reported by someone other than the witness) in the common-law courtroom. Pointing to the linguistic, socio-cultural and interactional complexity of the interpreter-mediated encounter, these authors challenge the prescriptive standard of literalism on principal grounds and argue instead for a redefinition of the (legal) interpreter as a more visible and accountable **communication facilitator** – a role description which had gained currency in the field of sign language interpreting by the 1980s (see McIntire and Sanderson 1995, Roy 1993/2002).

In other domains, too, normative discussions have emphasized a more broadly construed role for the interpreter. In the literature on interpreters in healthcare, Joseph Kaufert and associates (e.g. Kaufert and Koolage 1984), studying native Canadian interpreters from the perspective of medical anthropology, are frequently cited as representing the view of interpreters as **culture brokers** and patients' **advocates** working to redress power imbalances in cross-cultural clinical encounters (see Drennan and Swartz 1999). For the legal setting, particularly beyond the adversarial courtroom as such, authors such as Laster and Taylor (1994) and Mikkelson (1998) have highlighted the need for the interpreter to further the interests of the individual client in an unfamiliar institutional environment, and Barsky (1996) concluded from interviews with fifty-six applicants for refugee status in Canada that interpreters needed to empower the disadvantaged claimant by serving as **intercultural agents**. As summarized by Kondo and Tebble (1997), the need for the interpreter to make adjustments to 'smooth over cultural differences', if not 'bridge a wide cultural gap', has been discussed for virtually all domains of interpreting, essentially suggesting that "the ideal role of the interpreter is to serve not only as a linguistic but also as a cultural mediator" (1997: 158). Cutting across the various settings, authors in the field of sign language interpreting have contributed particularly actively to the debate on the interpreter's role (e.g. McIntire and Sanderson 1995, Page 1993, Pollitt 1997).

Some of the normative claims regarding the interpreter's role and power, which were first raised by R.B.W. Anderson (1976/2002) and Brislin (1976a), have been the subject of various types of **survey research**. Drennan and Swartz (1999) reported an evaluation study based on some thirty interviews with healthcare staff and interpreters in Cape Town and found rather mixed views on interpreter roles such as 'culture specialist' and 'patient advocate' among their informants. Though acknowledging the need for advocacy in response to South Africa's legacy of discriminiation, the authors point to the complex socio-political and structural issues weighing on the interactional 'micro-politics' of interpreting (» 8.2.2). In a questionnaire-based survey of more than 600 healthcare and social service providers in Vienna, Pöchhacker (2000b) found different expectation profiles among doctors, nurses, therapists and social workers with regard to such tasks as 'explaining technical terms for the client' and 'explaining foreign cultural references'. In a similar survey by Anne-Marie Mesa (2000) among community service providers in Canada, the expectation that the "cultural interpreter" should 'explain cultural values' ranked rather low, and even fewer respondents considered it very important to receive cultural explanations from the interpreter after the mediated exchange. In contrast, most of the twelve interpreters in Mesa's study considered it very important to be able to provide such explanations. This readiness among healthcare interpreters to adopt a more 'visible' role in the interaction is clearly reflected in the PhD research by Claudia Angelelli (2001), who used survey methods as well as extensive fieldwork to ascertain interpreters' role perceptions and role performance. Based on data from hundreds of questionnaires and interpreted interactions as well as eleven interviews, Angelelli concluded that interpreters perceived, enacted, and described their role as **visible agents** in the interaction.

In the legal sphere, Mira Kadric (2001) conducted a survey among some 200 local court judges in Vienna and found respondents rather accepting of tasks such as 'simplifying the judge's utterances' and 'explaining legal language' for the clients. In contrast to the study by Arlene Kelly (2000), who found that a majority of the fifty-three legal professionals in her survey were against a **cultural mediation** role for the interpreter, as many as 85% of the judges surveyed by Kadric (2001) expected the interpreter to explain cultural references for the court.

While the issue of cultural differences has been less prominent in the literature on conference interpreting (see e.g. Kondo 1990, Pöchhacker 1994b), role expectations have also been investigated for this professional domain. In a survey of users of conference interpreting in Poland, Kopczyński (1994) questioned a total of fifty-seven professionals with different academic backgrounds (humanities, science and technology, diplomacy) on their expectations regarding the interpreter's "visibility" or intrusiveness. Respondents generally preferred what Kopczyński calls the **ghost role** of the interpreter over the "intruder role," but would at the same time give interpreters licence to "correct the speaker" and "add his own explanations". Such varying and even contradictory views point to the limits of survey research on role expectations, and highlight the need for detailed descriptions of interpreters' actual performance.

7.4.2 Descriptions of performance

In his pioneering essay on the interpreter's role, R.B.W. Anderson (1976/2002: 211) observed that "the interpreter's role is always partially undefined – that is, the role prescriptions are objectively inadequate." With reference to the oath taken by interpreters in English courts, who swear to "well and faithfully interpret and true explanation make," Morris (1989) as well as Shlesinger (1991) drew attention to the 'fluidity' of the interpreter's role in their analyses of the Demjanjuk trial in Jerusalem, which involved an unprecedented complexity of interpreting arrangements (see Morris 1989, 1990). Based on an examination of the trial record and on participant observation, both authors found that the professional interpreters working between English and Hebrew were responsible for certain omissions and stylistic shifts which reflected a significant degree of **intrusiveness** (as perceived by the participants) or **latitude** (as perceived by the interpreters themselves). In Peter Jansen's (1995) case study of Spanish–Dutch court interpreting in a criminal case, the academically trained interpreter was found to simplify, adapt and explain complicated speech for the defendant and to filter out hesitations, errors and ambiguities. In her 1989 PhD thesis, Cynthia Roy (2000a) addressed the issue of intrusiveness, or **involvement**, by examining a (fully certified) sign language interpreter's turn-taking behavior in a videotaped meeting between a professor and her graduate student. Her micro-analysis of talk shows that the interpreter sometimes needs to take 'self-initiated turns' in order to manage the flow of communication. An instance of overlapping talk between the primary parties, for example, is resolved by a gesture signaling the student to "wait a minute," and a lengthy pause leads the interpreter to beckon the student to "say something" (see Roy 1996, 2000a).

That such interventions are not a matter of language modality was amply demonstrated by Wadensjö (1993/2002, 1998) on the basis of a large Swedish–Russian corpus of audiorecorded interpreter-mediated encounters in local police stations and healthcare clinics. Wadensjö showed that while much of the professional dialogue interpreter's work consists of 'relaying', in one way or another, other parties' talk, the translational function is inseparable from the function of **coordinating** the dynamics of the interaction. This is done by so-called "non-renditions", that is, interpreter-generated contributions or responses, which are described by Wadensjö (1998: 108ff) as either text-oriented (e.g. requests for clarification, comments on the substance or form of prior utterances) or interaction-oriented (e.g. requests to stop talking, requests to observe the turn-taking order). In a fine-grained analysis based on her model of the interpreter's multiple speaker–hearer roles in the 'participation framework' (« 5.3.1), Wadensjö shows these interpreter initiatives to be intricately interwoven with the variable and simultaneous 'speakership' and 'listenership' of the interlocutors. The fact that this **co-construction** of interactive spoken discourse involves the full range of communicative devices, from verbal and paralinguistic to kinesic and proxemic behaviors (see Poyatos 1987/2002), is highlighted in Wadensjö's (2001) analysis of the interpreter's spatial position and its impact on gaze behavior in therapeutic interviews – one of the few corpus-based studies on nonverbal communication in dialogue interpreting since the pioneering analysis of gaze behavior between court interpreters and defendants by Ranier Lang (1978).

The essentially qualitative descriptions of interpreting performance put forward by researchers like Roy (2000a) and Wadensjö (1998) have a valuable quantitative complement in the 2001 PhD research of Brett Rosenberg (2002), who analyzed eleven audiotaped English–Spanish medical interviews in a pediatric primary care clinic in which he was employed as an interpreter. Using five of Wadensjö's (1998) categories of interpreter renditions, Rosenberg found that some 40% of the 1334 interpreter utterances in his corpus were "close renditions" while "zero renditions" (i.e. utterances left untranslated) and "non-renditions", often involving short 'phatic' utterances, accounted for some 27% and 20%, respectively. Thus Rosenberg's **quantitative discourse analysis** reaffirms the dialogue interpreter's translational function while at the same time supplying clear evidence that "the interpreter is a full-fledged participant in the discourse whose responsibilities lie in the *skopos* of the interpreted speech event and in the expectations that the primary parties bring with them" (Rosenberg 2002: 222).

Primary parties' expectations are also foregrounded in Melanie Metzger's (1999) case study of a pediatric interview involving a professional sign language interpreter.

Drawing on concepts from the work of Goffman (e.g. 1981), Metzger examines her material for evidence of the 'frames' and 'schemas' that participants bring to the interpreted encounter. Her analysis of the interpreter's role performance reveals subtle changes in **footing** as reflected in the rendition of pronominal reference. When addressed directly by either party, the interpreter is seen as deliberately giving minimal responses, thereby limiting involvement as an active third party. On the whole, then, Metzger's study on the *Myth of Neutrality* again brings out the intrinsically dual role of interpreters as "both participants in the interaction and conveyors of discourse" (1999: 175). That this can apply even more strikingly in media settings was shown by Francesco Straniero Sergio (1999) in his case study of an interpreted talk show. With reference, again, to the notions of 'footing' and 'frame', the dialogue interpreter on the set is seen as (co-)structuring the interaction by turn-taking initiatives and actively participating in meaning negotiation and topic management, thus revealing the interpreter's neutrality and invisibility as an idealized fiction.

Nor are visibility and involvement limited to televised dialogue interpreting or interpreter-mediated face-to-face communication in general. As borne out by Ebru Diriker's (2001) ethnographic conference case study of English/Turkish simultaneous interpreting at a symposium on philosophy, the performance of conference interpreters is not limited to reproducing 'the meaning intended by the original speaker' but includes various forms of active involvement in the discourse. Having ascertained from on-site interviews that the interpreters in her study were neither neutral nor passive toward the social and interactional context, Diriker (2001) examined the transcribed audiorecording for what she calls "shifts in the speaking subject"; that is, shifts from the speaker's first person (or "alien I") to the 'I' of the interpreter. Diriker shows that the experienced professional interpreters in her study, in contrast to their idealized role in the meta-discourse of the profession, did not only 'speak on behalf of the original speakers' but also regulated turn-taking, resolved overlapping speech, addressed their listeners directly, disclosed the source of problems and interruptions, blended explanatory or compensatory remarks into the speaker's words, divulged their attitudes, voiced their comments and even criticism towards the speakers or other aspects of the interaction, and responded in self-defense to accusations of misinterpretation (see Diriker 2001: 269). Such departures from the professional norm of interpreting in the first person of the speaker (see Harris 1990) have also been discussed with reference to the Demjanjuk trial. As observed by Shlesinger (1991: 152), the use of third-person reference ("The witness says . . . ") indicates dissociation from the speaker and foregrounds the interpreter as "an independent persona". Shlesinger's observation that the courtroom interpreter may also use paralinguistic and prosodic shifts, and especially intonation, to indicate distance from what is being rendered, links up with the broader role issue raised by Collados Aís (1998/2002: 336), who called for more research on the extent of the interpreter's "active involvement in the communication process" by adopting an intonational 'persona' distinct from the original speaker.

7.4.3 Role and professionalism

The degree of the interpreter's involvement as an active participant intersects in a principal way with the issue of professional status. Indeed, features like the use of the speaker's first-person vs indirect speech have traditionally been cited to sharply distinguish professional from 'natural' or non-professional interpreting (see Harris 1990). Knapp-Potthoff and Knapp (1986), who were among the first to undertake discourse-analytical research on the subject, saw non-professional interpreting in informal ('everyday-life') settings as characterized by the **third-party status** adopted by untrained "linguistic mediators", and suggested that the resulting uncertainty regarding the authorship of mediator utterances necessitated the use of reported speech. And yet construing the interpreter's role as "located somewhere on a continuum between that of a mere medium of transmission and that of a true third party" (Knapp-Potthoff and Knapp 1986: 153) does not automatically address the issue of the interpreter's professionalism. Rather, the critical issue appears to be the tendency of interpreters without professional credentials to assume interactional tasks for which they lack training and expertise and which are liable to clash with the interpreting function entrusted to them.

The phenomenon of interpreters assuming an institutional **helper** role – in contrast to the role of helper or advocate for the individual client that was typical of early sign language interpreters – has been described for various community-based settings. In his ethnographic PhD research on communication and interpreting practices in a Californian outpatient clinic, Brad Davidson (1998, 2002) analyzed the behavior of Spanish/English interpreters who, though untrained, were employed by the hospital and hence referred to as 'professional'. Davidson's discourse-based analyses show the interpreters keeping the medical interview "on track" by asking their own follow-up questions and suppressing 'irrelevant' complaints, clearly in response to overriding institutional constraints (» 8.2.2). Similarly, Galina Bolden (2000), in her analysis of two history-taking interviews in a large US hospital in the Midwest, shows the Russian/English interpreter, a 25-year-old man with some training in community interpreting, acting as a **'pre-diagnostic agent'** who actively probes for medically relevant information while excluding the patient's narrative experiential accounts from his summary renditions. The same tendency was observed by Pöchhacker and Kadric (1999) in a case study of non-professional interpreting in a speech therapy session, in which the hospital cleaner serving as mediator sometimes assumed the role of **'co-therapist'**.

Similar findings have been reported in ethnographic studies of mediated police interrogations by German sociologists (e.g. Donk 1994, Scheffer 1997). As shown in the case study by Ute Donk (1994), the interpreter's initiatives in the role of **'deputy officer'**, though apparently ratified by the law enforcement agents, may both foil the interrogator's questioning strategy and alienate the suspect, who perceives the interpreter to be allied with the official. Such evidence of **role overload** and **role conflict**, as anticipated by R.B.W. Anderson (1976/2002), demonstrates that role performance is not only a matter of professionalism on the part of the interpreter. Rather, the latitude and power exercised by interpreters in carrying out their mediating function is subject to setting-specific higher-order constraints at the interactional, socio-professional and institutional levels (» 8.2.2).

7.5 Quality

While quality in interpreting has been a basic concern underlying the process of professionalization, its emergence as a topic of research dates back only to the 1980s. In conference interpreting, more and more attention has been paid to product-oriented analyses, whereas the issue of interpreters' abilities and qualifications (» 8.4.1) remains dominant for community-based domains, where the quest for professional standards is still under way and nowhere near as uniform. Whether the focus is on the 'product' or on the communicative service providers, however, quality is acknowledged as an essentially relative and multi-dimensional concept which can and must be approached with different evaluation methods from a variety of perspectives (see Pöchhacker 2002). Indeed, as presented here in the final section of this chapter, quality appears not as a self-contained topic but as a complex, overarching theme in which all aspects of the interpreter's product and performance – textuality, source–target correspondence, communicative effect, and role performance – play an integral part.

7.5.1 *Criteria and expectations*

As conference interpreting scholars went beyond the tradition of equating quality with the professional status afforded by university-level training and/or membership of AIIC or similar associations, there was a need for explicit criteria on which to base a precise definition. An initial step toward establishing criteria for the quality of interpreting and interpreters was taken by Hildegund Bühler (1986) in a survey of AIIC members. Using a list of sixteen criteria to be rated on a four-point scale ('highly important', 'important', 'less important', 'irrelevant'), Bühler asked her forty-seven respondents to indicate the relative importance of interpreter-related qualities (such as thorough preparation, endurance, poise, pleasant appearance, etc.) as well as nine features of the interpreter's output (native accent, pleasant voice, fluency of delivery, logical cohesion, sense consistency, completeness, correct grammar, correct terminology, appropriate style). Bühler found that most of the criteria were considered 'important' and suggested that the expectations of conference interpreters regarding the quality of professional output corresponded to the needs of those using their services – that is, to the "expectancy norms" (Chesterman 1993: 9) for what an interpretation should be like. Putting this assumption to an empirical test, Kurz (1989a) administered a bilingual (English/German) questionnaire with the first eight of Bühler's output-related criteria to delegates at a medical conference. High correlations with Bühler's results were found only for the criteria of **sense consistency**, **logical cohesion**, and **correct terminology**, whereas delivery-related aspects received lower ratings from the (forty-seven) respondents. Kurz (1993/2002) reported two follow-up surveys conducted in conferences involving engineers and diplomats, respectively. Converting the nominal assessment scale into a four-point metric scale, she observed that the average ratings by end-users were consistently lower than those of the interpreters in Bühler's study, and that users' expectation profiles differed according to their professional background. This was confirmed by a subsequent survey of nineteen 'users', if not end-users, of SI in media settings, who put considerably less emphasis on **completeness** while giving special importance to such criteria as **pleasant voice**, **native accent**, and **fluency of delivery** (Kurz and Pöchhacker 1995).

The variability of quality-related expectations among users of conference interpreting has been investigated and confirmed in a number of small-scale studies (as reviewed by Kurz 2001) and in a major international survey commissioned by AIIC. On the basis of 201 interviews conducted by ninety-four interpreters at eighty-four different meetings, Peter Moser (1996) reported **faithfulness** to the original as the most common expectation expressed spontaneously by the interviewees, followed by **content**, **synchronicity**, **rhetorical skills** and **voice quality**. Although the survey findings generally confirmed the importance given by users to criteria such as completeness, clarity of expression, and terminological precision, expectations tended to vary considerably depending on meeting type (large vs small, general vs technical), age, gender and previous experience with SI. Quite apart from the issue of **variability**, a number of authors have questioned the value of user expectation surveys on the grounds that hypothetical preferences may not reflect the way users actually respond to and judge a given interpretation (» 7.5.3).

Survey research on client expectations has also been carried out for community-based domains, albeit with an emphasis on criteria for a 'good interpreter' and desirable interpreter behavior. As part of a multi-perspective survey, Mesa (2000) asked 288 service providers from thirty different institutions in the Montreal region to rate the importance of over thirty interpreter qualities and behaviors on a three-point scale. The items which received the highest ratings ('very important') from most of the respondents included proficiency in the client's language (96%) and pointing out a client's lack of understanding' (92%). Kadric (2001), in her survey of judges in Vienna, also inquired about expectations regarding interpreters' qualifications and found that her 133 respondents rated 'interpreting skills' and 'linguistic and cultural competence' as more important in a good courtroom interpreter than 'basic legal knowledge' and 'knowledge of court organization and procedure'. Since the judges surveyed by Kadric are directly in charge of hiring interpreters when needed, the study also addresses the perspective of the 'client' in the broader sense of 'employer', which has received very little attention to date. Kadric highlights the specifics of this perspective by pointing to 're-hiring criteria' such as 'smooth facilitation of communication' and costs. As suggested by Moser-Mercer (1996: 50) for the employer's perspective in conference interpreting, criteria such as team discipline, adaptability, flexible scheduling and availability may be part of the quality of service expected of interpreters. Among the few initiatives in this area is a comprehensive 'total quality' study commissioned by the Joint Interpreting and Conference Service (SCIC) of the European Commission, the world's largest purchaser and provider of interpreting services.

7.5.2 *Measurement and judgment*

The need for measuring quality-related features of interpreting performance such as 'accuracy' and 'completeness' first arose in experimental research on SI and gave rise to various ways of scoring and assessing source–target correspondence (« 7.2). This 'inter-textual' perspective on quality has come to be relativized, however, by functional considerations. If, as maintained by Donovan-Cagigos (1990), fidelity cannot be quantified but is relative to the communicative situation, then findings from user expectation surveys, such as the preference for essentials rather than a complete rendition (Vuorikoski 1993: 321, P. Moser 1996: 163f), serve as higher-order principles which qualify accuracy and omission scores. In line with this 'client-centered' (or target-oriented) approach, various features of the interpreter's target text (« 7.1.3) have been examined and quantified as factors contributing to the quality or **acceptability** of the interpreter's product. Again, though, such measurements cannot be used to determine quality *per se*, without knowing when quantitative features begin to have a qualitative impact on audience perception and evaluation. In addition to establishing expectations and criteria as well as quantifying textual and paralinguistic features, researchers have thus relied on user judgments to gauge the effectiveness and quality of the interpeter's performance.

Aside from research to assess the cognitive and pragmatic effect of the interpreter's product (« 7.3), there have also been some fieldwork studies in which users were asked directly to judge the quality of the interpretation received. Gile (1990b) used a short bilingual questionnaire to elicit judgments from twenty-three participants in a medical conference with English/French SI. Asked to assess the interpretation received with regard to "general quality", "linguistic output quality", "terminological usage", "fidelity" and "quality of voice and delivery," respondents gave rather consistent – and favorable – overall ratings. Nevertheless, responses revealed differences between the two language groups (i.e. more critical ratings by French listeners) as well as a differential assessment of the two interpreters working into French with regard to voice and delivery.

For dialogue interpreting in various community settings, fieldwork on interpreting quality was done in Canada by Garber and Mauffette-Leenders (1997), who developed a cumulative case-based survey method to elicit evaluative feedback from service providers and non-English-speaking clients. Question items related to the interpreter's intelligibility, accuracy, confidentiality and impartiality, and responses from a total of thirty-four clients in three language groups (Vietnamese, Polish, Portuguese) indicated a high level of satisfaction with the seventeen interpreters involved. A similar evaluation was carried out by Mesa (2000), who asked sixty-six clients of eleven different language backgrounds to express their agreement (or disagreement) with ten evaluative statements on features of the interpreter's performance.

In an effort to relate text-bound measurements to **subjective performance assessment**, Strong and Rudser (1992) asked twelve deaf and hearing raters to assess the (videotaped) performance of twenty-five interpreters on a rating form which included a general assessment ("dislike" – O.K. – "like") as well as three criteria to be rated on a five-point scale ("low/high sign language ability", "hard/easy to follow", "unpleasant/pleasant to watch"). The authors found inter-rater correlation coefficients between 0.52 and 0.86 and concluded that the reliability of subjective ratings was considerably lower than that of accuracy scores obtained with a proposition-based assessment instrument (Strong and Rudser 1985). Indeed, the fact that raters or users are not very sensitive to such important components of quality as fidelity and linguistic correctness has been stressed by Gile (2003) on the basis of several studies, which clearly suggests a need for multiple approaches to quality-oriented investigations.

7.5.3 Multiple approaches

An initiative combining several perspectives on quality was taken by Anna-Riitta Vuorikoski (1993), who used fieldwork as well as survey techniques to investigate interpreting quality in five seminars with English–Finnish SI involving some 500 participants. With the help of a questionnaire and follow-up telephone interviews, Vuorikoski elicited both expectations and case-based quality judgments from a total of 177 respondents. Her findings included insights on **user motivation** and attitudes as well as a clear preference for a focus on essentials. Respondents had generally experienced the interpretation provided as "informed" and "coherent, or easy to follow" but felt more ambiguous about fluency and the interpreter's rhythm of speech. A similar combination of **expectations** and **judgments** was part of the study by Mesa (2000), who asked service providers in community settings to express their generic expectations and to state whether these had been met by the interpreter under evaluation.

As suggested by Kurz (2001: 405), the evaluative relationship between 'quality perceived' and 'quality expected' could be cast in the formula "Quality = Actual Service – Expected Service". However, several authors have pointed out that "user expectations are often unrealistic" (Bühler 1986: 233) and called for a shift from the concern with 'ideal quality' to "quality under the circumstances" (Pöchhacker 1994c: 242). In line with the assertion by Moser-Mercer (1996: 45) that "quality will always have to be evaluated against the background of the working conditions that prevail in the particular situation under observation", Pöchhacker's (1994a) conference-level case study addressed the issue of quality in an authentic setting by documenting preparatory, situational and text-delivery variables in addition to source- and target-text transcriptions. More recently, Kalina (2002) presented a contrastive analysis of two interpreted conferences in terms of the numerous factors described as relevant to interpreting quality in the literature (e.g. Altman 1990).

An alternative and more focused methodological option for combining different dimensions of quality is to relate specific features of performance to expectations and judgments in controlled experiments. Pioneering work in this regard was done by Collados Aís (1998/2002), who contrasted the expectations elicited from forty-two specialist interpretation users as well as fifteen professional interpreters with the actual assessment given by these subjects to a simulated interpreting performance delivered with either monotonous or lively intonation, with or without factual errors. Most strikingly, she found that subjects who, in line with previous findings, had given less importance to delivery features in the expectation survey, were nevertheless distinctly affected by monotonous intonation, as reflected in lower ratings for overall quality and several other criteria. In contrast, content errors in the 'melodic' interpretation did not result in lower scores, thus confirming that the criterion valued most highly by the users ('fidelity') is the one that they, by definition, fail to appreciate and are likely to judge by such 'secondary' criteria as fluency and lively delivery.

Adopting a similar approach, Giuliana Garzone (2003) collected expectation ratings for four of Bühler's (1986) output criteria from sixteen professional subjects (doctors, engineers) before asking them to judge a simultaneous interpreting performance delivered with or without hesitation and erratic prosody. Again, poor delivery had a marked impact on quality assessments, not only for the criterion of delivery but for voice quality, fidelity and coherence as well. This inter-dependence of quality criteria was confirmed also in an experiment by Andrew Cheung (2003), who asked 120 student subjects to rate the quality of a simultaneous interpretation (into Mandarin Chinese and Cantonese) delivered with either a native or a non native accent. Although the experimental material differed only with regard to accent, subjects, especially in the Cantonese group, gave lower ratings to the non native version for criteria like clarity, pacing, completeness, interference ('code-mixing'), fluency, and coherence.

This experimental evidence of the **interrelations** between various components of quality as perceived by users adds yet another layer of complexity to a topic that is unique for its multiple dimensions. Against this background, the evaluation of interpreting quality in the field suggests the need for a multi-method **case-study** approach which includes a thorough description of situational and interactional variables, inter- as well as intra-textual discourse-based analysis, subjective assessment by users, and insight into the attitudes and expectations of the various 'stakeholders', with particular regard for the perspectives of users (speakers/ listeners), interpreters and employers. As borne out by recent work on interpreting in psychotherapy (Bot 2003), "there are no absolute and unambiguous criteria for defining a mode of interpreting which would be 'good' across the board. Different activity-types with different goal structures, as well as the different concerns, needs, desires and commitments of primary parties, imply various demands on the interpreters" (Wadensjö 1998: 287).

Further reading

Discourse

Consorte (1999), Déjean le Féal (1982), Hatim and Mason (1997, 1997/2002), Mead (2000, 2002), Meyer (2002), Mizuno (1999), Pöchhacker (1994a, 1995b), Shlesinger (1994, 1995b), Taylor Torsello (1997), Tebble (1999); for general reference, see Beaugrande (1980, 1997), Clark (1996), Halliday (1985), Schiffrin *et al.* (2001), van Dijk (1997a, 1997b).

Source–target correspondence

Barik (1975/2002), Berk-Seligson (1990, 2000), Donovan-Cagigos (1990), Gerver (1976), Gile (1992b, 1995b), Hale (1997a, 1997b, 1999), Kopczyński (1980), Krouglov (1999), Kusztor (2000), Mason and Stewart (2001), Napier (2002), Schjoldager (1995/2002), Shlesinger (1995b), Strong and Rudser (1985), Tommola (2003), Tommola and Lindholm (1995), Wadensjö (1993/2002), and the papers in Lambert and Moser-Mercer (1994).

Effect

Berk-Seligson (1988/2002, 1990), Cokely (1990), Collados Aís (1998/2002), Gerver (1976), Livingston *et al.* (1994), Llewellyn-Jones (1981), Shlesinger (1994), Steiner (1998).

Role

R.B.W. Anderson (1976/2002), Bolden (2000), Davidson (2002), Donk (1994), Drennan and Swartz (1999), Kadric (2001), Knapp-Potthoff and Knapp (1986), Kondo and Tebble (1997), Kopczyński (1994), Laster and Taylor (1994), McIntire and Sanderson (1995), Metzger (1999), Mikkelson (1998), Morris (1989, 1990, 1995), Page (1993), Pöchhacker (2000b), Pollitt (1997), Rosenberg (2002), Roy (1993/2002, 1996, 2000a), Shlesinger (1991), Straniero Sergio (1999), Wadensjö (1993/2002, 1998, 2001).

Quality

Bühler (1986), Collados Aís (1998/2002), Garber and Mauffette-Leenders (1997), Gile (1990b, 1995b), Kalina (2002), Kurz (1989a, 1993/2002, 2001), Mesa (2000), Moser-Mercer (1996), Niska (1999), Pöchhacker (1994c, 2002), Shlesinger (1997), Vuorikoski (1993), and the papers in Collados Aís *et al.* (2003); see also the references for 'source–target correspondence' above.

8 Practice and profession

Beyond 'basic research' on the process and product, interpreting studies also addresses the concerns of those who practice interpreting as a profession. Given the deep roots of the academic field of study in the professional field of practice, the literature in the profession-oriented domain represents a continuum ranging from descriptions of personal experience to more detached empirical investigations. While the focus of the present review is on empirical research rather than professional argument, it must be acknowledged that there is no hard and fast line between 'professional writings' and 'academic research', and that the latter relies on the former for substantial input and inspiration.

8.1 History

History as a topic of research on interpreting, while never a priority concern, has received increasing attention ever since the early 1960s, when FIT envisaged a project to enhance the profession by revealing the contribution of translators to the history of humanity. Work to date includes contributions on interpreting as a millennial practice as well as studies on the more recent development of the profession(s).

8.1.1 History of practice

The historiography of interpreting is encumbered by some fundamental problems. Chief among them are the 'evanescence' of the activity, which does not leave any tangible trace, and its often low social esteem. For the most part, interpreting was a 'common' activity, in several respects, which did not merit special mention. With few exceptions, available sources are only marginally concerned with interpreting, making it an arduous task for the historian to locate references to the topic in chronicles, letters, autobiographies and literary works in a range of languages and cultures.

Pioneering attempts to gather together available sources on interpreting were made in the mid-1950s. Three 'Contributions to the History of Interpreting' by German scholars were published together in the same year as the French volume by Edmond Cary (1956), who offered much information of historical interest in his chapter on what he called 'official' translation and interpreting, including military, diplomatic, administrative and judicial settings. In the German volume by Thieme *et al.* (1956), the essay by Egyptologist Alfred Hermann (1956/2002) on "Interpreting in Antiquity" has proved particularly influential. His references to **Ancient Egypt**, **Greece** and **Rome** have been followed up and elaborated on by authors such as Kurz (e.g. 1985) and Vermeer (1992). This body of research also informs the comprehensive chapter on "Interpreters and the Making of History" by Margareta Bowen (1995), which serves as both a capstone to the work built up over four decades and a reference point for further investigations.

One way in which the state of the art has been extended is by adopting a less Eurocentric perspective and including **Asian** and **African** civilizations in the historian's purview (see e.g. Mason 2001). Much ground is also covered in the book by Ruth Roland (1999) on interpreting and translation in the field of **diplomacy** from ancient times up to the early 1980s. Other scholars have sought to develop a deeper historical understanding by narrowing the focus to particular events and persons. The biographical work of Frances Karttunen (1994) on **interpreter-guides** like Doña Marina and Sacajawea and other cultural mediators is a case in point. Other in-depth studies focus on developments in the twentieth century and are thus part of the history of the modern-day interpreting profession.

8.1.2 History of the profession

The most detailed and extensive study on the history of conference interpreting to date was undertaken in the late 1990s by Jesús Baigorri Jalón, a UN staff interpreter with an academic background in history. Based on personal files and administrative records in the Archives of the **League of Nations** and the **ILO** in Geneva, Baigorri Jalón (2000) gives a detailed description of interpreting and interpreters at the **Paris Peace Conference** in 1919. Working with original documents found in these archives, Baigorri Jalón also reconstructs the origins of simultaneous interpreting and provides a blow-by-blow account of the way the idea for a "telephonic translation system" was first implemented in the mid-1920s. Baigorri Jalón's history also covers the time between the wars and "the interpreters of the dictators" and leads up to the **Nuremberg Trials**, when simultaneous interpreting is generally said to have come of age. That crucial event is also the topic of an in-depth study by Francesca Gaiba (1998), who used both judicial records and interviews with interpreters to give a comprehensive description of the trials with a focus on interpreting arrangements and their effect on the proceedings. Apart from these two studies, parts of which are also included in the special issue of *Interpreting* (4:1, 1999) on *The History of Interpreting in the 20th Century*, few scholars have conducted similarly detailed historical research based on archival records and interviews. Wilss (1999), for one, offers a review of German translation and interpreting in the twentieth century, with particular emphasis on training programs, including the long-standing tradition of training in oriental languages in the context of diplomacy and foreign affairs.

Training as a cornerstone in the professionalization of interpreting has commanded particular attention among history-minded scholars, although only conference interpreter training in Europe goes back more than fifty years (e.g. Seleskovitch 1999, Mackintosh 1999). Other developments, such as sign language interpreter training in North America (e.g. Vidrine 1984) and the establishment of interpreter **training programs** throughout the world (see Harris 1997) are relatively recent and not yet the subject of archive-based historical research. A significant aspect of professionalization with somewhat deeper roots is the founding of **professional organizations** of interpreters, some of which date back to the early twentieth century. Paradigm cases in this regard are AIIC (see Keiser 1999) and the US Registry of Interpreters for the Deaf (RID), which is the subject of a 1979 doctoral thesis by Jacqueline Vidrine as well as a personal account by Lou Fant (1990). Similarly, descriptions of the interplay between such aspects of professionalization as legal provisions, professional bodies, training programs, and certification in a given national context and/or domain of interpreting are also part of the overall historical picture, reflecting the highly fragmented nature of the interpreting profession as it has emerged in various contexts and settings (» 8.2).

8.2 Settings

Professional interpreting is situated in a particular social context, which places certain constraints on the activity. It is the dialectic between institutional requirements and expectations on the one hand, and interpreters' performance standards on the other, that gives rise to the level of professionalism prevailing in a given institutional setting. By definition, interpreting in international settings is less constrained by socio-institutional factors than community-based interpreting, which is invariably set within a specific national, legal, political, economic, and cultural framework.

8.2.1 International settings

The emergence of interpreting as a recognized profession is closely associated with international conferencing in the first half of the twentieth century. The very first paper on the subject (Sanz 1931) described the work of interpreters at **multilateral conferences** on the basis of observations and personal interviews. Publications like Herbert's (1952) *Handbook* consolidated the profession's profile, and AIIC, founded in Paris in 1953, embarked on a successful drive to establish uniform standards for interpreting at international conferences, first in Western Europe and then throughout the world (see Keiser 1999). The AIIC Code of Professional Ethics (» 8.3.1) established standards of practice which became a widely accepted yardstick for consecutive and simultaneous interpreting in what remained loosely defined as **conference-like settings**. Indeed, it was these generic standards rather than the requirements of particular institutional settings that came to define the profession, and work in such diverse settings as international tribunals, private talks between heads of state, or television broadcasts is commonly seen as part of the professional territory of conference interpreters.

The uniform approach to conference interpreting standards may explain why the role of institutional constraints in international settings has received very little systematic attention. Among the few exceptions is an effort by Carlo Marzocchi (1998) to highlight the specifics of interpreting in the **European Parliament**. Work on user expectations (« 7.5.1) also points to setting-related constraints, particularly for interpreting in the **media** (see Kurz and Pöchhacker 1995). Media interpreting, however, while typically involving 'international' input, is essentially set within the institutional context of a specific socio-cultural community and is therefore community-based as well as international. Apart from the example of media interpreting in a transnational institutional setting (e.g. the European channel ARTE), socio-cultural specifics play a prominent role, as in the case of delayed-broadcast news interpreting in Japan (see Mizuno in Snelling 1997) and TV interpreting practices in various European countries (e.g. Alexieva 2001, Mack 2002). Most clearly a matter of language transfer in an intra-social context is the rendition of TV broadcasts for deaf viewers, which has been investigated in detail for Germany (Prillwitz 2001) and the UK (Steiner 1998).

8.2.2 Community-based settings

The most explicitly constrained community setting in which interpreters have played a significant role for centuries is the **courtroom**. Legal provisions establishing standards of practice for court interpreting in Spain's colonial empire were enacted as early as the sixteenth century (» 8.3.1), and there is a long, if problematic, tradition of interpreter use in English courts (see Morris 1995). As highlighted by Morris as well as other authors (e.g. Laster and Taylor 1994, Mikkelson 1998, Brennan 1999, Turner 2001), the constraints placed on interpreters in the legal system are often at odds with the standards promoted by the interpreting profession. Efforts have been made only recently, especially at European level (see Hertog 2001), to bridge the gap between unrealistic institutional demands for "verbatim translation" by 'invisible' interpreters on the one hand and a widespread lack of specific training and commonly accepted performance standards for judicial interpreting on the other. However, given the diversity of institutional settings in the **legal domain** (from police interrogations and asylum hearings to guardianship and domestic violence proceedings), the unique features of national legal traditions, and the great variety of languages involved, the goal of uniform professional standards comparable to those prevailing for international settings is not likely to be achieved in the near future. Without doubt, there is a significant role for systematic empirical research in this field along the lines of Berk-Seligson's (1990) pioneering ethnography of interpreting in US courtrooms, the British project on *Deaf People's Access to Justice* (see Brennan 1999), and the studies by Jansen (1995), Scheffer (1997), Kadric (2000), and Wadensjö (1998).

A comparable picture emerges for interpreting in **healthcare** settings, the second major domain of spoken-language interpreting in the community. Though not as tightly constrained by legal precepts and traditions as judicial interpreters, medical interpreters have similarly faced a powerful and highly structured institution in their efforts to promote professional standards. In fact, with few exceptions (see Puebla Fortier 1997), there are no specific legal provisions for an enforceable right to an interpreter in medical settings, nor is there a strong interest on the part of healthcare institutions to provide – and pay for – professional interpreting services. This lack of a well-defined 'market' has made it difficult for a profession to emerge even in the face of well-documented needs, and has favored *ad hoc* models of service provision relying on untrained or minimally trained bilinguals. Under these circumstances, professionalization has largely been "institution-driven" (Ozolins 2000), and research since the 1960s on inter-preting in healthcare strongly reflects the medical-institutional rather than the professional-translational perspective (see Drennan and Swartz 1999). Among the areas that have been given special attention are psychiatry (e.g. Marcos 1979) and psychotherapy (e.g. Bot 2003). In a broader perspective, recent work such as the ethnographic study by Davidson (1998) has highlighted the extent to which the diverse constraints of the healthcare setting impact on the standards of practice of more or less professional interpreters in this field.

While work in legal, medical and social service settings is no less important for sign language interpreters than for spoken-language interpreters, there are additional community-based settings which are unique to the practice of signed language interpreting. In countries with legislation providing for the 'main-streaming' of deaf students (as adopted in the US in the 1970s), **educational** interpreting is one of the chief professional domains of sign language interpreters. In the US, where schools, colleges and universities are the most important users of sign language interpreters, educational interpreting has been the subject of an impressive body of literature. There and elsewhere, research topics have included the cognitive effectiveness of interpreted lectures in various commu-nication modes (e.g. Cokely 1990, Livingston *et al.* 1994), the role of contextual constraints and strategies (e.g. Napier 2002), and the special qualifications required of educational interpreters (e.g. Hayes 1992, Harrington 2000).

Among the diverse institutional contexts in which sign language interpreters may be expected to work, special challenges have been described for **religious** settings and for interpreting in the **theater** (see Frishberg 1990).

8.3 Standards

More or less constrained by legal provisions, institutional requirements, educational opportunities, and mutual agreement, an 'occupation' takes shape as a 'profession' as the values and principles underlying expected and accepted behavior are codified and reaffirmed collectively by its practitioners. While most professional codes also specify performance levels, for example in terms of 'fidelity', 'accuracy' and 'completeness' (« 7.2.1), their main concern is with practitioners' ethical conduct as members of the interpreting profession and incumbents of a particular role (« 7.4).

8.3.1 Ethics

Written standards of conduct for interpreters can be traced back at least to the fourteen laws enacted by the Spanish Crown between 1529 and 1630 to regulate the behavior of interpreters in contacts between colonial officials and the native population (see Bowen 1995). In contrast to such rules imposed on practitioners by higher authority, international conference interpreters forging their profession some four hundred years later acted autonomously when they adopted the **AIIC Code of Professional Ethics** in early 1957. At the heart of this code of professional conduct and practice is a "Code of Honor" which consists of five articles, chief among them the principle of professional secrecy. The remainder contains detailed provisions concerning "Working Conditions", and these interrelate with the more specific "Professional Standards" formulated by AIIC to regulate the exercise of the profession. Thus settled, questions of ethics received little attention in the literature on conference interpreting until the 1990s. Since then, deregulation in the wake of the anti-trust case brought against AIIC in the US has given the topic of professional conduct and ethics new relevance among international conference interpreters. Even so, the AIIC Code remains silent about issues of role and performance quality (aside from the impact of working conditions) which have loomed large in other domains of the profession.

A trailblazing achievement in the professionalization of interpreting beyond international conferences and organizations was the adoption of the **RID Code of Ethics** in early 1965. Even though RID members at the time were less concerned with building a profession than with promoting the availability of competent interpreters (see Fant 1990), their Code of Ethics, revised and updated in the late 1970s, proved fundamental to the professional identity of sign language interpreters in North America. Indeed, the RID Code has served as the principal model for moves to establish professional standards in other countries and domains of interpreting. Since the RID Code of Ethics also addresses such principles as 'impartiality' and 'faithfulness', however, the approach to ethics in community-based domains inevitably intersects with the complex issue of the interpreter's role (« 7.4). Particularly in the field of sign language interpreting, problems of ethics (and role) have thus generated considerable debate and research. A number of authors have expressed dissatisfaction with the strictures of the Code. Tate and Turner (1997/2002), for instance, who surveyed some 100 British sign language interpreters about ethically challenging scenarios, proposed that the Code should be complemented by a kind of "case law" providing guidance on particularly complex situations. A more fundamental reorientation has been advocated by Cokely (2000), who has faulted the RID Code of Ethics for its deontological approach – that is, its focus on rigid limitations and prescriptions. Instead, Cokely proposes a "rights-based approach," which would give interpreters more freedom for professional decision-making in a given situation or case (see also Harrington and Turner 2001).

Following the RID example, efforts to codify professional practice in spoken-language community interpreting have been made particularly for legal and healthcare settings (see Mikkelson 2000/01). Whereas some codes – and authors – oriented towards court interpreting typically exhibit a more conservative, mechanistic attitude (e.g. Schweda Nicholson 1994), authors like Niska (1995) and Mikkelson (1998) have advocated the **emancipation**, if not 'empowerment', of the (court) interpreter as a responsible professional rather than an unobtrusive message converter. Similarly, the descriptive research by Wadensjö (1998) has pointed to the inadequacy of the Swedish Guide to Good Practice (*God tolksed*) in regulating the real-life dynamics of interpreter-mediated encounters. By the same token, standards of practice for healthcare interpreters in the US and Canada have been reviewed critically by Kaufert and Putsch (1997). Using case examples, these authors show how principles such as confidentiality, accuracy and completeness, and client self-determination are difficult to maintain in certain constellations of interaction. An effort to address these concerns while building on established traditions of codification was made by the California Healthcare Interpreters Association (CHIA), whose *Standards* document comprises six ethical principles as well as guidance on issues of intervention and advocacy.

8.3.2 *Certification*

Where explicit standards exist for such principles as confidentiality, integrity, and professionalism, some form of recognition is still needed to indicate whether a given practitioner can be expected to meet his or her ethical obligations toward society, employers, individual clients, and fellow professionals. One way of 'certifying' compliance with professional standards is membership in a professional organization that has adopted a code of conduct and practice. In the field of conference interpreting, the strict **admissions** policy of AIIC has served the purpose of a certification system, and the organization's directory of members has been regarded as a register of qualified professionals. For court interpreters, in contrast, some jurisdictions require no more than the swearing of an **oath**. As stated by Berk-Seligson (1990: 204), however, "No amount of oath-swearing can guarantee high quality interpreting from an interpreter who does not have the necessary competency." In domains for which professional training is either lacking or not well established, recourse is therefore made to certification procedures involving some form of **testing** or performance assessment. The model case, again, is the RID certification system. Launched in the early 1970s, the RID system and its assessment methods have been the subject of several studies addressing issues of validity and reliability (e.g. Strong and Rudser 1985, 1992). Other examples, and no less worth investigating in this regard, are the skills-based examinations conducted by NAATI, Australia's National Accreditation Authority for Translators and Interpreters (see Bell 1997), certification programs for US court interpreters at federal and state levels, healthcare interpreter certification in some parts of the US (e.g. Washington, Massachusetts), the Diploma of Public Service Interpreting administered by the Institute of Linguists in the UK, and efforts to certify providers of interpreting services according to 'standards' in the technical sense of the word. In any case, interpreter certification is closely intertwined with the topic of assessment (» 9.4) as well as with the levels of competence and expertise required of a professional (» 8.4).

8.4 Competence

For a practice or occupation to be acknowledged as a profession, it must be perceived to rest on a complex body of knowledge and skills, mastery of which can only be acquired by specialized training. Competence in interpreting can thus be defined as the congruence between task demands (performance standards) and qualifications, and an understanding of the latter is crucial to professionalization in general and interpreter training in particular. Chiefly informed by approaches from psychology, there is a growing body of research on the abilities and expertise which make up an interpreter's professional competence.

8.4.1 Personal qualities and abilities

Interpreters and psychologists have long pointed to a number of psychological prerequisites for those who would exercise the profession of interpreter. Based on interviews with twenty conference interpreters, whose performance he observed at the League of Nations and the ILO, Sanz (1931) listed a dozen qualities, including **cognitive** abilities (e.g. intelligence, intuition, memory) as well as **moral** and **affective** qualities (e.g. tact, discretion, alertness, poise). With an emphasis on the latter, the original RID Code of Ethics, adopted in 1965, required interpreters to be "of high moral character, honest, conscientious, trustworthy, and of emotional maturity" (Cokely 2000: 35), and similar requirements are often found in legal provisions for court interpreters. The list of personal prerequisites given by van Hoof (1962: 59ff) for court, military, liaison as well as conference interpreters includes **physical** qualities such as stamina and strong nerves, **intellectual** qualities, in particular language proficiency and wide general knowledge, and **mental** qualities such as memory skills, judgment, concentration and divided attention. With reference to conference interpreting, Keiser (1978: 17) emphasizes 'knowledge' (mastery of languages and general background knowledge) and 'personal qualities' including "the ability to intuit meaning," adaptability, concentration, memory skills, a gift for public speaking and a pleasant voice. For liaison interpreting, Gentile *et al.* (1996: 65ff) suggest language skills, cultural competence, interpreting techniques, memory skills and professional ethics as the main components of an interpreter's competence. For sign language interpreters, Frishberg (1990: 25ff) places particular emphasis on interpersonal and cross-cultural skills, whereas she subsumes interpreting skills under the heading of "language competencies".

Several attempts to profile interpreter personalities with the help of standard psychological instruments have yielded little conclusive evidence: examples include the neuroticism scale of the Eysenck Personality Inventory (Gerver 1976); the questionnaire for determining Type A (coronary-prone) behavior (Cooper *et al.*

1982); the Wechsler Adult Intelligence Scale and the California Personality Inventory (Strong and Rudser 1992); and the State-Trait-Anxiety Inventory (Kurz 1996). In a more specific line of investigation, **psychological tests** have been applied to discriminate between typical translator and interpreter personalities. Kurz *et al.* (1996) discussed previous studies as well as results from a student survey with reference to the model of communication value orientation by Casse. Whereas the dominant orientation for translators was toward 'process' and 'people', the typical interpreter was found to be 'people-oriented' and 'action-oriented'; that is, focusing on social interaction and 'getting things done'. Feldweg (1996), in an interview-based survey of thirty-nine German AIIC members, reaffirmed the consensus among professionals regarding the cognitive skills and affective disposition characteristic of a good interpreter (see also Bühler 1986). And yet the chief intellectual abilities required of interpreters – broad general education and knowledge, proficiency in working languages, cultural competence, analytic and memory skills – are difficult to establish as distinctive of interpreting. Researchers have therefore focused on the way this set of abilities evolves into the specific skills which make up an interpreter's expertise.

8.4.2 *Special skills and expertise*

The crucial starting point for the development of interpreting proficiency is bilingual skills (« 6.1.1), which, according to the theory of natural translation (Harris and Sherwood 1978), imply a rudimentary ability to translate. Just how this and other baseline abilities give rise to professional performance has been studied in the framework of expertise research – an area of cognitive psychology which has grown out of work on information processing and artificial intelligence since the 1970s (see Hoffman 1997). As has been established for a diverse range of domains, experts rely on richly integrated knowledge representations and elaborate mental models, and use advanced reasoning processes in perceptual and problem-solving tasks. Progressing beyond declarative ('rule-based') knowledge, experts have at their disposal flexible, context-sensitive strategies which have become automatic to the point of being regarded as intuition and tacit (procedural) knowledge. While this makes **knowledge elicitation** from expert interpreters a considerable challenge, a number of methodological approaches, including structured interviews, task analysis and contrastive performance analysis, have been suggested – and fit in well with previous studies on interpreting. The task analysis for consecutive interpreting described by Robert Hoffman (1997: 205), for instance, is reminiscent of the pioneering study by Seleskovitch (1975), and there is a long tradition of experimental research comparing the performance of professional subjects ('experts') with that of beginning students or bilingual controls ('novices'). Examples include Barik (1973, 1975/2002) on pauses and errors, Lambert (1989) on recall and recognition, Dillinger (1994) on comprehension, Padilla *et al.* (1995) on working memory capacity, Kurz (1996) on simultaneous listening and speaking, Andres (2002) on note-taking, and Mead (2002) on disfluencies in consecutive renditions.

Work set explicitly in the so-called **expert–novice paradigm** has been reported by Moser-Mercer *et al.* (2000), whose experiments focused on various language processing skills assumed to be part of expert proficiency in interpreting. However, while professionals were better able than students to avoid attentional disturbance in the 'delayed auditory feedback' task, neither the shadowing task nor a series of verbal fluency tasks yielded evidence discriminating between expert and novice performance. Similarly, the work of Liu (2001) suggests that expertise in simultaneous interpreting is not a function of discrete processing abilities (such as working memory capacity) but of task-specific skills (selective processing, efficient output monitoring and allocation of working memory resources in SI) which are acquired through extensive time-on-task, as in training and, in particular, real-life experience. Beyond cognitive processing and task performance as such, expertise in interpreting also includes assignment-related interactional skills (e.g. in briefings and the negotiation of working conditions) and strategies for knowledge acquisition, with or without the use of technological tools (» 8.5.2).

8.5 Technology

Technological advances since the early twentieth century have fueled the emergence of new forms of interpreting and extended the range of applications of interpreters' skills. Since the 1990s, the confluence of telecommunications and digital data processing systems has had a major impact on professional practice, particularly in multilingual conference settings, and has generated research needs that have yet to be more fully addressed.

8.5.1 Telecommunication

Spoken-language interpreting in multilingual conference settings was revolutionized by the application of **electro-acoustic transmission** systems to carry speech streams simultaneously and over a distance, but essentially 'on site', to the respective recipients. Whereas the electric circuitry involved in SI was still a novelty worth detailed description in the early 1960s (see van Hoof 1962: 119ff), it drew little further attention in subsequent decades. And yet, soon after the establishment of international standards governing signal quality in SI equipment (» 8.6.1), the first experiments with sound-and-picture teleconference interpreting, carried out by UN bodies in the late 1970s, heralded the fundamental challenge of remote conference interpreting that was to confront the profession two decades later. Thus problems with signal quality in **videoconferencing** via terrestrial (rather than satellite) links have led to renewed interest in transmission quality and the evolution of technological standards (see Mouzourakis 1996). Aside from technical reasons, conference interpreters have mainly cited psychological grounds for opposing 'tele-interpreting' or 'distance interpreting' – that is, 'off-site' videoconference interpreting, without a direct view of the speaker or of the audience. In surveys of conference interpreters to elicit their response to remote interpreting arrangements, problems like eye strain, fatigue, nervous tension and a sense of alienation, associated with a lack of motivation, are among the most common findings (e.g. UN 2001). Aside from such studies addressing issues of professional ecology (» 8.6), Braun and Kohn (2001), in one of the few linguistic-descriptive contributions on the subject, analyze discourse data from simulated videoconferences (via ISDN link) with tele-interpreting between German and English. Acknowledging the problems engendered by poor transmission quality, the authors nevertheless find evidence of efficient monitoring and adaptation strategies on the part of the interpreters, pointing to the potential rather than the limitations of such teleworking arrangements (see also Niska 1999, Stoll 2000).

Indeed, remote interpreting with an audio signal only has long been practiced in the form of telephone interpreting, which had been proposed as early as the 1950s (see Paneth 1957/2002). Even though used for dialogic communication, where the lack of access to nonverbal (visual) cues might be felt as a severe limitation, telephone interpreting services have enjoyed a high degree of acceptance (and commercial success), particularly in the US and the UK. **Over-the-phone** interpreting is also used to serve deaf people, sometimes with the use of videotelephony (see Niska 1999), but very little research on the subject has been carried out. Aside from an experimental study contrasting a monolingual (English) to an interpreted (English–Japanese) telephone conversation (see Niska 1999: 112), the research potential of telephone interpreting has been explored in particular by Wadensjö (1999). Analyzing authentic discourse data from two interpreter-mediated encounters involving the same participants (a Russian-speaking woman and a Swedish police officer), Wadensjö showed that the participants' audiovisual co-presence in on-site interpreting facilitated a shared conversational rhythm, permitting more talk and interaction in less time. Conversely, an initiative launched in California to introduce **remote simultaneous** dialogue interpreting in healthcare settings yielded more favorable evaluations than on-site consecutive interpreting (see Niska 1999: 112f). In a similar vein, simultaneous telephone interpreting has been introduced in some US federal courts. This and other innovations, such as the use of hand-held wireless SI equipment, are likely to have a decisive impact on interpreters' working conditions (» 8.6.1).

8.5.2 Tools

Ever since the 1920s, conference interpreters working in the consecutive mode have made do with such simple 'tools' as a notepad and a pen. A variant of the simultaneous mode involving the conversion of source-language speech into target-language writing on an overhead projector was described by Paneth (1990), who suggested that projection from a PC might enhance the potential of this technique. While such "projected interpretation" has received little attention, it bears a relation to both the technique of 'live subtitling' and the idea of employing interpreters for the on-line rendition of messages in multilingual Internet chats, as practiced in the SCIC.

A radical innovation involves the use of **digital recording** technology to replace note-taking for consecutive interpreting. In what has been called the "consecutive simultaneous" mode (Ferrari 2001), interpreters use portable PC equipment to record the source speech on digital tape and then, replaying it into a headset, render it in the simultaneous mode. Similarly, digital memory has been employed for short-term processing support in the simultaneous interpreting booth. A repeat function included in some SI consoles allows the interpreter to replay the previous seconds of the source speech from a buffer memory and then catch up with the speaker's real-time delivery. Here again, technology-driven developments are under way that await systematic research.

More than digital speech processing, though, PC-based word processing, particularly of terminological and textual data, has been changing the working environment and techniques of simultaneous conference interpreters in their booths. Moser-Mercer (1992) carried out a first survey of more than 100 AIIC members to establish their needs and preferences regarding terminology management software. PC-based tools tailored to the workflow in simultaneous interpreting for technical conferences have since been developed, including LookUp®, a modular resource system designed for use in both off-line preparation and on-line search (Stoll 2002). This kind of multi-functional "Conference Interpreter's Workbench," which combines disk-based language support and Internet access from the booth, represents an important step in the direction of computer-assisted interpreting.

8.5.3 *Automation*

At considerable remove from the interests of professional interpreters, researchers in such fields as computer science, linguistics, speech processing and artificial intelligence have made substantial efforts to implement systems for **speech-to-speech machine translation**, or 'automatic interpreting'. All of the major research prototypes developed since the 1990s – in the US, Japan and several European countries – are restricted in both mode and domain; that is, limited to consecutive dialogue interpreting in such specific communicative genres as appointment scheduling and travel information. Some researchers, particularly in Japan, have placed the emphasis on **interpreting telephony**, which is a central system for machine interpreting of telephone conversations (see LuperFoy 1996). In contrast, the German ***Verbmobil*** project, a multi-center undertaking which received nearly €60 million in public funds between 1993 and 2000, was aimed at building a portable machine interpreting system for face-to-face dialogue (see Wahlster 2000). Aside from achievements in the area of speech recognition and language processing, *Verbmobil* research has yielded insights into 'dialogue acts' which are highly germane to the study of human interpreting. The work of Susanne Jekat (Jekat and Klein 1996) and Birte Schmitz (1998), for instance, highlights the inadequacy of a close ('semantic') rendition of spontaneous speech and argues for a translational approach based on the 'intended interpretation', as determined with reference to the dialogic context and the communicative purpose of a given dialogue act.

8.6 Ecology

Interpreters are essentially involved in interaction and are therefore subject to a variety of constraints arising from the communicative situation and the environment in which they perform their work. Interpreters' working conditions, which are increasingly shaped by technology (« 8.5) and involve a number of stressors, have given rise to concerns about occupational health, some of which have been addressed by research.

8.6.1 Working conditions

In the broader sense of 'employment conditions', investigations of professional practice focus on such **industrial issues** as level of compensation, treatment by employers, and amount of work – both in the sense of excessive work-load and underemployment. In conference interpreting, such issues have been addressed rather effectively by AIIC, which was after all conceived as a hybrid between a professional body and a trade union (see Keiser 1999: 84). More recently, community-based interpreters have followed a similar course, either through professional associations or trade unions. An example of the latter is the British National Union of Professional Interpreters and Translators (NUPIT), which aspires to represent public service interpreters and has surveyed its members on employment conditions (NUPIT 2001).

In a more specific sense, interpreters' working conditions in a given assignment are shaped by the physical environment, including time and place; by task-related factors such as preparation, cognitive workload, and various input variables (« 6.6); and by inter-personal factors (e.g. relations with team members, client feedback). Many of these have been the subject of further investigation, particularly among international conference interpreters. With an emphasis on booth size and the quality of sound transmission, Walter Jumpelt (1985) described the working environment of conference interpreters under international standards: ISO 2603 (first adopted in 1974) for built-in (permanent) booths and ISO 4043 for mobile booths as well as IEC 60914 for sound systems equipment. Janet Altman (1990) surveyed both Brussels-based staff interpreters and freelance AIIC members on factors which have an impact on performance quality, including the quality of sound transmission, availability of documents, density and delivery of the source speech, and visual access to the proceedings. The latter has emerged as a principal challenge with the spread of remote interpreting arrangements, both in conference interpreting and in legal and healthcare settings (« 8.5.1). The most comprehensive investigation into conference interpreters' working conditions is the **Workload Study** commissioned by AIIC (2002), which included on-site measurements of such physical factors as air quality, temperature and humidity in the booth in the course of a workday. In this study CO_2 levels and temperatures were found to exceed ISO recommendations, particularly in mobile booths, and a number of other shortcomings were noted.

8.6.2 Stress and health

The AIIC Workload Study, which addressed **physical** as well as **physiological** and **psychological** parameters in the professional practice of conference interpreting, was fundamentally concerned with sources of occupational stress and their impact on professional performance. A previous AIIC-supported study, by Cooper *et al.* (1982), had involved thirty-three interviews in Strasbourg, Brussels and Geneva as well as a world-wide mail survey, in which a total of 826 AIIC members responded to a fourteen-page questionnaire on issues such as job satisfaction, sources of stress, mental health status, and cardiovascular risk factors (Type A behavior). As part of their more complex investigation, the authors of the Workload Study (AIIC 2002) surveyed some 600 (mainly freelance) AIIC members, whose responses indicated high levels of work-related fatigue, exhaustion and mental stress, and pointed to difficult source texts and speaker delivery, poor booth conditions and insufficient preparation as the most important stressors. The perception by interpreters that theirs is a highly stressful occupation was matched by objective measures such as hormone levels (cortisol) and cardiovascular activity (blood pressure and heart rate). However, the feeling, expressed by 40–60% of respondents, that work-related stress causes a drop in performance quality, was not substantiated by an assessment of interpretation samples for meaning correspondence, linguistic correctness, and delivery. There is, however, experimental evidence that the fatigue resulting from excessively long turns in SI (up to 60 minutes) has a significant detrimental effect on performance (see Moser-Mercer *et al.* 1998, Zeier 1997).

The types and levels of stress experienced by interpreters on the job are clearly subject to a variety of **situational** and **personal** factors. Whereas the Workload Study was geared to on-site interpreting in conference settings, its survey component also touched on videoconference interpreting, of which 61% of respondents had at least some experience. Asked about the effects of remote interpreting arrangements, the interpreters in the sample indicated that it resulted in higher stress levels, less physical comfort, and lower performance quality. While this is in line with the responses of interpreters participating in the UN remote interpreting trial (UN 2001), there is little evidence of lower output quality as judged from the perspective of interpretation users. Higher stress levels compared to conventional conference interpreting have also been reported for media interpreting. Kurz (2002a) used cardiovascular indicators as well as sweat gland activation, measured by reduced galvanic skin resistance, to show different physiological stress responses when working during a technical conference and a live-broadcast interpreting assignment.

While most stress research has focused on spoken-language SI in conference settings, sign language interpreting has been shown to involve high levels of task-related stress as well. Peper and Gibney (1999) traced respiration rates, skin conductance, and upper extremity electromyographic activity in nine experimental subjects and found elevated levels of physiological arousal which they concluded were conducive to a deleterious cycle of pain. This relates in particular to educational settings (« 8.2.2), where turns may be as long as an entire class period, with little recovery time, and where thorough preparation of the subject matter is hardly feasible. Several authors have shown educational interpreters to be particularly at risk from repetitive strain injury, or 'upper extremity cumulative trauma disorders' like tendinitis and carpal tunnel syndrome. Feuerstein *et al.* (1997) surveyed some 1400 sign language interpreters and found the prevalence of upper extremity disorders (up to 32%) to be associated with a combination of work demands, psychosocial stressors, and workstyle (e.g. excessive hand/wrist deviations from the neutral position as the sign equivalent of shouting).

Occupational health **hazards** for interpreters in the community also include the risk of infection in medical settings and threats to personal safety, as in police settings and legal cases (see NUPIT 2001). A survey by Karen Baistow (1999) of nearly 300 community interpreters in five European countries highlighted the role of psychologically troubling experiences, and more than half of respondents in the NUPIT survey reported "significant emotional stress" arising from their work or the circumstances of their clients. Most acutely, post-traumatic stress has been described for interpreting in the hearings of the South African Truth and Reconciliation Commission (see Wiegand 2000). Such health risks, together with low levels of compensation, have been cited as reasons for interpreter **burnout**, one of the key issues addressed in the AIIC Workload Study.

8.7 Sociology

As a more or less clearly defined professional group in society, interpreters can be studied from a variety of sociological angles. In addition to the aspects touched on in previous sections of this chapter, some of the rather scattered research findings on the profession in society, and on individuals in the profession, can be discussed under the broad headings of status and demographic composition.

8.7.1 Status

One of the most comprehensive reviews of the conference interpreting profession is offered, from a German perspective, by Feldweg (1996), who touches on such issues as recognition and the public image of conference interpreters as reflected in literary works and in the mass media. Kondo (1988) described the socio-cultural context of conference interpreters in Japan, suggesting reasons for the rather modest status of the profession in that country. An empirical finding that has emerged in various surveys, including the AIIC Workload Study, is the perception that the **prestige** of the profession has declined over the years, though this appears to have little effect on the high level of job satisfaction among conference interpreters. With regard to the status of individuals in the profession, discussion focuses on issues such as access to the profession, employment status, career opportunities, and equality of the sexes, on which few systematic data are available outside the realm of professional associations. This lack of data is particularly acute for community-based interpreting, which is still characterized in many countries by a lack of recognition and a low degree of organization.

A major issue which brings out some distinctive features of different sectors of the profession is the **cultural identity** and status of interpreters. Historically, it was mainly immersion in more than one cultural community that qualified individuals to assume the role of interpreter, and this applied to the pioneers of conference interpreting in the early twentieth century as much as to early sign language interpreters. The consequences of academization are well known and appreciated for the field of conference interpreting – and are similarly desired by community interpreters. However, the fact that access to the profession is now mainly via the academic route rather than through cultural immersion and interaction may be problematic for sign language interpreters, who are invariably seen by the deaf community as members of the majority culture responsible for their marginalization and oppression (see e.g. Cokely 2000). For spoken-language community interpreters, in contrast, the fact that they often belong to the ethnic minority or migrant culture of the individual client is likely to color the attitudes towards them in the mainstream society. The cultural hybrid status and variable alliances with dominant powers that have been typical of dragomans and interpreters throughout their millennial history (see Karttunen 1994, Cronin 2002) thus remain a live issue in parts of the profession today.

8.7.2 Demographics

Apart from the impressive growth of the profession since the 1950s and 1960s, as reflected in the membership figures of professional bodies like AIIC and RID, the most striking demographic phenomenon has been the growing presence of women, who have come to outnumber men in the profession at a ratio of roughly 3 : 1. Among the explanations advanced for the **feminization** of the profession has been a superior aptitude for languages and communication in women. Less flatteringly, the high percentage of women, who first outnumbered men within AIIC in 1967 (see Feldweg 1996: 82), has also been associated with declining prestige and the increasing image of interpreting as a service or helping profession. The latter is particularly pronounced in community-based settings, not least in sign language interpreting, where low rates of pay have been cited as a disincentive for men to enter the profession. Following an early survey effort of US sign language interpreters by Cokely (1981), Stauffer *et al.* (1999) reported a demographic profile of some 200 attendees of the 1997 RID Convention. In addition to evidence of more formal training in interpreting, the authors found their sample to be predominantly female (79%) and middle-aged, with over 70% of respondents in their thirties or forties. Among conference interpreters, a significant number of long-time practitioners are close to retirement age, thus pointing to the crucial importance of interpreter training programs in ensuring an adequate supply of competent professionals.

Further reading

History

Baigorri Jalón (2000), Bowen (1995), Cary (1956), Fant (1990), Gaiba (1998), Herbert (1978), Hermann (1956/2002), Karttunen (1994), Keiser (1999), Kurz (1985), Roland (1999), Thieme *et al.* (1956), van Hoof (1962), Vidrine (1984), Wilss (1999), and the papers in the special issue of *Interpreting* (4:1, 1999).

Settings

Alexieva (2001), Berk-Seligson (1990), Brennan (1999), Chiaro (2002), Davidson (1998), Frishberg (1990), Gentile *et al.* (1996), Harrington (2000), Hayes (1992), Hertog (2001), Jansen (1995), Kadric (2000, 2001), Laster and Taylor (1994), Mack (2002), Marzocchi (1998), Morris (1995), Puebla Fortier (1997), Seal (1998), Turner (2001).

Standards

Bell (1997), Cokely (2000), Harrington and Turner (2001), Kaufert and Putsch (1997), Mikkelson (2000/01), Morris (1995, 2000), Niska (1995), Pollitt (1997), Roy (1993/2002), Schweda Nicholson (1994), Tate and Turner (1997/2002); for ethics in Translation studies, including specific domains of interpreting, see the special issue of *The Translator* (7:2, 2001).

Competence

Feldweg (1996), Gentile *et al.* (1996), Gerver (1976), Hoffman (1997), Keiser (1978), Kurz (1996), Kurz *et al.* (1996), Moser-Mercer (2000), Moser-Mercer *et al.* (1997, 2000), Strong and Rudser (1992), van Hoof (1962); see also the references for 'selection' and 'assessment' in Chapter 9.

Technology

Braun and Kohn (2001), Ferrari (2001), Jekat and Klein (1996), LuperFoy (1996), Mouzourakis (1996, 2000), Niska (1999, 2002), Schmitz (1998), Stoll (2000, 2002), Wadensjö (1999), Wahlster (2000); see also the papers in Hauenschild and Heizmann (1997) and web pages at http://www.aiic.net, http://europa.eu.int/comm/scic/, http://www.lookup-online.de, http://www.is.cs.cmu.edu/js/, http://verbmobil.dfki.de.

Ecology

AIIC (2002), Altman (1990), Baistow (1999), Cooper *et al.* (1982), Feuerstein *et al.* (1997), Jumpelt (1985), Kurz (2002a), Moser-Mercer *et al.* (1998), NUPIT (2001), Zeier (1997); see also relevant pages on the AIIC website (http://www.aiic.net).

Sociology

Cokely (1981, 2000), Feldweg (1996), Kondo (1988), Stauffer *et al.* (1999); see also relevant pages on the AIIC website (http://www.aiic.net).

9 Pedagogy

From the earliest writings on interpreting in the 1950s, imparting the requisite knowledge and skills on to the next generation of professionals has stood out as an overriding concern in the literature. Assuming that teaching presupposes a thorough understanding of what is to be taught, much research on interpreting, as presented in previous chapters, has been carried out in the context and, more or less directly, in the service of interpreter training. Indeed, most authors in interpreting studies are involved in interpreter education, as teachers or as students completing a thesis requirement, and many studies have been carried out on student subjects. Nevertheless, as a research topic as such, the pedagogy of interpreting has generated little systematic investigation but a comparatively large body of experiential description. Apart from basic curricular issues, prominent themes in the literature on interpreter training include student selection and performance assessment as well as teaching methods for developing the skills that make up the interpreter's core competence (« 8.4).

9.1 Curriculum

While courses for the development of interpreting-specific skills date back to the early twentieth century, systematic reflection on curricular issues remained very limited until the 1980s and 1990s, when the strongly profession-based tradition of conference interpreter training was complemented by a scientific, process-oriented approach, and new training needs for interpreting in community-based settings highlighted the role of the curriculum as an organizational structure framing and guiding teaching practice.

9.1.1 Approaches

For most of the twentieth century, nearly all training programs and institutions were geared to spoken-language interpreting in multilingual international settings. With the clear goal of developing professional skills in consecutive and simultaneous interpreting, first-generation teachers of interpreting, themselves accomplished professionals, established a lasting tradition of training by **apprenticeship**; that is, transfer of know-how and professional knowledge from master to student, mainly by exercises modeled on real-life tasks. In the face of expansive growth in interpreter training in Europe in the 1950s and 1960s, and the growing influence of foreign-language pedagogy on training, the conference interpreting profession as represented by AIIC reaffirmed the apprenticeship approach in a series of meetings and asserted its influence on university-level interpreter training by a **school policy** (see Seleskovitch 1999: 58). The single most important force shaping what Mackintosh (1995) described as the "training paradigm" for conference interpreting was the strongly profession-based program at ESIT, Paris. Underpinned by the holistic theory of Seleskovitch (« 4.2, « 5.4.1), the Paris School's pedagogy was laid down in a comprehensive training manual (Seleskovitch and Lederer 1989) which was not only co-published and endorsed by the European institutions but also, through an English translation published by the RID (Seleskovitch and Lederer 1995), was made directly available to the American sign language interpreting community.

As the certainties of the Paris School paradigm came to be questioned in the 1980s (« 4.4), calls for a more **scientific approach** were also made for interpreter training (see Gran and Dodds 1989). Representatives of the cognitive process-oriented paradigm have applied their models to skill training for interpreters, highlighting aspects such as component skills (e.g. Lambert 1988), strategies (e.g. Riccardi 1996, Kalina 1998), processing capacity management (Gile 1995b) and the development of expertise (Moser-Mercer 2000, Moser-Mercer *et al.* 2000). As an early advocate of a more scientific, theory-driven training paradigm, Arjona (1978, 1984) has been among the few interpreter educators who have not only turned to fields like psycholinguistics and cognitive psychology for insights on the interpreting process, but also drawn on the theory of education as such to address issues of curriculum. In her 1990 PhD thesis on curriculum policy-making, Arjona-Tseng demonstrated, on the basis of an ethnographic case study in Taiwan, how socio-cultural, political and institutional constraints impact on curriculum design and implementation. With a more specific focus, David Sawyer (2001) similarly leveraged advances in curriculum theory for a case study of curriculum and assessment at a US T/I school. Sawyer shows how, alongside a scientific approach centered on processing-skill components and stages of expertise, a **humanistic** approach to curriculum foregrounds the personal and social aspects of instructional interaction and the process of socializing students into a "community of professional practice" (see 2001: 93ff). Thus concepts such as 'situated cognition', 'reflective practice' and 'cognitive apprenticeship' can be used to underpin a more student-oriented and interaction-oriented refinement of established interpreter training practices.

9.1.2 *Levels and formats*

Rather than philosophical foundations, most of the literature on training, particularly in less well-established domains, is devoted to **organizational issues** like the level, duration and intensity of training programs. In conference interpreting, curricular formats range from six-month postgraduate courses, such as the in-house training formerly offered by the European Commission or the course at the former Polytechnic of Central London (Longley 1978), to four- or five-year university degree courses for comprehensive T/I training. Of the various models described in the literature (e.g. Arjona 1984, Mackintosh 1999, Sawyer 2001), trends in the organization of higher education (« 2.1.3) have favored conference interpreter training in graduate (master's level) degree programs of one or two years' duration, depending on the relative weight of **professional vs academic** course content. The latter issue remains as controversial as the role of translation in the curriculum, and the study by Sawyer (2001) is exceptional in addressing this issue on the basis of quantitative empirical data.

The master's degree courses that have emerged as the rule in conference interpreter education have rather been the exception for sign language interpreting (see Isham 1998). Given the variety and heterogeneity of the courses offered, the Conference of Interpreter Trainers (CIT), a professional body founded in 1979, developed "Interpreter Education Standards" as a basis for accreditation in the US (see Patrie 1995). Understandably, the field of sign language interpreter training has traditionally been associated with sign language studies rather than T/I education. Nevertheless, signed languages have come to be accepted among the working languages offered in CIUTI-type T/I programs, and the second edition of the interpreter training manual by Seleskovitch and Lederer (1989), published in 2002, features a section devoted to the pedagogy of interpreting with sign languages.

With few exceptions, spoken-language community interpreters do not (yet) have the option of dedicated master's or even bachelor's degree programs. According to Roberts (2002: 169f), "Much, if not most, community interpreter training is provided by organizations which hire community interpreters". With little involvement of higher-education institutions, training courses offered by interpreting agencies or user organizations like hospitals are usually limited in duration (from one-day orientation workshops up to some 100 hours of basic-level training) and geared to specific settings. Research in this context, often unpublished, primarily relates to needs assessment and program evaluation, but also to the general issue of selecting candidates for training (» 9.2).

9.1.3 *Content and structure*

Most interpreter training courses established since the 1940s have featured roughly similar curricular **components**: basic concepts of language and communication, language enhancement (e.g. specialized terminology), 'area studies' (i.e. socio-cultural background knowledge), skill training in consecutive and simultaneous interpreting, and professional ethics (see Arjona 1984). In addition to a focus on international institutions and their terminology, conference interpreter training has also involved specialized subjects like law, economics, science and technology, either explicitly or indirectly through the choice of source texts (see Kurz 2002b). In curricula for community-based interpreters, the orientation toward particular **settings** is much more prominent. More often than not, training is geared to specific domains, such as legal interpreting or medical interpreting, either in the program as a whole or in a specialization following basic-level training (e.g. Corsellis 1999).

The relative effectiveness of various curricular arrangements is difficult to assess, since many aspects of implementation are not manifested in the 'official curriculum'. As emphasized by Sawyer (2001), researchers need access to the **hidden curriculum**, that is, the curriculum as experienced by the individual student and teacher. Among the **contentious issues** that have been discussed in the literature, but not resolved, are SI training into the B-language and the requirement of proficiency in consecutive before simultaneous interpreting (see Mackintosh 1999: 70). For spoken-language community interpreters, in particular, the share of generic (monolingual) vs language-pair-specific instruction has been an important concern, not least in the light of organizational and financial considerations. In general, the role of the theoretical component in the curriculum is not clearly defined and depends on the underlying educational philosophy as well as the relative weight of profession-oriented training and academic content (see Harris 1992, Pöchhacker 1992, Mackintosh 1999).

9.2 Selection

The selection of suitable candidates for training has been a prime concern to interpreter educators across the different professional domains. While there is considerable consensus regarding the nature and extent of the abilities to be demonstrated on entry into a training program, there is little certainty regarding objective ways of testing candidates for the requisite knowledge and skills.

9.2.1 Entry requirements

In line with the widely accepted **competence profile** of professional interpreters (« 8.4.1), knowledge (of languages and of the world), cognitive skills (relating to analysis, attention and memory) and personality traits (including stress tolerance and intellectual curiosity) are expected of candidates for interpreter training to varying degrees, depending on the level and duration of a given training program. For conference interpreting, the basic tenet is that language acquisition must precede training in interpreting (e.g. Arjona 1984), which makes the would-be interpreter's degree of bilingual or multilingual competence a fundamental criterion for admission. Although given less explicit attention, cultural knowledge and competence are generally considered equally indispensable, and indeed viewed as closely interrelated with high-level language proficiency (e.g. Arjona 1978). More so than in international conference interpreting, where the focus tends to be on cognitive-linguistic skills, issues of socio-cultural identity and attitude may come to the fore in community-based interpreting and require special consideration (e.g. Cokely 2000, Bot 2003).

There is some uncertainty regarding the level of **written language skills** as an entry requirement in interpreter training. Translation tests, in particular, have been rejected outright as a component of interpreter aptitude tests by some, defended by others, or questioned in hindsight (e.g. Lotriet 2002). In many university-level programs, the acquisition of translation skills prior to interpreter training remains built into the curriculum, suggesting a need for studies along the lines of Sawyer (2001) on the relationship between modality-specific translational skills.

9.2.2 Aptitude testing

Subject to legal provisions governing access to higher education in particular countries, a variety of procedures have been adopted by different institutions to test candidates for the knowledge, skills and personal qualities considered necessary to successfully acquire professional competence in interpreting. As reviewed by Keiser (1978) and Moser-Mercer (1994b) for conference interpreting, traditional examination methods include **holistic communicative tasks** such as bilingual or multilingual interviews, impromptu speech production, and oral summary rendition in another language. Notwithstanding their validity for ascertaining a candidate's general knowledge and communicative language use (i.e. comprehension and expressive skills), such aptitude tests have been criticized for their strong subjective component and, hence, lack of reliability (e.g. Dodds 1990). On the other hand, the use of **translational tasks** such as written translation («9.2.1), sight translation and written summary in another language have been challenged for lack of validity as well as poor reliability (see Dodds 1990, Gringiani 1990).

Despite their appeal as efficient screening procedures, standardized test instruments for **personality traits** («8.4.1) have proved of very limited use in predicting interpreting proficiency (see Longley 1989: 106). Reporting on attempts in the 1970s to link student interpreters' performance to personality traits, Frishberg (1990: 36) concluded for the field of sign language interpreting that "no objective tools have been found to predict who will succeed in the profession of interpreting." And yet, with less attention to personality than linguistic aptitude, Carroll (1978) had proposed a number of **psychometric tools**, especially for "verbal intelligence" and "verbal fluency", some of which were indeed, literally, put to the test. In a seminal study carried out at the Polytechnic of Central London in the late 1970s (see Longley 1989), Gerver *et al.* (1989) explored the value of various tests assumed to address the "ability to grasp rapidly and to convey the meaning of spoken discourse." Recall, cloze and error detection tests as well as "subskill-based" tests of verbal fluency and comprehension (see Carroll 1978) and a generic speed-stress test were administered to a total of thirty students enrolled for six-month postgraduate training in conference interpreting. When related to students' final examination ratings, seven out of the twelve tests, mainly of the text-based type, showed significantly higher scores for students who had passed the course compared to the twelve who had failed. In a similar vein, Mariachiara Russo (1993) used a simultaneous paraphrasing task to test the interpreting aptitude of a group of twenty students who then began a two-year training course in conference interpreting.

Scores based on a detailed multi-parameter analysis of syntactic, semantic and pragmatic correspondence (Pippa and Russo 2002) were subsequently related to students' successful completion of the course and were found to have greater predictive value for students with a good chance of success than for those assessed as less promising.

A different approach was taken by Moser-Mercer (1985), who developed a ten-week monolingual **screening course** on the basis of her process model of simultaneous interpreting (« 5.4.3). Students were given exercises in shadowing, dual-tasking (speech comprehension while counting aloud), paraphrasing and number processing, and received a positive, conditional or negative recommendation for further training based on their performance in the course as well as additional criteria (e.g. English language skills, coping with stress, assertiveness). A significant relationship was found between the type of recommendation given and students' pass/fail rates in the mid-term and final (second-year) examinations.

With particular emphasis on shadowing exercises and recall tests for evaluating interpretation-related skills, S. Lambert (1991) described a battery of selection instruments which combines cognitive processing skills with sight translation and interviewing. This approach also informed the oral screening of candidates for an intensive two-week training course in simultaneous interpreting for community interpreters in South Africa (see Lotriet 2002). More comprehensively, Arjona-Tseng (1994) developed and implemented a two-day **screening procedure** for admission to a two-year graduate program. Following a five-part written test for language proficiency and general knowledge, final selection was based on a series of oral tests, including written recall of a recorded passage, error detection, and sight translation. Out of a total of 565 applicants over three years, eleven candidates were selected as 'trainable' in conference interpreting between English and Mandarin Chinese.

Similarly elaborate and rigorous screening procedures are difficult to find in the literature on community-based interpreting, not least because most training courses are less formally structured and less institutionalized. Penney and Sammons (1997: 69) deplore "the low level of formal education achieved by enrolling students" and speak of the need to ensure "at least minimal competency requirements in both languages," while Carr and Steyn (2000) find that "bilingual pre-screening procedures, written and oral, are time-consuming and costly to prepare and administer". Although standardized **language grades**, such as those used for NATO peacekeeping interpreters (Monacelli 2002) or formulated in the Common European Framework of Reference for Languages, may facilitate screening for linguistic aptitude, interpreting-related entry requirements of a cognitive and affective nature remain difficult to address. As acknowledged in the literature (e.g. Dodds 1990, Frishberg 1990: 36, Moser-Mercer 1994b), personal qualities such as motivation, learning style, and coping with physical as well as emotional stress have not been objectively assessed in entrance examinations to date and may indeed elude any one-time selection procedure.

9.3 Teaching

In line with the overall teaching and learning goal of developing task-specific expert skills, most of the literature on interpreter training falls into three prototypical subdivisions: consecutive interpreting with note-taking; simultaneous interpreting for international conference settings; and dialogue interpreting in the community. Contributions to the didactic literature tend to take the form of reports by teachers willing to share their particular approach, and range from the descriptive ('How I do it') to the prescriptive ('How it should be done'). The latter orientation is inherent in textbooks on interpreter training (e.g. Seleskovitch and Lederer 1995, Gile 1995b, Kautz 2000), whereas few authors have followed the pioneering example of Eva Paneth (« 2.2.1) and collected systematic data on teaching practices in different courses or programs.

9.3.1 Didactic issues

Beyond the focus on specific interpreting skills, a number of broader didactic issues have been raised, if not systematically addressed, in the literature, mostly with regard to conference interpreter training. These include the use of theoretical models in the teaching of interpreting (e.g. Seleskovitch and Lederer 1989, Gile 1995b, Pöchhacker 1992); the value of subskill-oriented drill exercises vs holistic 'real-life' methods (e.g. Kurz 1992, 2002b); the causes and management of stress (e.g. Kellett 1995, Russo 1995); and the use of technology (e.g. Kurz 1989b, Gran *et al.* 2002).

A number of authors have described teaching approaches for various **preliminary** and **ancillary skills** for interpreting in general. These relate in particular to analytical skills in text comprehension (e.g. Seleskovitch and Lederer 1989, Kalina 1992, Setton 1994, Winston and Monikowski 2000), expressive skills for 'public speaking' (e.g. Weber 1990), situation analysis (e.g. Thiéry 1990), and assignment preparation, with special regard to terminology research and documentation (e.g. Schweda Nicholson 1989). Other 'pre-interpreting skills' have mostly been discussed in connection with the two major working modes, that is, as preparatory exercises for either consecutive or simultaneous interpreting.

9.3.2 Consecutive interpreting

While no hard and fast line can be drawn between short consecutive (as used in dialogue interpreting) and the 'classic' form of consecutive implying the rendition of at least five to ten minutes of uninterrupted discourse (« 1.4.2), consecutive interpreting skills are usually taken to be synonymous with the latter and thus closely linked to **note-taking** skills. Indeed, most publications on the teaching of consecutive interpreting – as reviewed by Ilg and Lambert (1996) – are mainly concerned with note-taking. Nevertheless, authors describing their teaching approaches (e.g. Seleskovitch and Lederer 1989, 1995; Kalina 1998) usually stress the need for preliminary exercises to enhance 'active listening', message analysis, and recall, including such techniques as 'clozing', 'chunking' and visualization.

Though few systematic studies on the pedagogy of consecutive interpreting have been carried out, the interaction between memory and note-taking stands out as a focus of investigation. The experimental study by Andres (2002) has supplied particularly detailed evidence of **processing overload** in student interpreters during the listening and note-taking phase. With regard to note-taking techniques as such, there are few descriptive data documenting the practical application of the approaches put forward by various authors – from the seminal proposal by Rozan (1956) to the elaborate symbol-based system developed by Heinz Matyssek (1989). Here again, the data on student interpreters' notes in Andres' (2002) corpus are a rare exception.

Another area of emphasis has been **public speaking** skills for the production phase of consecutive interpreting. Didactic suggestions include sight translation exercises (e.g. Weber 1990, Ilg and Lambert 1996) and the use of videotapes for feedback on student performance (e.g. Kellett 1995). In an effort to test the effectiveness of public speaking exercises in the curriculum, Lorena Bottan (2000) carried out an experimental study comparing skill development in students who had taken a thirty-hour public speaking course with those of a control group. Focusing on frequent faults of presentation, Bottan found clear evidence that specific training in public speaking (including breathing, voice control, eye contact) raised students' awareness of their delivery and enhanced their presentation in consecutive interpreting.

9.3.3 Simultaneous interpreting

Much more than training in the complex skill of simultaneous interpreting as such, it is **preliminary exercises** that have commanded prime attention in the pedagogical literature. Most authors have suggested introducing students to the crucial task demand of simultaneity, perceived as the skill of listening and speaking at the same time, by way of 'dual-task' exercises. These involve a listening task in combination with a second, different task, such as simultaneously counting backwards or reading aloud (see Moser 1978: 363, Seleskovitch and Lederer 1989: 168). The usefulness of dual-tasking as an introductory exercise has been questioned on the grounds that the performance of cognitively unrelated tasks does not approximate the processing demands of SI (e.g. Déjean le Féal 1997, Kalina 1998).

A specific exercise in simultaneous verbal processing is **shadowing**, which is the immediate repetition of auditory input in the same language with either minimal delay ('phoneme shadowing') or at greater latencies ('phrase shadowing'). As possibly the most contentious issue in interpreter pedagogy to date, the shadowing task has both fervent advocates (e.g. Lambert 1991) and staunch opponents (e.g. Seleskovitch and Lederer 1989: 168), and exemplifies the division between the holistic training approach championed by ESIT and the 'cognitive approach' based on the identification and separate practice of component skills (see Lambert 1988). Unlike most other didactic issues, the case for or against shadowing has been made not only by statements of faith but also with reference to research. Kurz (1992), citing neuropsychological findings, characterizes mono-lingual repetitive speech production as a poor approximation to simultaneous interpreting, pointing out that "a crucial element is missing in those exercises: the *active analysis of the speech input*" (1992: 248). In a longitudinal study, Kurz (1992, 1996) tested five first-year students on a shadowing task and two simultaneous question and answer tasks at the beginning and at the end of one semester of regular training in simultaneous interpreting. While test results were significantly better on all three tasks, Kurz found the most pronounced improvements for the more demanding task (i.e. answering a why question while listening to the next question). This is in line with the results of the pioneering study by Moser (1978), who found that a program of introductory exercises (including abstraction of ideas, message prediction, dual-tasking and shadowing) resulted in the least significant difference between the test performance of course participants and a control group for the shadowing task, whereas the most pronounced difference was found for the '*décalage*' or extended lag test, which required subjects to repeat or translate input sentences while staying one or two sentences behind. Moser's (1978) conclusion that shadowing requires less processing for meaning was confirmed in a recent expert–novice study: Moser-Mercer *et al.* (2000) found that their five student subjects were more efficient shadowers than the five professional interpreters, who presumably brought their acquired content-processing strategies to bear on the task. Similarly, Elisabetta Sabatini (2000/01) found that the near-professional student subjects in her experiment adopted a meaning-oriented approach to the shadowing task, thus obscuring the performance difference expected between shadowing and SI.

Much less controversial than shadowing have been preliminary exercises with a focus on content processing, such as simultaneous **paraphrasing**, shadowing tasks combined with **cloze** exercises (see Kalina 1992, 1998) or simultaneous interpreting of well-known **fairy tales** (see Seleskovitch and Lederer 1989). Russo (1995), who had proposed paraphrasing as a test for aptitude in simultaneous interpreting (see Russo 1993), used a questionnaire to elicit students' perception of difficulties and found that the paraphrasing task was experienced as particularly taxing. Moser-Mercer (2000) asked beginning students to keep a journal recording their difficulties with introductory exercises (including shadowing and interpreting a fairy tale) and found "concentration" to be the crucial problem area. Still, as pointed out by Déjean le Féal (1997), it has proved difficult, if not impossible, to measure the effectiveness of any one training method for simultaneous interpreting, including her own proposal, in line with the ESIT approach, to take the route via consecutive interpreting.

Beyond the first stage of training designed to familiarize students with the technique of SI, didactic proposals have emphasized the need to focus on the **process** rather than the product (e.g. Gile 1995b); to teach **strategies**, particularly for coping with lexical and structural difficulties (e.g. Kirchhoff 1976/2002, Riccardi 1996, Kalina 1998); and to create a training environment that is as close to **real-life conditions** as possible (e.g. Kurz 1989b, 2002b). Apart from what is described by various authors, however, little is known about actual teaching practices adopted by individual instructors or institutions. Dodds and Katan (1997), for instance, have expressed serious doubts regarding the impact that the literature on interpreting and interpreter training has had on teaching practices. This was confirmed in a questionnaire-based classroom survey by Pöchhacker (1999), who found highly varied approaches to input text presentation, media use, and correction in a total of twenty-five SI courses given by twenty-two teachers within the same institution.

The teaching of **sight translation** as a special form of interpreting in the simultaneous mode has received very little attention. With few exceptions (e.g. Weber 1990), most authors have discussed interpreting at sight as a preliminary exercise, or even an aptitude test, rather than a curricular component in its own right. From a process-oriented perspective, Viezzi (1990) questioned the similarity of task demands assumed for sight translation and SI. Although the implications of input processing by reading rather than listening remain unclear, there is no doubt that sight translation is an integral part of an interpreter's translational competence. Indeed, interpreting at sight in combination with SI, as in the case of a speaker reading a text that the interpreter has available in the booth, involves a high degree of complexity that has yet to be addressed in detail from a didactic perspective. The same holds true for spoken-language simultaneous interpreting practiced in the whispering and the relay mode (see Seleskovitch and Lederer 1989) as well as in remote conferencing, for which special training needs are gradually being acknowledged (see Kurz 2002b).

Since sign language interpreters are trained mainly to work in the simultaneous mode, much of the didactic literature on spoken-language conference interpreting also has a bearing on interpreting with signed languages, especially on voice-to-sign interpreting in educational settings or in the media. (Consecutive interpreting, in contrast, has largely been viewed only as a propaedeutic stage, roughly in line with the training approach of ESIT.) Nevertheless, training for sign language interpreters needs to give special attention to dialogic settings, where, as in the case of spoken-language community interpreting, the focus is less on processing skills for high information loads than on interactive skills in interpersonal dialogue.

9.3.4 Dialogue interpreting

The skills required for dialogue interpreting ('liaison interpreting', 'bilateral interpreting'), which may be practiced in the short consecutive or simultaneous (signed or whispered) modes, have more to do with the dynamics of **inter-personal interaction** than with 'content processing' as such (see Roy 2000b). Hence the teaching methods developed for consecutive and simultaneous interpreting apply only to a limited extent. Areas of shared ground include note-taking (e.g. González *et al.* 1991, Schweda Nicholson 1990), whispered simultaneous interpreting, and intercultural communication (e.g. Arjona 1978), though the latter has not acquired a distinct profile as a didactic approach. A more specific, and unique, didactic focus has been the management of interactive discourse, with particular regard to turn-taking and role performance. On the theoretical foundation provided by discourse analytical concepts and descriptions (e.g. Zimmer 1989, Englund Dimitrova 1997, Wadensjö 1998, Metzger 1999, Roy 2000a), **role-plays** and simulations of interpreting scenarios have emerged as the key method for developing interpreting and discourse management skills which are sensitive to the purpose of the interaction and the constraints of a particular communicative context (e.g. Zimman 1994, Metzger 2000). The pedagogical focus on contextualized decision-making is particularly important because most training in dialogue interpreting is geared to specific institutional settings. Ultimately, then, the pedagogy of liaison interpreting in the community shares with the – distinctly mode-oriented – teaching approach to conference interpreter training an appreciation for expertise-building on tasks which approximate real-life conditions.

9.4 Assessment

Assessment in interpreter training is a highly complex subject, since it is not only linked to curricular and didactic issues as covered so far but also closely inter-dependent with topics such as 'professional standards' (« 8.3) and 'competence' (« 8.4) as well as the multi-dimensional theme of 'quality' addressed in much of Chapter 7. Within the pedagogical context, 'assessment' covers a range of approaches for evaluating student performance and educational attainment, few of which have been thoroughly treated in the literature.

9.4.1 *Types and levels*

In the most substantial contribution on assessment in interpreter education to date, Sawyer (2001) discusses the scant literature on the subject within a systematic framework of concepts and principles derived from the fields of language testing and educational assessment. Including entry-level assessment (aptitude testing) in his purview, he highlights the distinction between intermediate and final assessment in a given curriculum and between **formative** assessment by the instructor as part of the teaching and learning process, and **summative** assessment by one or more examiners at the end of a program. For in-training evaluation, some authors (e.g. Kellett 1995, Schjoldager 1996, Riccardi 2002) have proposed checklists and evaluation sheets with regard to mode-specific components. As a complement to 'traditional' interpreter testing, some authors (e.g. Humphrey 2000, Sawyer 2001) have suggested the use of **portfolio** assessment – that is, the systematic collection and evaluation of student products to document progress and learning outcomes – which allows for self-assessment, peer review and extensive instructor feedback.

Final examinations at the end of a program not only test students' educational attainment – and the effectiveness of training – but also serve as a gateway to the professional interpreting market; hence the special significance of the methodology used for such **professional-level** testing, which bears a crucial relation to the testing done by certifying bodies and by institutions hiring staff interpreters (see

Frishberg 1990, Repa 1991). The examination practices described in the literature (e.g. Seleskovitch and Lederer 1989, Dubrovsky and Weller 1990, Lotriet 2002) involve **realistic** consecutive and simultaneous interpreting tasks and **holistic** assessment by a panel of instructors and, where admissible, external examiners (e.g. from employer organizations). From his detailed examination of assessment practices, Sawyer (2001) concludes that **professional judgment** clearly prevails over systematic approaches to test design and evaluation. Acknowledging professional judgment as necessary but not sufficient, he calls for a standardization of test parameters, or 'test method facets,' and more transparent assessment criteria and procedures so as to ensure maximum validity and reliability.

9.4.2 *Parameters and criteria*

The key issues in final testing (and, by the same token, in competence testing by employers or certifying bodies) are the **tasks** on which candidates are to be examined and the criteria by which their performance is to be evaluated. Would-be conference interpreters are generally expected to give a consecutive rendition with notes of a speech lasting up to ten minutes, working both into their A- and their B-language, and to perform simultaneous interpreting in the booth for up to twenty minutes, working into the A-language and, though controversial, sometimes also into the B-language. The status of interpreting at sight ('sight translation'), either as part of SI testing in the booth or as a separate task, and of bilateral interpreting remains unclear in programs geared to conference interpreting, whereas sight translation and dialogue interpreting are seen as principal components of examinations for community-based interpreters (e.g. Roberts 2000).

Even for prototypical components in tests for interpreting skills, there is little systematic information on parameters such as the mode and context of source-text delivery, text type, authenticity, level of technicality, or the time and resources allowed for preparation. It is largely left to the professional judgment of the examiner(s) to gauge the combined impact of these variables on the level of difficulty and to make appropriate allowance for it in assessing a candidate's performance.

Considerably more published information than on the methods of test administration is available on performance targets and assessment **criteria**, not least because these link up with the more extensive literature on professional standards and quality assessment (see Riccardi 2002). There is widespread agreement that performance must be assessed for both **content** (i.e. source–target correspondence) and target-language **presentation** (i.e. expression and delivery), but little consensus on whether or how these notions can be operationalized for a transparent assessment procedure. The use of **error counts** is notoriously problematic even in transcript-based descriptive research, and impractical in on-the-spot judgments on several grounds, including the lexical variability of interpreters' output (e.g. Lamberger-Felber 2003), the variable information value of individual text components, the variability of error ratings between different assessors (Gile 1999c), and the impact of norms and expectations (Shlesinger

2000b). Similarly, output features such as clarity, style, fluency, rhythm, intonation, and so on largely elude an itemized assessment, notwithstanding the various lists of relevant features that have been proposed for use in student assessment (e.g. Kellett 1995, Schjoldager 1996, Riccardi 2002). Several authors have indeed expressed their disappointment with detailed scoring systems (e.g. Longley 1978, Dubrovsky and Weller 1990, Roberts 2000) and have reaffirmed the more holistic approach relying on the professional judgment of experienced interpreters. The latter is no doubt vital for evaluating the **overall impression** made by an interpreter in terms of professionalism, credibility, poise, technical skill, and so on, particularly in consecutive and in dialogue interpreting.

9.5 Meta-level training

In addition to 'primary' interpreter training as reviewed so far, educational efforts which go beyond the focus on would-be interpreters' professional skills have emerged as important complementary pathways toward the goal of professionalization and improved professional standards. These include continuing education for practicing interpreters, training for teachers of interpreting, user education, and training in research skills, and are variously connected with the primary level of interpreter pedagogy.

9.5.1 Continuing education

Although not often reflected in the pedagogical literature, continuing education for practicing interpreters has become increasingly significant even in the most highly professionalized domains of interpreting. Courses offered for conference interpreters within or outside AIIC focus on particular working languages or subject areas (e.g. medicine, law) and aspects of technological support, particularly for documentation and terminology. A highly institutionalized approach has been developed by American Sign Language interpreters, for whom **continuing professional development** is part of the code of ethics and a requirement for maintaining professional certification (« 8.3). Given the limited scope and institutionalization of community interpreter training, continuing education needs are particularly acute in this domain, and many training initiatives are indeed geared to the professionalization of working (and even 'natural') interpreters rather than novice students.

9.5.2 Training of trainers

As early as the mid-1960s, AIIC stipulated that courses in consecutive and simultaneous interpreting should be "designed and taught by practicing conference interpreters, preferably AIIC members" (Mackintosh 1995: 124). Nevertheless, it was only a quarter of a century later that the profession began actively to address the need for training of trainers. The symposia on the teaching of interpreting convened in the late 1980s at Trieste (Gran and Dodds 1989) and Monterey set clear signals for a more systematic approach to interpreter pedagogy. AIIC has since offered a series of **workshops**, on topics such as instruction methods and testing, which have met with a highly favorable response (see Mackintosh 1995, 1999). Among the university institutions for (conference) interpreter training that are joined together in CIUTI, few have been as committed to pedagogical skill development as ETI in Geneva, where a biennial **trainers course** leading to the award of a certificate was launched in 1996 (see Moser-Mercer and Setton 2000).

Similar initiatives have been taken by educators of American Sign Language interpreters in the framework of the **CIT**, which has organized numerous conferences and published proceedings reflecting the exchange and development of pedagogical expertise among its members (e.g. McIntire 1984). At Western Maryland College, a master's degree program for teachers of ASL and ASL/English interpreting was set up in the late 1980s (see Baker-Shenk 1990). At around the same time, New Jersey educators charged with training (spoken-language) legal interpreters pioneered a four-week team-taught **Pedagogical Institute** on curriculum design and methods of teaching and testing (see Roberts and Tayler 1990). At a more academic than organizational, hands-on level, the Critical Link conference series (« 2.5.2) has yielded a wealth of literature relevant to training, pointing to the obvious role of academic conferences in the continuing education of those involved in university-level interpreter training.

9.5.3 *User education*

The professional literature on interpreting is rife with complaints about the lack of appreciation and understanding of the interpreter's job on the part of clients. With the exception perhaps of conference interpreters working for international organizations, informing users and clients about the nature and constraints of the interpreter's work is therefore considered a vital task of individual practitioners as well as their professional associations. And yet, while **advice for conference organizers** and **guidelines for conference speakers** are readily available, little is known about the delivery and effectiveness of this type of user-oriented material. The best documented initiatives to date have addressed client education needs in community-based domains. Ann Corsellis (1997: 78) formulated training needs for public service personnel, emphasizing "understanding and practice in the communicative processes required to work through, and with, interpreters". Based on data from a survey of officers, interpreters and clients of a British probation service, Corsellis (2000) developed detailed recommendations for a **modular training course**. Tebble (1998), drawing on her research on the discourse structure of medical consultations (« 7.1.1), developed a videotape and book on *Medical Interpreting* to be used in training courses for healthcare personnel. Moreover, involving staff from prospective user institutions in role-play-based training sessions for dialogue interpreters has been described as an effective way of both raising client understanding of interpreter-mediated encounters and creating more realistic interpreting scenarios in the classroom (e.g. Metzger 2000).

9.5.4 Research training

In his efforts to promote higher scientific standards in interpreting research, Daniel Gile (« 4.4.1) has identified research training as a crucial requirement for progress in interpreting studies. Mindful of the lacunae in this respect even in graduate-level university curricula for interpreter education, Gile has played a leading role in a number of initiatives designed to develop methodological expertise among interpreting scholars. This goal has also been pursued by Barbara Moser-Mercer (« 4.4.1), whose **Ascona workshops** were designed to foster interaction between interpreting researchers and leading scientists from related disciplines (see *Interpreting* 2:1/2, 1997 and 5:2, 2000/01). Focusing less on interdisciplinary expertise than on hands-on tuition by members of the wider Translation studies community, a group of scholars at the Aarhus School of Business, in cooperation with Gile, organized a one-week seminar on interpreting research in early 1997. This **PhD school** eventually gave rise to the publication of a collective volume (Gile *et al.* 2001) offering guidance to would-be researchers – an objective which also informs the present textbook as a whole and will be addressed in the last section of Chapter 10.

Further reading

Curriculum

Arjona (1978, 1984), Baker-Shenk (1990), Corsellis (1999), Harris (1992, 1997), Mackintosh (1995, 1999), Repa (1991), Roberts (2002), Roberts and Tayler (1990), Roy (1984), Sawyer (2001); see also the web sites of institutions such as AIIC, CIT, CIUTI and the Institute of Linguists.

Selection

Arjona-Tseng (1994), Carroll (1978), Dodds (1990), Gerver *et al.* (1989), Gringiani (1990), Keiser (1978), Lambert (1991), Longley (1989), Lotriet (2002), Moser-Mercer (1985, 1994b), Niska (2002), Pippa and Russo (2002), Seleskovitch and Lederer (1989, 1995).

Teaching

Andres (2002), Arjona (1978), Bottan (2000), Déjean le Féal (1997), Dodds and Katan (1997), Gile (1995b), Gran *et al.* (2002), Ilg and Lambert (1996), Kalina (1992, 1998), Kautz (2000), Keiser (1978), Kellett (1995), Kurz (1989b,

1992, 2002b), Lambert (1988), Metzger (2000), Moser (1978), Moser-Mercer (2000), Moser-Mercer *et al.* (2000), Pöchhacker (1992, 1999), Riccardi (1996), Russo (1995), Schweda Nicholson (1989, 1990), Seleskovitch and Lederer (1989, 1995), Setton (1994), Thiéry (1990), Weber (1990), Winston and Monikowski (2000), Zimman (1994); and see in particular the contributions in Gran and Dodds (1989).

Assessment

Dubrovsky and Weller (1990), Gile (1999c), Kellett (1995), Lotriet (2002), Moser-Mercer (1996), Riccardi (2002), Roberts (2000), Sawyer (2001), Schjoldager (1996), Seleskovitch and Lederer (1989, 1995).

Meta-level training

Baker-Shenk (1990), Corsellis (1997, 2000), Gile *et al.* (2001), Mackintosh (1995, 1999), Roberts and Tayler (1990), Tebble (1998); see also papers in Gran and Dodds (1989) and the web sites of institutions such as AIIC, CIT and CIUTI.

Part III

Directions

10 Directions

This chapter, which is offered as a conclusion to the survey of interpreting studies presented in Parts I and II, reviews major trends in the evolution of the field to date, and identifies some of the critical issues that have been confronting the young discipline for some time. With a look to the future, attention is drawn to a number of developments which are likely to shape the professional practice of interpreting as well as the theoretical and methodological foundations of its systematic study. In view of the old and new challenges for research and the various directions the field may take, the final section is an attempt to provide would-be researchers with some more concrete orientation for taking their first steps and actively contributing to this field of study.

The **main points** covered in this chapter are

· aspects of growth and expansion in interpreting studies as a discipline
· individual, institutional and international manifestations of convergence
· major obstacles and opportunities for disciplinary progress
· socio-cultural and technological developments likely to shape the future course of research
· theoretical and methodological perspectives for the development of the field
· basic guidance for those 'getting started' in interpreting studies

---

10.1 Trends

Looking back over the development of research on interpreting since the mid-twentieth century, one easily appreciates that the field has expanded in various ways and developed a more broadly shared sense of identity. Since the early 1990s, in particular, the overall trends of growth and convergence have manifested themselves at institutional and international levels as well as in the realm of theory and methodology.

10.1.1 Growth

The most important growth trend underlying the evolution of interpreting studies as a discipline has been the **academization of training**, primarily for the domain of international conference interpreting (« 2.1.3). From a dozen or so committed professionals writing in the 1950s and 1960s to pass on their know-how to the next generation of practitioners, the **number of authors** contributing to the systematic study of (conference) interpreting has increased manifold, mainly as a result of the growing recognition of academic work as a complement to profession-oriented training in university-level T/I schools. Aside from a large number of MA-level **graduation theses**, the literature has been enriched especially by doctoral dissertations. Although the academic infrastructure for **PhD research** in interpreting studies as such remains tenuous, the field's global output of doctoral theses has clearly been on the rise, even when looking only at the more established field of international conference interpreting. When the focus is widened to include all other domains of practice, the volume of doctoral research on interpreting, often launched from neighboring academic disciplines, is much more impressive still.

The **diversification** of the field, which began to make itself felt in the 1980s (« 2.4.1) and was widely accepted by the turn of the millennium (« 2.5.2), has not only brought new **interpreting types and settings** into the researcher's purview, but also extended, by necessity more than by choice, the range of **theoretical and methodological approaches** brought to bear on the phenomenon under study. Having emerged within the humanities (« 4.2) in a tense relationship with the linguistic and behavioral sciences (« 4.3), interpreting studies received a major impetus from the analysis of interpreting as discourse in social interaction (« 4.6), which has broadened and diversified its disciplinary foundations.

No less importantly, diversification has gone hand in hand with growing **internationalization**, as reflected in the pursuit of post-graduate interpreting research in an increasing number of academic **institutions** throughout the world, and in the creation of international **journals** and publications available to the global interpreting studies community in English, the field's international language since the 1990s.

As in many other fields, the use of a **common language** for academic communication and exchange, together with world-wide **electronic access** via the Internet, has opened up new channels for networking and cooperation. This communicative linkage has been essential to turning quantitative progress – more authors, 'centers', theses, domains, approaches, countries, and so on – into qualitative changes in the field's structure and interrelations.

10.1.2 Convergence

Growth and diversification often come with the risk of fragmentation along diverging lines of specialization, but this is rather a 'natural' process in the evolution of human science – witness, for instance, the development of linguistics from Saussure's lectures in the early twentieth century to the conglomerate of sub-disciplines and applied extensions a hundred years later. For a field as small and specialized as the study of interpreting, however, which is at an early stage in its institutional development, growth is first of all a matter of **growing together** rather than growing apart. While an overall assessment of convergence or divergence is also a matter of attitude and perspective (i.e. of preferring to see the glass half full or half empty), it is nevertheless possible to note a pattern of convergence at an individual and institutional as well as an international level: more and more authors with a home base in conference interpreting are doing and promoting research also on **community-based** domains (e.g. Dam, Kalina, Pöchhacker); interaction between research(ers) on **signed and spoken**-language interpreting has intensified, not least within the Critical Link community but also involving scholars of the Paris School and other CIUTI institutions; several members of the interpreting studies community have made substantial con-tributions to the field in more than one of its **paradigms** (e.g. Shlesinger) or have worked toward a dialectic synthesis of different paradigms (e.g. Setton); a number of leading (conference) interpreting researchers (e.g. Gile, Gran, Kurz) have forged **interdisciplinary** ties with non-interpreter specialists in fields like cognitive psychology and neurophysiology, while maintaining and asserting a sense of identity for their own field, more and more T/I schools, whose teaching staff and students constitute the main intellectual infrastructure for interpreting studies, have been opening up their **training programs** for newly emerging profes-sional domains; international **conferences** on interpreting (e.g. Turku, Forlì, Almuñécar) have increasingly featured a broader range of interpreting types, questioning the dominant perspective of what UN interpreter and interpreting scholar Sergio Viaggio self-critically called the "boothed gentry"; *Interpreting*, the field's top international **journal**, though apparently springing from a cognitive-psychological foundation, has provided a forum for work on all types of interpreting; and conferences and publishing ventures in Asian countries (e.g. China, Korea) have sought the active involvement of 'western' scholars, who have in turn benefited from the momentum generated by **inter-continental cooperation**.

Such highlights in the process of expansion and convergence notwithstanding, there remain a number of critical areas in which growth and development will be needed if interpreting studies is to continue its progress in the future. One set of critical factors, which may manifest themselves as either obstacles or oppor-tunities, will briefly be discussed.

10.1.3 Critical issues

To facilitate a summary discussion of problem areas and weaknesses that have plagued interpreting studies as a discipline, six critical issues can be singled out and examined with regard to their mutual impact and interdependence (Figure 10.1).

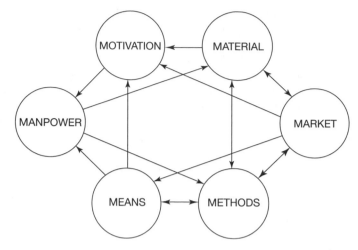

Figure 10.1 Critical issues for progress in interpreting studies (from Pöchhacker 2000a: 106)

The essential prerequisite for the field's continued capacity to generate research is an intellectual labor force with the requisite knowledge and skills. Such **manpower** (or, rather, 'womanpower', considering the female predominance in this field) is mainly available in academic institutions for (translator and) interpreter training, where teaching staff are called on to further their understanding of the subject, and students are initiated into the discipline by guided reflection on their skill-oriented practice. Instructors as well as established professionals may decide to undertake research toward a higher academic degree, joining graduate students committed enough to continue their studies up to doctoral level. It is easy to see how such factors as curricular requirements, tuition fees, charismatic role models, research funding and scholarships, employment opportunities, and so on may variously affect both the **motivation** for engaging in research as well as the **means** (in terms of time and money) available for sustaining a research project over several months or years.

A key to expanding the pool of able and willing research workers is what has been labeled in Figure 10.1 as '**market**' – that is, a sense that research is indeed needed to address a particular problem in the 'real world', and that those sponsoring such research will get their money's worth. In the broadest sense, this applies to the interest of society at large in cultivating state-of-the-art academic expertise in any field of learning, hence the existence of T/I departments in (often publicly funded) universities. Notwithstanding the increasing claims by interpreting scholars to their parcel of 'basic research', most of this public need – and much of the research output addressing it – has been of an educational nature and ultimately geared to the question as to how interpreting can best be taught. While this has generated substantial attention to the process of (simultaneous) interpreting as a human skill ('How does it work?'), it has tended to leave the communicative and institutional implications of interpreting as a social practice largely unexplored. In this regard, the increasing prominence of community-based interpreting opens up a wide field for research on the function, effect and (cost) effectiveness of interpreting in its social context of interaction. This broadens the market for interpreting research to include institutional 'stakeholders' such as courts, hospitals, broadcasters, and advocacy groups for migrants and deaf people, and also generates educational research needs for previously neglected types of practice such as whispered interpreting, over-the-phone interpreting and sight translation. By the same token, institutional users of conference interpreter services as well as the conference interpreting profession have a growing need for research findings on the effects of new technology-based forms of practice on performance quality and professional ecology. And yet major studies commissioned by AIIC and SCIC so far have been entrusted to social science research consultants rather than interpreting scholars, possibly for lack of confidence in the latter's methodological expertise. Indeed, the research **methods** used in interpreting studies to date, typically involving simple experimental designs, small samples of student subjects, and single-judge output analysis, leave plenty of room for innovation and improvement. The fact that several international research training initiatives have been undertaken since the 1990s shows that the interpreting studies community is aware of the challenge and has recognized methodology as vital to the future progress of the discipline. Moreover, the emergence of new research problems in new areas of study is likely to facilitate methodological diversification (» 10.2.3), including the honing of computer-supported analytical tools on a broader range of **material**. Here again, the problem of access to data, 'subjects' and informants 'in the field', which has long been regarded as a critical bottleneck in conference interpreting research, may be resolved as the need for 'applied research', once accepted, leads various kinds of stakeholders to offer more support and cooperation.

The six critical issues for progress in the discipline, which have been discussed here only in very general terms without fully exploring their multiple interrelations, can serve as a framework for the analysis of past and present trends as well as an assessment of future potential. A more global view of future directions will be taken in the next section, which examines some overarching developments for their potential impact on the future course of interpreting studies.

10.2 Perspectives

Although it seems reasonable to project the trends of diversified growth and disciplinary convergence into the foreseeable future, the variable interplay of the factors shaping the academic infrastructure and research environment of the field (« 10.1.3) makes it difficult to predict its future direction(s). Indeed, much more powerful variables, such as globalization and technological progress, need to be reckoned with as well. These 'mega-trends' are likely to have a forceful impact on the development of interpreting studies, both via changes in the profession and by their more direct implications for theory and methodology. The latter will in turn be subject to some strong currents in the postmodern context of scientific endeavor which are likely to steer the field toward the social sciences and qualitative methods of inquiry.

10.2.1 Globalization

In line with the basic assumption that interpreting must be viewed first and foremost with regard to the social context of interaction (« 1.3.1), the ubiquitous theme of globalization is of prime relevance to interpreting studies. For international conference interpreting, itself an early example of a 'global profession', globalization is a mixed blessing. While the trend to carry out transactions in business, politics, arts, and science on a world-wide scale could be assumed to boost the role of interpreters in international communication, the **spread of English** as a *lingua franca* (mentioned above as a boon to interpreting studies) largely offsets this potential need. As much as the official language policy, and **interpreting policy**, of the EU will preserve Europe's heritage as the heartland of multilateral conference interpreting, the spread of international English is likely to shrink the market for conference interpreters there as well.

At the same time, the related trend of 'localization' makes more international (usually English) informational input available to more local and diverse recipients (as in the case of 'glocalized' training of sales personnel). This tends to sustain the need for conference interpreting services, either in bilingual meetings involving English and the local language, or in events with asymmetrical (one-to-many) language arrangements. The former case highlights the role of **bilateral interpreting**, not only in the traditional **liaison** mode but especially in the **simultaneous** mode (including simultaneous dialogue interpreting), for which the implications of A-to-B interpreting have yet to be addressed more fully. In the case of meetings with only English spoken on the floor and interpreted into a range of languages, more fundamental issues of **power relations** and **cultural adaptation** arise, as captured in Vincent Buck's (2002) valid concern that interpreters may be "relegated to mere localisers of dominant ideologies".

Another significant development of a global nature is the increasing presence of China and other Asian countries on the international stage. Although subject to the same pattern of language policy as already described, **developments in Asia** have some broader implications for interpreting practice and interpreting studies. These include the enormous quantitative growth potential of the profession, and hence of training (and research); more pronounced cross-cultural, and not least ideological, differences; and particular cross-linguistic challenges which are likely to give a more prominent role in interpreting research to specialists in linguistics, foreign-language teaching and bilingualism studies.

Beyond the spread of a global language and the world-wide movement of goods, services and capital, globalization of course also applies to the movement, or **migration**, of people, which manifests itself in increasingly multi-ethnic and linguistically diverse societies. As witnessed in recent decades, public institutions in host countries are thus faced with a growing need for intercultural communication, or, more generally, for **policies** to ensure **access**, regardless of language or cultural background, for those entitled to their services or under their jurisdiction. Subject to complex political, ideological and economic constraints, the **role** of interpreting and interpreters in a given context and setting is constantly in need of definition and analysis. Evaluating the **effectiveness** and implications of interpreting services will thus command particular interest and attention, not least with regard to efficiency and cost compared to other institutional arrangements. To the extent that policy-makers envisage a role for professional interpreters, new **training needs** would suggest an acute demand for research, mainly in the form of 'action research' by teachers on such issues as student selection and assessment as well as effective methods of instruction.

The relative effectiveness of interpreting services presents itself as a major research challenge in community-based and international settings alike. Speakers with a limited command of the host-country language or of international English, respectively, may try to get by without relying on an interpreter. At technical conferences, in the reception of foreign-language broadcasts, or in institutional settings such as courts and hospitals, the crucial question is whether **limited-proficiency speakers** can achieve a sufficient **degree of understanding** for their communicative purpose. This, apart from various pragmatic considerations, will decide whether there is a role for an interpreter in a given encounter – and a role for professional interpreting in a given socio-cultural context.

10.2.2 Technologization

The role of technology is no less a long-standing issue in interpreting than globalization. Indeed, the field might not exist as such if it had not been for the use of electro-acoustic transmission equipment to allow for simultaneous interpreting in the 1920s. Half a century later, advances in telecommunications and digital data processing technology began to usher in developments which stand to profoundly transform the way interpreting is practiced in the twenty-first century. The most visible manifestation of 'the technologizing of interpreting', to adapt Ong's (1982) phrase, is **remote interpreting** in international conference settings – and **videoconferences** (« 8.5.1). Its effect on simultaneous interpreters' working conditions and on the profession in general will be a focus of research for years to come, with issues such as **stress**, **visual access** and **psycho-social factors** requiring particular attention (« 8.6). More generally, the impact on the **ergonomics** of SI of digital tools for terminology management, instant knowledge access and speech recognition awaits substantial research, as does the potential of portable wireless equipment for pushing the limits of the **'wired interpreter'** (« 8.5.2). The latter is likely to appear in force beyond the conference hall (e.g. in tourist centers, courts and hospitals), also using equipment to perform in the **consecutive simultaneous** mode or via **videophone** links.

In communication involving **deaf** and hearing-impaired people, the increasing availability of **audiovisual telecommunications** equipment is likely to facilitate remote interpreting arrangements, whereas more efficient technologies for converting speech to text, and written (or even manually coded) input into spoken output, may favor the use of script-based communication and make interpreters redundant. As in the limited-proficiency spoken mode, research will need to establish the comparative effectiveness of one mode or another for a given interactional purpose. In the long term, advanced prosthetic technology (cochlear implants) made available to – or imposed on – deaf people may well make the community of signed-language users even more heterogeneous, and the market for sign language interpreters more fragmented. The same could apply to the substitution of spoken-language community interpreting in routine communication (e.g. administrative information, appointment scheduling) by **speech-to-speech translation** systems.

Whatever the direction and impact of technological progress, and however it is taken up in the profession, there can be little doubt that the increasing role of technology will have strong repercussions on interpreter **training**, including the need to introduce would-be conference interpreters to the efficient use of state-of-the-art electronic equipment in and outside the booth; the need to prepare trainees for various types of remote interpreting arrangements; and the deployment of digital training stations and web-based source-text archives for classroom instruction as well as self-study. These and other pedagogical innovations ought to be accompanied by a concerted effort at action research by interpreting teachers so as to assess needs and effects on an ongoing basis.

Not only will technology transform intercultural communication arrangements and professional practice, which will in turn generate new phenomena requiring systematic study; interpreting researchers will also benefit directly from the availability of new equipment and **tools** to enhance the efficiency of empirical **data collection and analysis**. Survey research, for instance, may increasingly be done over the Internet, and powerful software facilitates the processing of quantitative as well as qualitative data. Fieldwork involving discourse data can rely on digital, and less obtrusive, **recording** equipment, and subsequent **transcription** will be aided by specialized software and speech recognition systems. This will also enhance the feasibility of applying corpus-linguistic methods to **large corpora** of source, target and parallel texts from authentic interpreted events. Aside from high-volume discourse data processing, computer equipment and software for digitized speech data analysis will permit investigations of **paralinguistic phenomena** such as intonation contours and pauses with incomparably more precision than the measurements taken by the pioneers of experimental interpreting research. Indeed, some of the present-day experimental methods for the study of interpreting, particularly from the realm of cognitive neuropsychology, can be expected to benefit most spectacularly from the application of imaging technologies pioneered in biomedical research. This will ensure continued interest in neurolinguistic approaches to interpreting, and promise unprecedented insights into its **neurophysiological underpinnings**.

10.2.3 Cognitive / linguistic / qualitative orientation

Notwithstanding the significant role of technology in providing interpreting researchers with more effective tools, progress in interpreting studies will need to be shaped, first and foremost, by innovation in the realm of theory and methodology. Considering the field's short tradition and limited institutionalization in academia, such analytical momentum is not likely to be generated entirely from within the discipline's existing paradigms. Rather, interpreting scholars will continue to look to other disciplinary frameworks for relevant concepts, models and methods. But look where?

Since interpreting crucially involves complex forms of intellectual activity, a logical source of inspiration is the **cognitive sciences**. Even the label used for that cluster of disciplines suggests that there is more than one cognitive-scientific paradigm to keep in view. What is more, the various subfields and paradigms have undergone major reorientations since they first came together under the heading of 'cognitive science' in the mid-1970s. Interpreting scholars hitching their wagon to the driving forces in cognitive psychology, artificial intelligence or cognitive linguistics thus need to keep track of the course being taken. One example of new and promising paths is **situated cognition**, also known as 'situated action' or 'embodied cognition.' This cognitive-science paradigm, which followed 1980s connectionism and proved particularly fertile in the context of education, rejects the concern with mental plans and symbolic structures in favor of interaction with a given environment and social context, regarding the person and the environment as parts of a mutually constructed whole. The view of context as part of cognition is in turn strikingly congenial with **cognitive pragmatics**, a cognitive approach to linguistics based on Relevance Theory. In its cognitive as well as linguistic ramifications, the methodology of this recent orientation in the study of human performance emphasizes **processes** rather than structures. Researchers consequently prefer to observe and reconstruct dynamic changes rather than to search for quantifiable categories and patterns. The essentially **qualitative** study by Setton (1999), who applied the cognitive-pragmatic approach to a corpus of simultaneous conference interpreting from Mandarin Chinese, is a case in point.

The work of Setton, incidentally, also illustrates the renewed interest in **linguistic** analyses that will be associated with the increasing prominence in interpreting studies of non-European languages. On the understanding that 'linguistic' refers not to an abstract system but to the 'use of language in context', to **discourse** as a 'situated process', the linguistic orientation can also be said to underlie discourse-analytical studies of interpreting in face-to-face interaction (e.g. Wadensjö 1998). Here, however, the notion of **context**, which is no less interaction-based than in the situated-cognitive approach, extends far beyond the immediate communicative environment to a broadly sociological dimension. While the study of discourse also includes a strong psychological orientation which connects the linguistic to the cognitive (e.g. Graesser *et al.* 1997), viewing interpreting as a discourse process in society foregrounds issues such as **roles**, **power** and **ideology** which lead the interpreting scholar into the domain of sociology, cultural anthropology, and social psychology.

It is these disciplines in the **social sciences** in particular that have been experiencing revolutionary changes in the area of research **methodology**. Having come a long way from nineteenth-century positivism, the wide range of qualitative social-science approaches that had become more established by the early 1990s underwent even more profound transformations in the course of that decade (see Denzin and Lincoln 2000). The basic lesson to be drawn for interpreting studies from this methodological evolution is the need for a heightened awareness of the inextricable relationship between theoretical frameworks and methods of inquiry. As postmodern epistemologies and qualitative research approaches, not least in the field of education, continue to assert themselves, research on interpreting is set to take a **qualitative turn**, moving away from an empiricist belief in apparently unproblematic factual explanations toward a greater readiness to engage with various types of qualitative data which force the researcher to become aware of the theories needed to impose a personal interpretation. At the same time, a greater readiness to accept that there is no objective reality to be captured, and to engage with various theoretical interpretations, highlights the need for methodological triangulation – that is, the use of multiple sources of data – and gives qualitative research an inherently multi-method focus. Accepting the linkage of **theory grounded in data organized by theories**, which is the hallmark of qualitative research, rules out both an empiricist view relying fundamentally on 'factual evidence' and a rationalist position which disregards data-based evidence in favor of theorizing. This kind of epistemological middle ground can profitably be aimed at by researchers in interpreting studies, where relevant sources of data range from brain scans and pause measurements to discourse transcriptions and critical-case narratives, and where such diverse paradigms as connectionism, functional grammar, expertise studies, social field theory and gender studies may prove useful in describing and explaining some of the many facets of the object of study.

It is clear from these reflections and from the review of selected models and research presented in this book that the study of interpreting does not fit neatly into any of the fields from which it has received, and may continue to receive, significant contributions. As a disciplinary entity which is more than the sum of its parts, interpreting studies is free to develop along various pathways. Indeed, as suggested in this section and its heading, it is likely to do so simultaneously, 'pushing the envelope', as it were, in several inter-connected directions. If it needed an epistemological and methodological point of reference between such traditional assignations as the natural sciences and liberal arts (« 4.4.1), it might well be close to the social sciences and their rich arsenal of qualitative as well as quantitative methods of inquiry.

10.3 Orientation

Having reflected on some basic options for the future orientation of interpreting studies as a discipline, it is time to stress that the future starts . . . HERE! However fascinating and inspiring it may be to speculate broadly about long-range directions of research, the process and progress of science, although inherently a collective enterprise, takes place in small, individual steps. Where, then, could YOU make your contribution?

Assuming that most readers of this introductory book will be rather new to the field and near the beginning of their career in academic research, this final section endeavors to provide those taking their first steps in the practice of research with some basic orientation regarding where to go and how.

10.3.1 Getting started

Orientation for those getting started in interpreting studies is of course the fundamental purpose of this book, which is offered essentially as a **map** of the interpreting studies **landscape**. Building on the basic understanding and broad overview of the terrain provided in Part I, students and would-be interpreting researchers are pointed to areas of study which merit their attention in Part II and in section 10.2. The following paragraphs provide more specific pointers, hopefully amounting to a sort of **compass** for scholars to get their bearings in the **field**. There is no list, however, of particular research questions, nor a description of the methods to be adopted. The field is indeed wide open, and the plurality of domains and paradigms makes it impossible to compile a systematic and balanced research agenda and methodological inventory. The latter will require a separate book introducing and illustrating research methods in interpreting studies.

How, then, to take one's first steps toward the goal of completing an interpreting research project? Having gained an **overview** of the territory (step 1), it is vital to find your bearings and reflect on your '**position**'; that is, where you stand, with regard to both your professional and your institutional (academic) environment (step 2). These contextual factors, including in particular the prevailing research paradigm(s) as well as your relevant personal experience, will largely determine your area(s) of interest in terms of interpreting **type and domain** as well as your underlying '**model**', or theory, of interpreting (step 3). A number of illustrative case studies of this fundamental stage in the process of *Getting Started in Interpreting Research* are included in the very useful book by that title (Gile *et al.* 2001) which resulted from the 1997 Aarhus Seminar on Interpreting Research.

In the present volume, the thematic organization of Part II, with its section headings and subheadings, should be instrumental in choosing a **topic** (step 4), with the text links and the subject index directing you to additional references for the topic and interpreting type in question. There are of course many additional and related concepts and issues on which you may want to build a research idea of your own. The structure offered in this book is really meant to serve as a scaffolding for further access rather than a rigidly constraining grid. By the same token, the subject index of the *Reader* (Pöchhacker and Shlesinger 2002) provides a particularly rich inventory of key terms which you can mine for further ideas and references.

Having found the place you want to explore in depth, you need to 'dig deeper'; that is, "read, read, read," as Miriam Shlesinger had memorably impressed on participants in the Aarhus Seminar. Thorough coverage of the literature is vital in order to observe that fundamental principle of science, as a collective and cumulative process, which requires the researcher to build on and add to the state of the art. Your **reading** (step 5) is thus designed to establish, in detail, the state of the art in your topic area, and may well begin with the sources listed at the end of each chapter in Part II, starting with the material made accessible – and contextualized with numerous further references – in the *Reader*. Purposeful reading of the literature is a significant part of a researcher's specialized skills. It requires both the sound intellectual processing of content, the critical appraisal of the author's perspective, aims, and methodology, and an appropriate way of documenting the information and insights gained from one's sources. On this the chapter on "critical reading" in Gile *et al.* (2001) provides valuable guidance and advice, and should be read, critically of course, before you delve into the literature.

The reading process will go a long way toward helping you to formulate a specific **research question** (step 6) and consider ways in which it might be addressed. It is at this (early) stage that the way to proceed hinges on your basic choice of **methodological approach**, which is not so much a stage in the research process as a fundamental orientation to 'doing science' (« 3.3.1, « 3.3.2): your affinities with regard to modern or postmodern epistemologies; your focus on data in search of a theory ('induction') vs theories from which to derive testable hypotheses ('deduction'); your preference for quantitative (numerical) vs qualitative (nonnumerical) data; and the purpose you have set yourself for your study will shape your methodological orientation and **strategy**. Making your basic stance as explicit as possible for yourself, and for others, is an important step after all (step 7) because it largely informs the way you will design and implement your study.

Deciding on a **research design** (step 8), for instance, may not mean the same to someone testing a causal hypothesis in a laboratory as it does to someone wishing to understand how participants behave in a real-life event. In the former case, a number of standard designs with certain types of experimental conditions, subjects, materials and methods may be available to **choose** from. In the latter, preparing to 'go into the field' may require a complex process to **develop** an appropriate design under a particular set of (often unknown) circumstances and constraints. The **context** of research, broadly speaking, includes a number of factors which may have a significant influence on the design of a study. With special regard to qualitative research, but not limited to it, some of the relevant contextual factors which variously impact on the main components of research design are depicted graphically in Figure 10.2.

Apart from drawing explicit attention to such factors as personal goals, ethical concerns, research skills, personal experience, and prevailing paradigms, Figure

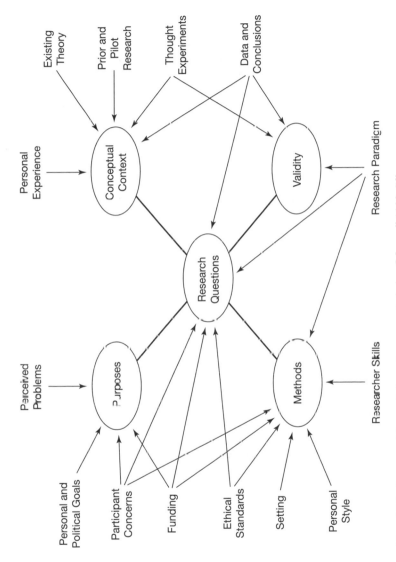

Figure 10.2 Contextual factors influencing research design (Maxwell 1998: 73)

10.2 is also valuable for highlighting the inherent interdependence of the principal components of design. At the upper level, the **purposes** – that is, the object and goal(s) of a study, including pragmatic considerations and personal motivation – and the **conceptual context** – that is, the theoretical assumptions and frameworks informing or guiding the study – are linked up to the **research question(s)** as the central component, which is in turn closely interrelated with the **methods** and techniques to be used and the **validity** issues bearing on the study.

This basic orientation to critical issues of methodology, and the present book as a whole, mainly address the interaction between conceptual contexts (foundations, models, theories) and research questions within a particular environment. There is no scope for offering hands-on advice on more concrete methodological matters such as how to **plan** and organize your study (step 9), how to **implement** your research design by collecting, processing and analyzing various types of data (step 10), how to **evaluate** and interpret your findings in relation to the research question and the underlying theoretical framework (step 11), and how to **report** on your study in an appropriate way, be it in the form of a conference presentation, a journal article, or an academic thesis (step 12).

Help with the more detailed and practical issues in the process of empirical research is available from a variety of publications and sources, as indicated in the final paragraphs that follow. Nevertheless, in research on interpreting as in interpreting as such, no amount of reading and good advice can replace experiential, case-based learning 'on the job'. Quite often it is only when actually **doing it** that questions, doubts and problems arise, prompting the junior researcher to oscillate between trying out solutions and seeking advice.

10.3.2 Getting help

Ideally, students of interpreting can acquire the necessary research skills in graduate-level seminars under the guidance of an experienced researcher and teacher. Where curricular provisions and staff resources fall short of this ideal, there are several ways for would-be interpreting researchers to get help. As mentioned above, the volume by Gile *et al.* (2001) on *Getting Started* is a rich source of information and advice tailored especially to the needs of graduate students and PhD candidates. The initial chapter by Gile on "selecting a topic" and the report by Čeňková on "MA theses in Prague" offer helpful guidance on the early stages of developing a research project. In a similar vein, Shlesinger (2002) provides inspiring orientation in a paper on "choosing a research topic" which includes a list of twenty examples from such subject areas as interpreting mode and modality, working conditions, stress, fatigue, and teaching methods. Shlesinger shows how research questions can usefully be formulated as hypotheses and suggests possible methodologies for testing them. Further along these lines, the book by Gile *et al.* (2001) contains several illustrative examples of PhD research in interpreting studies, with particular emphasis on methodological problems and solutions. Much practical advice can also be found in the *Beginner's Guide to Doing Research in Translation Studies* by Williams and Chesterman (2002).

Though designing and implementing an inquiry is a personal, creative process and as such not really amenable to recipe-like instructions, researchers in other disciplines, with more consolidated paradigms and an established canon of methods, usually dispose of handbooks providing comprehensive methodological guidance. To the extent that concepts and methods from fields such as anthropology, discourse analysis, ethnography, linguistics, psychology and sociology (« 3.1.2, « 3.1.3) can help interpreting researchers address some of the diverse aspects of their multi-faceted object of study, the methodological literature for the respective paradigms can provide important inspiration.

For the **social sciences**, an impressive range of standard texts on research methodology can be found in the "Applied Social Research Methods Series" published since the early 1980s by Sage Publications, Inc. The series, which runs to dozens of titles, includes books by leading authors on survey and case-study research, participant observation, ethnography, sampling, research ethics, and basic design issues. A digest of eighteen volumes was published by the series editors as a compact resource under the title *Handbook of Applied Social Research Methods* (Bickman and Rog 1998). The same publisher also offers a series on "Qualitative Research Methods" and a large number of individual introductory texts as well as the most advanced and comprehensive reference on qualitative research currently available: the *Handbook of Qualitative Research* was first published in 1994 and was followed only six years later by an expanded and revised second edition which runs to more than 1000 pages (Denzin and Lincoln 2000). Such overwhelming collections are hardly recommendable as introductory reading, however, and there are many useful books for that more modest purpose (e.g. Babbie 1999).

A concise and reader-friendly introduction to basic research strategies and techniques, from single-case studies to experimental hypothesis-testing in **psychology**, is Robson's (1993) *Real World Research*. Expressly catering for "practitioner–researchers", the book provides clear explanations as well as annotated bibliographies for each topic and technique, thus serving as a gateway to more specialized sources. A similar gateway function for methodological orientations in the area of **linguistics** and **discourse studies** is served by the interdisciplinary survey by Titscher *et al.* (2000) on *Methods of Text and Discourse Analysis*. With annotated references to the respective paradigms' original sources, the book presents and compares a dozen methodologies, including approaches such as grounded theory, functional pragmatics, and critical discourse analysis, which have informed recent PhD research on community-based interpreting. From the multitude of textbooks on linguistic methodology, special mention might be made of the introduction to *Corpus Linguistics* by Biber *et al.* (1998) and the volume by McDonough and McDonough (1997) on *Research Methods for English Language Teachers*, with special emphasis on action research in the classroom.

From the many reference works on the principles of **sampling**, **data analysis** and **statistics**, one might mention the classic text on *Statistical Methods* by Snedecor and Cochran (1980), which is cited in some papers on research methodology in interpreting studies, and the "Sourcebook" on *Qualitative Data Analysis* by Miles and Huberman (1994).

Even this sparse selection of references to the methodological literature in established disciplines is enough to demonstrate how much ground there is to cover, and how much there is to learn for researchers in interpreting studies. Whereas it is certainly desirable for everyone doing empirical research to 'go to the source' and become thoroughly familiar with methodological choices and their implications, such effort may not always be commensurate with the projects at hand. In such a case, fledgling researchers may find it safe to follow the model provided by published empirical studies such as those introduced in Part II. An existing survey instrument may be applied to a different study population, for instance, and a tested experimental design may be implemented with different subjects or different input material. Such **replication**, which is recommended particularly at the level of graduation theses, is of substantial value, regardless of whether it confirms previous findings or leads to different results – and thus raises further questions. An alternative, or complementary, approach is to rely on one or more **consultants** with relevant experience in research design and data analysis.

Consulting other experts is generally a good idea, and it may be particularly efficient to obtain feedback and advice from interpreting researchers who have done related kinds of work. You can usually find and approach them via the Internet, and you may count on a rather cooperative attitude, provided that you have 'done your homework' and have gone as far as you could with the means and sources available – locally, through inter-library exchange, and in cyberspace (see the Internet links provided after the Bibliography). In e-mail correspondence and, if possible, in personal contacts at conferences, new members of the interpreting studies community will interact with some old hands. It is when the latter find that the questions being asked are too clever and difficult for them to answer that all of us in this field may take heart from the realization that progress in interpreting studies is set to continue.

Bibliography

Agger-Gupta, N. (2001) "From 'Making Do' to Established Service, the Development of Health Care Interpreter Services in Canada and the United States of America: A Grounded Theory Study of Health Organization Change and the Growth of a New Profession," PhD dissertation, The Fielding Graduate Institute.

AIIC (2002) "Workload Study," Geneva: AIIC (http://www.aiic.net.ViewPage.cfm/article467).

Alexieva, B. (1983) "Compression as a Means of Realisation of the Communicative Act in Simultaneous Interpreting," *Fremdsprachen* 27 (4): 233–8.

—— (1985) "Semantic Analysis of the Text in Simultaneous Interpreting," in H. Bühler (ed.) *Xth World Congress of FIT. Proceedings*, Vienna: Wilhelm Braumüller, pp. 195–8.

—— (1994) "Types of Texts and Intertextuality in Simultaneous Interpreting," in Snell-Hornby *et al.* (eds) (1994), pp. 179–87.

—— (1997/2002) "A Typology of Interpreter-mediated Events," in Pöchhacker and Shlesinger (eds) (2002), pp. 219–33.

—— (1999) "Understanding the Source Language Text in Simultaneous Interpreting," *The Interpreters' Newsletter* No. 9: 45–59.

—— (2001) "Interpreter-mediated TV Live Interviews," in Y. Gambier and H. Gottlieb (eds) *(Multi)Media Translation: Concepts, Practices, and Research*, Amsterdam and Philadelphia: John Benjamins, pp. 113–24.

Alonso Bacigalupe, L. (1999) "Visual Contact in Simultaneous Interpretation: Results of an Experimental Study," in Álvarez Lugrís and Fernández Ocampo (eds) (1999), pp. 123–37.

Alpbach (1968) Report on Session "Interpreters and Interpreting," European Forum Alpbach, 19–24 August 1968, unpublished typescript.

Altman, J. (1990) "What Helps Effective Communication? Some Interpreters' Views," *The Interpreters' Newsletter* No. 3: 23–32.

Álvarez Lugrís, A. and Fernández Ocampo, A. (eds) (1999) *Anovar/Anosar estudios de traducción e interpretación*, vol. 1, Vigo: Universidade de Vigo.

Anderson, J.R. (1990) *Cognitive Psychology and Its Implications*, 3rd ed, New York: Freeman.

Anderson, L. (1994) "Simultaneous Interpretation: Contextual and Translation Aspects," in Lambert and Moser-Mercer (eds) (1994), pp. 101–20.

Anderson, R.B.W. (1976) "Perspectives on the Role of Interpreter," in Brislin (ed.) (1976b), pp. 208–28.

—— (1976/2002) "Perspectives on the Role of Interpreter," in Pöchhacker and Shlesinger (eds) (2002), pp. 209–17.

Andres, D. (2002) *Konsekutivdolmetschen und Notation*, Frankfurt: Peter Lang.

Angelelli, C.V. (2001) "Deconstructing the Invisible Interpreter: A Critical Study of the Interpersonal Role of the Interpreter in a Cross-cultural/linguistic Communicative Event," PhD dissertation, Stanford University.

Apfelbaum, B. (1995) "Interaktive Verfahren der Disambiguierung in Situationen des Gesprächsdolmetschens," *Kognitionswissenschaft* 5 (3): 141–50.

Arjona, E. (1978) "Intercultural Communication and the Training of Interpreters at the Monterey Institute of Foreign Studies," in Gerver and Sinaiko (eds) (1978), pp. 35–44.

—— (1984) "Issues in the Design of Curricula for the Professional Education of Translators and Interpreters," in McIntire (ed.) (1984), pp. 1–35.

Arjona-Tseng, E. (1994) "A Psychometric Approach to the Selection of Translation and Interpreting Students in Taiwan," in Lambert and Moser-Mercer (eds) (1994), pp. 69–86.

Babbie, E. (1999) *The Basics of Social Research*, Belmont, CA: Wadsworth.

Baddeley, A. (2000) "Working Memory and Language Processing," in Englund Dimitrova and Hyltenstam (eds) (2000), pp. 1–16.

Baigorri Jalón, J. (2000) *La interpretación de conferencias: el nacimiento de una profesión. De París a Nuremberg*, Granada: Comares.

Baistow, K. (1999) "The Emotional and Psychological Impact of Community Interpreting," in *1st BABELEA Conference on Community Interpreting* (Vienna, 3–5 November 1999), London: Language Line.

Bajo, M.T., Padilla, F. and Padilla, P. (2000) "Comprehension Processes in Simultaneous Interpreting," in A. Chesterman, N. Gallardo San Salvador and Y. Gambier (eds) *Translation in Context. Selected Papers from the EST Congress, Granada 1998*, Amsterdam and Philadelphia: John Benjamins, pp. 127–42.

Baker, M. (1997) "Non-cognitive Constraints and Interpreter Strategies," in K. Simms (ed.) *Translating Sensitive Texts: Linguistic Aspects*, Amsterdam and Atlanta: Rodopi, pp. 111–29.

—— (ed.) (1998) *Routledge Encyclopedia of Translation Studies*, London and New York: Routledge.

Baker-Shenk, C. (ed.) (1990) *A Model Curriculum for Teachers of American Sign Language and Teachers of ASL/English Interpreting*, Silver Spring, MD: RID Publications.

Balzani, M. (1990) "Le contact visuel en interprétation simultanée: resultats d'une expérience (Français–Italien)," in Gran and Taylor (eds) (1990), pp. 93–100.

Barik, H.C. (1972) "Interpreters Talk a Lot, Among Other Things," *Babel* 18 (1): 3–10.

—— (1973) "Simultaneous Interpretation: Temporal and Quantitative Data," *Language and Speech* 16 (3): 237–70.

—— (1975/2002) "Simultaneous Interpretation: Qualitative and Linguistic Data," in Pöchhacker and Shlesinger (eds) (2002), pp. 79–91.

Barsky, R. (1996) "The Interpreter as Intercultural Agent in Convention Refugee Hearings," *The Translator* 2 (1): 45–63.

Beaugrande, R. de (1980) *Text, Discourse, and Process*, Norwood, NJ: Ablex.

—— (1997) "The Story of Discourse Analysis," in van Dijk (ed.) (1997a), pp. 35–62.

—— and Dressler, W.U. (1981) *Introduction to Text Linguistics*, London: Longman.

Bell, S.J. (1997) "The Challenges of Setting and Monitoring the Standards of Community Interpreting: An Australian Perspective," in Carr *et al.* (eds) (1997), pp. 93–108.

Berk-Seligson, S. (1988/2002) "The Impact of Politeness in Witness Testimony: The Influence of the Court Interpreter," in Pöchhacker and Shlesinger (eds) (2002), pp. 279–92.

—— (1990) *The Bilingual Courtroom: Court Interpreters in the Judicial Process*, Chicago and London: The University of Chicago Press.

—— (2000) "Interpreting for the Police: Issues in Pre-trial Phases of the Judicial Process," *Forensic Linguistics* 7 (2): 212–37.

Biber, D., Conrad, S. and Reppen, R. (1998) *Corpus Linguistics: Investigating Language Structure and Use,* Cambridge: Cambridge University Press.

Bickman, L. and Rog, D.J. (eds) (1998) *Handbook of Applied Social Research Methods,* Thousand Oaks, London and New Delhi: Sage.

Blum-Kulka, S. (1986/2000) "Shifts of Cohesion and Coherence in Translation," in Venuti (ed.) (2000), pp. 298–313.

Bolden, G.B. (2000) "Toward Understanding Practices of Medical Interpreting: Interpreters' Involvement in History Taking," *Discourse Studies* 2 (4): 387–419.

Bot, H. (2003) "Quality as an Interactive Concept: Interpreting in Psychotherapy," in Collados Aís *et al.* (eds) (2003), pp. 33–45.

Bottan, L. (2000) "La présentation en interprétation consecutive: comment développer une habileté de base," *The Interpreters' Newsletter* No. 10: 47–67.

Bowen, D. and Bowen, M. (eds) (1990) *Interpreting – Yesterday, Today, and Tomorrow,* Binghamton, NY: SUNY.

Bowen, M. [*et al.*] (1995) "Interpreters and the Making of History," in Delisle and Woodsworth (eds) (1995), pp. 245–73.

Braun, S. and Kohn, K. (2001) "Dolmetschen in der Videokonferenz. Kommunikative Kompetenz und Monitoringstrategien," in G. Thome, C. Giehl and H. Gerzymisch-Arbogast (eds) *Kultur und Übersetzung. Methodologische Probleme des Kulturtransfers,* Tübingen: Gunter Narr, pp. 1–32.

Brennan, M. (1999) "Signs of Injustice," *The Translator* 5 (2): 221–46.

Brislin, R.W. (1976a) "Introduction," in Brislin (ed.) (1976b), pp. 1–43.

—— (ed.) (1976b) *Translation: Applications and Research,* New York: Gardner Press.

Broadbent, D.E. (1952) "Speaking and Listening Simultaneously," *Journal of Experimental Psychology* 43: 267–73.

—— (1958) *Perception and Communication,* London: Pergamon Press.

Bros-Brann, E. (1975) "Critical Comments On H.C. Barik's Article 'Interpreters Talk a Lot, Among Other Things', *Babel*, no. 1, 1972, Vol. XVIII," *Babel* 21 (2): 93–4.

Buck, V. (2002) "One World, One Language?" in *Communicate!* April–May 2002 (http://www.aiic.net/ViewPage.cfm/article520)

Bühler, H. (1985) "Conference Interpreting – a Multichannel Communication Phenomenon," *Meta* 30 (1): 49–54.

—— (1986) "Linguistic (Semantic) and Extra-linguistic (Pragmatic) Criteria for the Evaluation of Conference Interpretation and Interpreters," *Multilingua* 5 (4): 231–5.

Carr, S.E. and Steyn, D. (2000) "Distance Education Training for Interpreters: An Insurmountable Oxymoron?" in Roberts *et al.* (eds) (2000), pp. 83–8.

—— Roberts, R., Dufour A. and Steyn, D. (eds) (1997) *The Critical Link: Interpreters in the Community. Papers from the First International Conference on Interpreting in Legal, Health, and Social Service Settings (Geneva Park, Canada, June 1–4, 1995),* Amsterdam and Philadelphia: John Benjamins.

Carroll, J.B. (1978) "Linguistic Abilities in Translators and Interpreters," in Gerver and Sinaiko (eds) (1978), pp. 119–29.

Cary, E. (1956) *La traduction dans le monde moderne,* Geneva: Georg.

Cencini, M. and Aston, G. (2002) "Resurrecting the Corp(us|se): Towards an Encoding Standard for Interpreting Data," in Garzone and Viezzi (eds) (2002), pp. 47–62.

Čeňková, I. (1988) *Teoretické aspekty simultánního tolumočení,* Prague: Charles University.

Chernov, G.V. (1978) *Teoriya i praktika sinkhronnogo perevoda* [Theory and Practice of Simultaneous Interpretation], Moscow: Mezhdunarodnyye otnosheniya.

—— (1979/2002) "Semantic Aspects of Psycholinguistic Research in Simultaneous Interpretation," in Pöchhacker and Shlesinger (eds) (2002), pp. 99–109.

—— (1994) "Message Redundancy and Message Anticipation in Simultaneous Interpretation," in Lambert and Moser-Mercer (eds) (1994), pp. 139–53.

Chesterman, A. (1993) "From 'Is' to 'Ought': Laws, Norms and Strategies in Translation Studies," *Target* 5 (1): 1–20.

—— (1997) *Memes of Translation: The Spread of Ideas in Translation Theory*, Amsterdam and Philadelphia: John Benjamins.

—— and Arrojo, R. (2000) "Shared Ground in Translation Studies," *Target* 12 (1): 151–60.

Cheung, A. (2003) "Does Accent Matter? The Impact of Accent in Simultaneous Interpretation into Mandarin and Cantonese on Perceived Performance Quality and Listener Satisfaction Level," in Collados Aís *et al.* (eds) (2003), pp. 85–96.

Chiaro, D. (2002) "Linguistic Mediation on Italian Television. When the Interpreter Is Not an Interpreter: A Case Study," in Garzone and Viezzi (eds) (2002), pp. 215–25.

Clark, H.H. (1996) *Using Language*, Cambridge: Cambridge University Press.

Cokely, D. (1981) "Sign Language Interpreters: A Demographic Survey," *Sign Language Studies* No. 32: 261–86.

—— (1990) "The Effectiveness of Three Means of Communication in the College Classroom," *Sign Language Studies* 69: 415–42.

—— (1992a) *Interpretation: A Sociolinguistic Model*, Burtonsville, MD: Linstok Press.

—— (ed.) (1992b) *Sign Language Interpreters and Interpreting*, Burtonsville, MD: Linstok Press.

—— (2000) "Exploring Ethics: A Case for Revising the Code of Ethics," *Journal of Interpretation* 2000: 25–57.

Collados Aís, A. (1998/2002) "Quality Assessment in Simultaneous Interpreting: The Importance of Nonverbal Communication," in Pöchhacker and Shlesinger (eds) (2002), pp. 327–36.

—— Fernández Sánchez, M.M. and Gile, D. (eds) (2003) *La evaluación de la calidad en interpretación: Investigación*, Granada: Comares.

Consorte, C. (1999) "Thematic Structure and Simultaneous Interpretation: Some Experimental Evidence," *The Interpreters' Newsletter* No. 9: 99–124.

Cooper, C.L., Davies, R. and Tung, R.L. (1982) "Interpreting Stress: Sources of Job Stress among Conference Interpreters," *Multilingua* 1 (2): 97–107.

Corina, D.P. and Vaid, J. (1994) "Lateralization for Shadowing Words versus Signs: A Study of ASL–English Interpreters," in Lambert and Moser-Mercer (eds) (1994), pp. 237–48.

Corsellis, A. (1997) "Training Needs of Public Personnel Working with Interpreters," in Carr *et al.* (eds) (1997), pp. 77–89.

—— (1999) "Training of Public Service Interpreters," in Erasmus (ed.) (1999), pp. 197–205.

—— (2000) "Turning Good Intentions into Good Practice: Enabling the Public Services to Fulfil their Responsibilities," in Roberts *et al.* (eds) (2000), pp. 89–99.

Cronin, M. (2002) "The Empire Talks Back: Orality, Heteronomy and the Cultural Turn in Interpreting Studies," in Pöchhacker and Shlesinger (eds) (2002), pp. 387–97.

Dam, H.V. (1993) "Text Condensing in Consecutive Interpreting," in Gambier and Tommola (eds) (1993), pp. 297–313.

—— (1998) "Lexical Similarity vs Lexical Dissimilarity in Consecutive Interpreting," in Pöchhacker and Shlesinger (eds) (2002), pp. 267–77.

—— (2001) "On the Option Between Form-based and Meaning-based Interpreting: The Effect of Source Text Difficulty on Lexical Target Text Form in Simultaneous Interpreting," *The Interpreters' Newsletter* No. 11: 27–55.

Danks, J.H., Shreve, G.M., Fountain, S.B. and McBeath, M.K. (eds) (1997) *Cognitive Processes in Translation and Interpreting*, Thousand Oaks, London and New Delhi: Sage.

Darò, V. (1994) "Non-linguistic Factors Influencing Simultaneous Interpretation," in Lambert and Moser-Mercer (eds) (1994), pp. 249–71.

—— (1997) "Experimental Studies on Memory in Conference Interpretation," *Meta* 42 (4): 622–8.

Davidson, B. (1998) "Interpreting Medical Discourse: A Study of Cross-linguistic Communication in the Hospital Clinic," PhD dissertation, Stanford University.

—— (2002) "A Model for the Construction of Conversational Common Ground in Interpreted Discourse," *Journal of Pragmatics* 34: 1273–300.

de Bot, K. (2000) "Simultaneous Interpreting as Language Production," in Englund Dimitrova and Hyltenstam (eds) (2000), pp. 65–88.

de Groot, A.M.B. (1997) "The Cognitive Study of Translation and Interpretation: Three Approaches," in Danks *et al.* (eds) (1997), pp. 25–56.

Déjean le Féal, K. (1982) "Why Impromptu Speech is Easy to Understand," in Enkvist (ed.) (1982), pp. 221–39.

—— (1990) "Some Thoughts on the Evaluation of Simultaneous Interpretation," in Bowen and Bowen (eds) (1990), pp. 154–60.

—— (1997) "Simultaneous Interpretation with 'Training Wheels'," *Meta* 42 (2): 616–21.

Delisle, J. and Woodsworth, J. (eds) (1995) *Translators through History*, Amsterdam and Philadelphia: John Benjamins.

Denzin, N.K. and Lincoln, Y.S. (2000) *Handbook of Qualitative Research*, 2nd edn, Thousand Oaks, London and New Delhi: Sage.

Dillinger, M. (1994) "Comprehension during Interpreting: What do Interpreters Know that Bilinguals Don't?" in Lambert and Moser-Mercer (eds) (1994), pp. 155–89.

Diriker, E. (2001) "De-/Re-contextualising Simultaneous Interpreting: Interpreters in the Ivory Tower?" PhD dissertation, Boğaziçi University, Istanbul.

Dodds, J.M. (1990) "On the Aptitude of Aptitude Testing," *The Interpreters' Newsletter* No. 3: 17–22.

—— and Katan, D. [*et al.*] (1997) "The Interaction between Research and Training," in Gambier *et al.* (eds) (1997), pp. 89–107.

Dollerup, C. and Appel, V. (eds) (1996) *Teaching Translation and Interpreting 3: New Horizons*, Amsterdam and Philadelphia: John Benjamins.

Dollerup, C. and Lindegaard, A. (eds) (1994) *Teaching Translation and Interpreting 2: Aims, Insights, Visions*, Amsterdam and Philadelphia: John Benjamins.

Dollerup, C. and Loddegaard, A. (eds) (1992) *Teaching Translation and Interpreting: Training, Talent and Experience*, Amsterdam and Philadelphia: John Benjamins.

Donk, U. (1994) "Der Dolmetscher in kriminalpolizeilichen Vernehmungen. Eine ethnographische Strukturrekonstruktion," in N. Schröer (ed.) *Interpretative Sozialforschung*, Opladen: Westdeutscher Verlag, pp. 130–50.

Donovan-Cagigos, C. (1990) "La fidélité en interprétation," doctoral dissertation, Université de la Sorbonne Nouvelle/Paris III.

Drennan, G. and Swartz, L. (1999) "A Concept Over-burdened: Institutional Roles for Psychiatric Interpreters in Post-Apartheid South Africa," *Interpreting* 4 (2): 169–98.

Dubrovsky, R. and Weller, G. (1990) "Curriculum Review at the ISIT (Mexico City)," in Bowen and Bowen (eds) (1990), pp. 61–9.

Englund Dimitrova, B. (1997) "Degree of Interpreter Responsibility in the Interaction Process in Community Interpreting," in Carr *et al.* (eds) (1997), pp. 147–64.

—— and Hyltenstam, K. (eds) (2000) *Language Processing and Simultaneous Interpreting: Interdisciplinary Perspectives*, Amsterdam and Philadelphia: John Benjamins.

Enkvist, N.E. (ed.) (1982) *Impromptu Speech: A Symposium*, Åbo: Åbo Akademi.

Erasmus, M. [*et al.*] (ed.) (1999) *Liaison Interpreting in the Community*, Pretoria: Van Schaik.

Ericsson, K.A. and Kintsch, W. (1995) "Long-term Working Memory," *Psychological Review* 102 (2): 211–42.

Ervin, S.M. and Osgood, C.E. (1965) "Second Language Learning and Bilingualism," in C.E. Osgood and T.A. Sebeok (eds) *Psycholinguistics: A Survey of Theory and Research Problems*, Bloomington and London: Indiana University Press, pp. 139–46.

Fabbro, F. and Gran, L. (1994) "Neurological and Neuropsychological Aspects of Polyglossia and Simultaneous Interpretation," in Lambert and Moser-Mercer (eds) (1994), pp. 273–317.

—— (1997) "Neurolinguistic Research in Simultaneous Interpretation," in Gambier *et al.* (eds) (1997), pp. 9–27.

Fabbro, F., Gran, L., Basso, G. and Bava, A. (1990) "Cerebral Lateralization in Simultaneous Interpretation," *Brain and Language* 39: 69–89.

Fant, L. (1990) *Silver Threads: A Personal Look at the First Twenty-five Years of the Registry of Interpreters for the Deaf*, Silver Spring, MD: RID Publications.

Feldweg, E. (1996) *Der Konferenzdolmetscher im internationalen Kommunikationsprozeß*, Heidelberg: Groos.

Fenton, S. (1993) "Interpreting in New Zealand: An Emerging Profession," *Journal of Interpretation* 6: 155–65.

Ferrari, M. (2001) "Consecutive simultaneous?" SCIC*News* No. 26, 21 November 2001 (http://scic.cec.eu.int/scicnews/2001/011121/news05.htm)

Feuerstein, M., Carosella, A.M., Burrell, A.L., Marshall, L. and DeCaro, J. (1997) "Occupational Upper Extremity Symptoms in Sign Language Interpreter: Prevalence and Correlates of Pain, Function, and Work Disability," *Journal of Occupational Rehabilitation* 7 (4): 187–205.

Flores d'Arcais, G.B. (1978) "The Contribution of Cognitive Psychology to the Study of Interpretation," in Gerver and Sinaiko (eds) (1978), pp. 385–402.

Frishberg, N. (1990) *Interpreting: An Introduction*, rev. edn, Silver Spring, MD: RID Publications.

Fukuii, H. and Asano, T. (1961) *Eigotsûyaku no jissai* [An English Interpreter's Manual], Tokyo: Kenkyusha.

Gaiba, F. (1998) *The Origins of Simultaneous Interpretation: The Nuremberg Trial*, Ottawa: University of Ottawa Press.

Gambier, Y. and Tommola, J. (eds) (1993) *Translation and Knowledge: SSOTT IV*, Turku: University of Turku, Centre for Translation and Interpreting.

Gambier, Y., Gile, D. and Taylor, C. (eds) (1997) *Conference Interpreting: Current Trends in Research*, Amsterdam and Philadelphia: John Benjamins.

Garber, N. and Mauffette-Leenders, L.A. (1997) "Obtaining Feedback from Non-English Speakers," in Carr *et al.* (eds) (1997), pp. 131–43.

García-Landa, M. (1981) "La 'théorie du sens', théorie de la traduction et base de son enseignement," in J. Delisle (ed.) *L'enseignement de l'interprétation et de la traduction: de la théorie à la pédagogie*, Ottawa: University of Ottawa Press, pp. 113–32.

—— (1998) "A Theoretical Framework for Oral and Written Translation Research," *The Interpreters' Newsletter* No. 8: 5–40.

Garnham, A. (1994) "Future Directions," in Gernsbacher (ed.) (1994), pp. 1123–44.

Garzone, G. (2003) "Reliability of Quality Criteria Evaluation in Survey Research," in Collados Aís *et al.* (eds) (2003), pp. 23–30.

—— and Viezzi, M. (eds) (2002) *Interpreting in the 21st Century: Challenges and Opportunities*, Amsterdam and Philadelphia: John Benjamins.

—— Mead, P. and Viezzi, M. (eds) (2002) *Perspectives on Interpreting*, Bologna: CLUEB.

Gentile, A., Ozolins, U. and Vasilakakos, M. (1996) *Liaison Interpreting: A Handbook*, Melbourne: Melbourne University Press.

Gernsbacher, M.A. (ed.) (1994) *Handbook of Psycholinguistics*, San Diego, CA: Academic Press.

Gerver, D. (1969/2002) "The Effects of Source Language Presentation Rate on the Performance of Simultaneous Conference Interpreters," in Pöchhacker and Shlesinger (eds) (2002), pp. 53–66.

—— (1971) "Aspects of Simultaneous Interpretation and Human Information Processing," D Phil thesis, Oxford University.

—— (1974a) "Simultaneous Listening and Speaking and Retention of Prose," *Quarterly Journal of Experimental Psychology* 26 (3): 337–41.

—— (1974b) "The Effects of Noise on the Performance of Simultaneous Interpreters: Accuracy of Performance," *Acta Psychologica* 38 (3): 159–67.

—— (1975) "A Psychological Approach to Simultaneous Interpretation," *Meta* 20 (2): 119–28.

—— (1976) "Empirical Studies of Simultaneous Interpretation: A Review and a Model," in Brislin (ed.) (1976b), pp. 165–207.

—— and Sinaiko, H.W. (eds) (1978) *Language Interpretation and Communication. Proceedings of the NATO Symposium, Venice, Italy, September 26–October 1, 1977*, New York and London: Plenum Press.

—— Longley, P.E., Long, J. and Lambert, S. (1989) "Selection Tests for Trainee Conference Interpreters," *Meta* 34 (4): 724–35.

Gile, D. (1984) "Les noms propres en interprétation simultanée," *Multilingua* 3 (2): 79–85.

—— (1985) "Le modèle d'efforts et l'équilibre en interprétation simultanée," *Meta* 30 (1): 44–8.

—— (1988) "An Overview of Conference Interpretation Research and Theory," in Hammond (ed.) (1988), pp. 363–71.

—— (1990a) "Scientific Research vs. Personal Theories in the Investigation of Interpretation," in Gran and Taylor (eds) (1990), pp. 28–41.

—— (1990b) "L'évaluation de la qualité de l'interprétation par les délégués: une étude de cas," *The Interpreters' Newsletter* No. 3: 66–71.

—— (1992a) "Predictable Sentence Endings in Japanese and Conference Interpretation," *The Interpreters' Newsletter*, Special Issue 1: 12–23.

—— (1992b) "Basic Theoretical Components for Interpreter and Translator Training," in Dollerup and Loddegaard (eds) (1992), pp. 185–94.

—— (1993) "Translation/Interpretation and Knowledge," in Gambier and Tommola (eds) (1993), pp. 67–86.

—— (1994a) "Opening Up in Interpretation Studies," in Snell-Hornby *et al.* (eds) (1994), pp. 149–58.

—— (1994b) "Methodological Aspects of Interpretation and Translation Research," in Lambert and Moser-Mercer (eds) (1994), pp. 39–56.

—— (1995a) *Regards sur la recherche en interprétation de conférence*, Lille: Presses Universitaires de Lille.

—— (1995b) *Basic Concepts and Models for Interpreter and Translator Training*, Amsterdam and Philadelphia: John Benjamins.

—— [*et al.*] (1997) "Methodology," in Gambier *et al.* (eds) (1997), pp. 109–22.

—— (1997/2002) "Conference Interpreting as a Cognitive Management Problem," in Pöchhacker and Shlesinger (eds) (2002), pp. 163–76.

—— (1998) "Observational Studies and Experimental Studies in the Investigation of Conference Interpreting," *Target* 10 (1): 69–93.

—— (1999a) "Doorstep Interdisciplinarity in Conference Interpreting Research," in Álvarez Lugrís and Fernández Ocampo (eds) (1999), pp. 41–52.

—— (1999b) "Testing the Effort Models' Tightrope Hypothesis in Simultaneous Interpreting – A Contribution," *Hermes. Journal of Linguistics* 23: 153–72.

—— (1999c) "Variability in the Perception of Fidelity in Simultaneous Interpretation," *Hermes. Journal of Linguistics* 22: 51–79.

—— (2000) "The History of Research into Conference Interpreting: A Scientometric Approach," *Target* 12 (2): 297–321.

—— (2003) "Quality Assessment in Conference Interpreting: Methodological Issues," in Collados Aís *et al.* (eds) (2003), pp. 109–23.

—— Dam, H.V., Dubslaff, F., Martinsen, B. and Schjoldager, A. (eds) (2001) *Getting Started in Interpreting Research: Methodological Reflections, Personal Accounts and Advice for Beginners*, Amsterdam and Philadelphia: John Benjamins.

Glémet, R. (1958) "Conference Interpreting," in Smith (ed.) (1958), pp. 105–22.

Göhring, H. (2002) *Interkulturelle Kommunikation: Anregungen für Sprach- und Kulturmittler*, Tübingen: Stauffenburg.

Goffman, E. (1981) *Forms of Talk*, Oxford: Basil Blackwell.

Goldman-Eisler, F. (1967) "Sequential Temporal Patterns and Cognitive Processes in Speech," *Language and Speech* 10 (3): 122–32.

—— (1972/2002) "Segmentation of Input in Simultaneous Translation," in Pöchhacker and Shlesinger (eds) (2002), pp. 69–76.

González, R.D., Vásquez, V.F. and Mikkelson, H. (1991) *Fundamentals of Court Interpretation: Theory, Policy, and Practice*, Durham, NC: Carolina Academic Press.

Graesser, A.C., Gernsbacher, M.A. and Goldman, S.R. (1997) "Cognition," in van Dijk (ed.) (1997a), pp. 292–319.

Gran, L. (1989) "Interdisciplinary Research on Cerebral Asymmetries: Significance and Prospects for the Teaching of Interpretation," in Gran and Dodds (eds) (1989), pp. 93–100.

—— and Dodds, J. (eds) (1989) *The Theoretical and Practical Aspects of Teaching Conference Interpretation*, Udine: Campanotto.

—— and Taylor, C. (eds) (1990) *Aspects of Applied and Experimental Research on Conference Interpretation*, Udine: Campanotto.

—— Carabelli, A. and Merlini, R. (2002) "Computer-assisted Interpreter Training," in Garzone and Viezzi (eds) (2002), pp. 277–94.

Green, A., Vaid, J., Schweda Nicholson, N., White, N. and Steiner, R. (1994) "Lateralization for Shadowing vs. Interpretation: A Comparison of Interpreters with Bilingual and Monolingual Controls," in Lambert and Moser-Mercer (eds) (1994), pp. 331–55.

Gringiani, A. (1990) "Reliability of Aptitude Testing: A Preliminary Study," in Gran and Taylor (eds) (1990), pp. 42–53.

Grosjean, F. (1997) "The Bilingual Individual," *Interpreting* 2 (1/2): 163–87.

Gumperz, J.J. and Hymes, D. (1972) *Directions in Sociolinguistics*, New York: Holt, Rinehart and Winston.

Hale, S. (1997a) "The Interpreter on Trial: Pragmatics in Court Interpreting," in Carr *et al.* (eds) (1997), pp. 201–11.

—— (1997b) "The Treatment of Register Variation in Court Interpreting," *The Translator* 3 (1): 39–54.

—— (1999) "Interpreters' Treatment of Discourse Markers in Courtroom Questions," *Forensic Linguistics* 6 (1): 57–82.

Halliday, M.A.K. (1985) *An Introduction to Functional Grammar*, London: Edward Arnold.

Hamers, J.F. and Blanc, M.H.A. (2000) *Bilinguality and Bilingualism*, 2nd edn, Cambridge: Cambridge University Press.

Hammond, D.L. (ed.) (1988) *Languages at Crossroads: Proceedings of the 29th Annual Conference of the American Translators Association*, Medford, NJ: Learned Information.

—— (ed.) (1989) *Coming of Age: Proceedings of the 30th Annual Conference of the American Translators Association*, Medford, NJ: Learned Information.

Harrington, F.J. (2000) "Sign Language Interpreters and Access for Deaf Students to University Curricula: The Ideal and the Reality," in Roberts *et al.* (eds) (2000), pp. 219–38.

—— and Turner, G.H. (2001) *Interpreting Interpreting: Studies and Reflections on Sign Language Interpreting*, Coleford: Douglas McLean.

Harris, B. (1990) "Norms in Interpretation," *Target* 2 (1): 115–19.

—— (1992) "Teaching Interpreting: A Canadian Experience," in Dollerup and Loddegaard (eds) (1992), pp. 259–68.

—— (1997) "Language International" *World Directory of Translation and Interpreting Schools*, Amsterdam and Philadelphia: John Benjamins.

—— and Sherwood, B. (1978) "Translating as an Innate Skill," in Gerver and Sinaiko (eds) (1978), pp. 155–70.

Hatim, B. and Mason, I. (1997) *The Translator as Communicator*, London and New York: Routledge.

—— (1997/2002) "Interpreting: A Text Linguistic Approach," in Pöchhacker and Shlesinger (eds) (2002), pp. 255–65.

Hauenschild, C. and Heizmann, S. (eds) (1997) *Machine Translation and Translation Theory*, Berlin and New York: Mouton de Gruyter.

Hayes, P.L. (1992) "Educational Interpreters for Deaf Students: Their Responsibilities, Problems, and Concerns," *Journal of Interpretation* 5: 5–23.

Herbert, J. (1952) *The Interpreter's Handbook: How to Become a Conference Interpreter*, Geneva: Georg.

—— (1978) "How Conference Interpretation Grew," in Gerver and Sinaiko (eds) (1978), pp. 5–9.

Hermann, A. (1956/2002) "Interpreting in Antiquity," in Pöchhacker and Shlesinger (eds) (2002), pp. 15–22.

Hertog, E. (ed.) (2001) *Aequitas: Access to Justice across Language and Culture in the EU*, Antwerp: Lessius Hogeschool.

Hoffman, R.R. (1997) "The Cognitive Psychology of Expertise and the Domain of Interpreting," *Interpreting* 2 (1/2): 189–230.

Holmes, J.S (1972/2000) "The Name and Nature of Translation Studies," in Venuti (ed.) (2000), pp. 172–85.

Humphrey, J.H. (2000) "Portfolios. One Answer to the Challenge of Assessment and the 'Readiness to Work' Gap," in Roy (ed.) (2000c), pp. 153–75.

Hung, E. (ed.) (2002) *Teaching Translation and Interpreting 4: Building Bridges*, Amsterdam and Philadelphia: John Benjamins.

Ilg, G. and Lambert, S. (1996) "Teaching Consecutive Interpreting," *Interpreting* 1 (1): 69–99.

Ingram, R.M. (1978) "Sign Language Interpretation and General Theories of Language, Interpretation and Communication," in Gerver and Sinaiko (eds) (1978), pp. 109–18.

—— (1985) "Simultaneous Interpretation of Sign Languages: Semiotic and Psycholinguistic Perspectives," *Multilingua* 4 (2): 91–102.

—— (1992) "Interpreters' Recognition of Structure and Meaning," in Cokely (ed.) (1992b), pp. 99–119.

Isham, W.P. (1994) "Memory for Sentence Form after Simultaneous Interpretation: Evidence both For and Against Deverbalization," in Lambert and Moser-Mercer (eds) (1994), pp. 191–211.

—— (1998) "Signed Language Interpreting," in Baker (ed.) (1998), pp. 231–5.

—— and Lane, H. (1994) "A Common Conceptual Code in Bilinguals: Evidence from Simultaneous Interpretation," *Sign Language Studies* 85: 291–317.

Ishikawa, L. (1999a) "Strategies for Interpreting a Japanese Complex Sentence into English – A Linguistic Study," *Interpreting Research* 8 (2): 74–95.

—— (1999b) "Cognitive Explicitation in Simultaneous Interpreting," in Álvarez Lugrís and Fernández Ocampo (eds) (1999), pp. 231–57.

Jansen, P. (1995) "The Role of the Interpreter in Dutch Courtroom Interaction: The Impact of the Situation on Translational Norms," in Tommola (ed.) (1995), pp. 11–36.

Jekat, S. and Klein, A. (1996) "Machine Interpretation: Open Problems and Some Solutions," *Interpreting* 1 (1): 7–20.

Jones, R. (1998) *Conference Interpreting Explained*, Manchester: St Jerome Publishing.

Jörg, P. (2001) "Das Dolmetschprodukt als Reflexion von translations- und produktionsbedingten 'feature-shifts': Eine empirische Korpusanalyse englisch–deutsch," diploma thesis, University of the Saar.

Jörg, U. (1997) "Bridging the Gap: Verb Anticipation in German–English Simultaneous Interpreting," in M. Snell-Hornby, Z. Jettmarová and K. Kaindl (eds) *Translation as Intercultural Communication*, Amsterdam and Philadelphia: John Benjamins, pp. 217–28.

Jumpelt, W. (1985) "The Conference Interpreter's Working Environment under the New ISO and IEC Standards," *Meta* 30 (1): 82–90.

Kade, O. (1967) "Zu einigen Besonderheiten des Simultandolmetschens," *Fremdsprachen* 11 (1): 8–17.

—— (1968) *Zufall und Gesetzmäßigkeit in der Übersetzung*, Leipzig: Verlag Enzyklopädie.

—— and Cartellieri, C. (1971) "Some Methodological Aspects of Simultaneous Interpreting," *Babel* 17 (2): 12–16.

Kadric, M. (2000) "Interpreting in the Austrian Courtroom," in Roberts *et al.* (eds) (2000), pp. 153–64.

—— (2001) *Dolmetschen bei Gericht. Erwartungen, Anforderungen, Kompetenzen*, Vienna: WUV-Universitätsverlag.

Kalina, S. (1992) "Discourse Processing and Interpreting Strategies – an Approach to the Teaching of Interpreting," in Dollerup and Loddegaard (eds) (1992), pp. 251–7.

—— (1998) *Strategische Prozesse beim Dolmetschen: Theoretische Grundlagen, empirische Fallstudien, didaktische Konsequenzen*, Tübingen: Gunter Narr.

—— (2002) "Quality in Interpreting and its Prerequisites: A Framework for a Comprehensive View," in Garzone and Viezzi (eds) (2002), pp. 121–30.

Karttunen, F. (1994) *Between Worlds: Interpreters, Guides, and Survivors*, New Brunswick, NJ: Rutgers University Press.

Kaufert, J.M. and Koolage, W.W. (1984) "Role Conflict among 'Culture Brokers': The Experience of Native Canadian Medical Interpreters," *Social Science & Medicine* 18 (3): 283–6.

Kaufert, J.M. and Putsch, R.W. (1997) "Communication through Interpreters in Healthcare: Ethical Dilemmas Arising from Differences in Class, Culture, Language, and Power," *Journal of Clinical Ethics* 8 (1): 71–87.

Kautz, U. (2000) *Handbuch Didaktik des Übersetzens und Dolmetschens*, Munich: Iudicium.

Keiser, W. (1978) "Selection and Training of Conference Interpreters," in Gerver and Sinaiko (eds) (1978), pp. 11–24.

—— (1999) "L'Histoire de l'Association Internationale des Interprètes de Conférence (AIIC)," *Interpreting* 4 (1): 81–95.

Kellett, C.J.M. (1995) "Video-aided Testing of Student Delivery and Presentation in Consecutive Interpretation," *The Interpreters' Newsletter* No. 6: 43–66.

Kelly, A.M. (2000) "Cultural Parameters for Interpreters in the Courtroom," in Roberts *et al.* (eds) (2000), pp. 131–48.

Kintsch, W. (1998) *Comprehension: A Paradigm for Cognition*, Cambridge: Cambridge University Press.

—— and van Dijk, T.A. (1978) "Toward a Model of Text Comprehension and Production," *Psychological Review* 85 (5): 363–94.

Kirchhoff, H. (1976) "Das dreigliedrige, zweisprachige Kommunikationssystem Dolmetschen," *Le Langage et l'Homme* 31: 21–7.

—— (1976/2002) "Simultaneous Interpreting: Interdependence of Variables in the Interpreting Process, Interpreting Models and Interpreting Strategies," in Pöchhacker and Shlesinger (eds) (2002), pp. 111–19.

Kitano, H. (1993) "La traduction de la langue parlée," in A. Clas and P. Bouillon (eds) *La traductique: Études et recherches de traduction par ordinateur*, Montréal: Presses de l'Université de Montréal, pp. 408–22.

Knapp-Potthoff, A. and Knapp, K. (1986) "Interweaving Two Discourses – The Difficult Task of the Non-professional Interpreter," in J. House and S. Blum-Kulka (eds) *Interlingual and Intercultural Communication*, Tübingen: Gunter Narr, pp. 151–68.

—— (1987) "The Man (or Woman) in the Middle: Discoursal Aspects of Non-professional Interpreting," in K. Knapp and W. Enninger (eds) *Analyzing Intercultural Communication*, The Hague: Mouton, pp. 181–211.

Kohn, K. and Kalina, S. (1996) "The Strategic Dimension of Interpreting," *Meta* 41 (1): 118–38.

Kondo, M. (1988) "Japanese Interpreters in Their Socio-cultural Context," *Meta* 33 (1): 70–8.

—— (1990) "What Conference Interpreters Should Not Be Expected To Do," *The Interpreters' Newsletter* No. 3: 59–65.

—— (2003) "3-Party 2-Language Model of Interpreting Revisited," *Forum* 1 (1): 77–96.

—— and Tebble, H. [*et al.*] (1997) "Intercultural Communication, Negotiation, and Interpreting," in Gambier *et al.* (eds) (1997), pp. 149–66.

Kopczyński, A. (1980) *Conference Interpreting: Some Linguistic and Communicative Problems*, Poznań: A. Mickiewicz University Press.

—— (1982) "Effects of Some Characteristics of Impromptu Speech on Simultaneous Interpreting," in Enkvist (ed.) (1982), pp. 255–66.

—— (1994) "Quality in Conference Interpreting: Some Pragmatic Problems," in Snell-Hornby *et al.* (eds) (1994), pp. 189–98.

Krouglov, A. (1999) "Police Interpreting: Politeness and Sociocultural Context," *The Translator* 5 (2): 285–302.

Kuhn, T.S. (1962/1996) *The Structure of Scientific Revolutions*, 3rd edn, Chicago and London: The University of Chicago Press.

Kurz, I. (1985) "The Rock Tombs of the Princes of Elephantine. Earliest References to Interpretation in Pharaonic Egypt," *Babel* 31 (4): 213–18.

—— (1989a) "Conference Interpreting: User Expectations," in Hammond (ed.) (1989), pp. 143–8.

—— (1989b) "The Use of Video-tapes in Consecutive and Simultaneous Interpretation Training," in Gran and Dodds (eds) (1989), pp. 213–15.

—— (1992) "'Shadowing' Exercises in Interpreter Training," in Dollerup and Loddegaard (eds) (1992), pp. 245–50.

—— (1993/2002) "Conference Interpretation: Expectations of Different User Groups," in Pöchhacker and Shlesinger (eds) (2002), pp. 313–24.

—— (1994) "A Look into the 'Black Box' – EEG Probability Mapping during Mental Simultaneous Interpreting," in Snell-Hornby *et al.* (eds) (1994), pp. 199–207.

—— (1996) *Simultandolmetschen als Gegenstand der interdisziplinären Forschung*, Vienna: WUV-Universitätsverlag.

—— (2001) "Conference Interpreting: Quality in the Ears of the User," *Meta* 45 (2): 394–409.

—— (2002a) "Physiological Stress Responses during Media and Conference Interpreting," in Garzone and Viezzi (eds) (2002), pp. 195–202.

—— (2002b) "Interpreting Training Programmes: The Benefits of Coordination, Cooperation, and Modern Technology," in Hung (ed.) (2002), pp. 65–72.

—— and Pöchhacker, F. (1995) "Quality in TV Interpreting," *Translatio. Nouvelles de la FIT – FIT Newsletter* N.s. 14 (3/4): 350–8.

—— Basel, E., Chiba, D., Patels, W. and Wolfframm, J. (1996) "Scribe or Actor? A Survey Paper on Personality Profiles of Translators and Interpreters," *The Interpreters' Newsletter* No. 7: 3–18.

Kusztor, M. (2000) "Darstellung von Kohärenz in Original und Verdolmetschung," in S. Kalina, S. Buhl and H. Gerzymisch-Arbogast (eds) *Dolmetschen: Theorie – Praxis – Didaktik*, St Ingbert: Röhrig Universitätsverlag, pp. 19–44.

Lamberger-Felber, H. (2003) "Performance Variability among Conference Interpreters: Examples from a Case Study," in Collados Aís *et al.* (eds) (2003), pp. 147–68.

Lambert, S. (1988) "A Human Information Processing and Cognitive Approach to the Training of Simultaneous Interpreters," in Hammond (ed.) (1988), pp. 379–87.

—— (1989) "Information Processing among Conference Interpreters: A Test of the Depth-of-Processing Hypothesis," in Gran and Dodds (eds) (1989), pp. 83–91.

—— (1991) "Aptitude Testing for Simultaneous Interpretation at the University of Ottawa," *Meta* 36 (4): 586–94.

—— (1994) "Foreword," in Lambert and Moser-Mercer (eds) (1994), pp. 5–14.

—— and Moser-Mercer, B. (eds) (1994) *Bridging the Gap: Empirical Research in Simultaneous Interpretation*, Amsterdam and Philadelphia: John Benjamins.

Lambert, W.E. (1978) "Psychological Approaches to Bilingualism, Translation and Interpretation," in Gerver and Sinaiko (eds) (1978), pp. 131–43.

—— Havelka, J. and Gardner, R.C. (1959) "Linguistic Manifestations of Bilingualism," *American Journal of Psychology* 72 (1): 77–82.

Lang, R. (1978) "Behavioral Aspects of Liaison Interpreters in Papua New Guinea: Some Preliminary Observations," in Gerver and Sinaiko (eds) (1978), pp. 231–44.

Laplace, C. (1994) *Théorie du langage et théorie de la traduction. Les concepts-clefs de trois auteurs: Kade (Leipzig), Coseriu (Tübingen), Seleskovitch (Paris)*, Paris: Didier Érudition.

Laster, K. and Taylor, V. (1994) *Interpreters and the Legal System*, Leichhardt, NSW: The Federation Press.

Lederer, M. (1978/2002) "Simultaneous Interpretation – Units of Meaning and Other Features," in Pöchhacker and Shlesinger (eds) (2002), pp. 131–40.

—— (1981) *La traduction simultanée – Expérience et théorie*, Paris: Minard Lettres Modernes.

—— (1990) "The Role of Cognitive Complements in Interpreting," in Bowen and Bowen (eds) (1990), pp. 53–60.

Lee, T. (1999) "Simultaneous Listening and Speaking in English into Korean Simultaneous Interpretation," *Meta* 44 (4): 560–72.

Levelt, W.J.M. (1989) *Speaking: From Intention to Articulation*, Cambridge, MA: MIT Press.

Linell, P. (1997) "Interpreting as Communication," in Gambier *et al.* (eds) (1997), pp. 49–67.

Liu, M. (2001) "Expertise in Simultaneous Interpreting: A Working Memory Analysis," PhD dissertation, University of Texas at Austin.

Livingston, S., Singer, B. and Abramson, T. (1994) "Effectiveness Compared: ASL Interpretation vs. Transliteration," *Sign Language Studies* 82: 1–53.

Llewellyn-Jones, P. (1981) "Simultaneous Interpreting," in B. Woll, J. Kyle and M. Deuchar (eds) *Perspectives on British Sign Language and Deafness*, London: Croom Helm, pp. 89–104.

Longley, P. (1978) "An Integrated Programme for Training Interpreters," in Gerver and Sinaiko (eds) (1978), pp. 45–56.

—— (1989) "The Use of Aptitude Testing in the Selection of Students for Conference Interpretation Training," in Gran and Dodds (eds) (1989), pp. 105–8.

Lonsdale, D. (1997) "Modeling Cognition in SI: Methodological Issues," *Interpreting* 2 (1/2): 91–117.

Lotriet, A. (2002) "Can Short Interpreter Training Be Effective? The South African Truth and Reconciliation Commission Experience," in Hung (ed.) (2002), pp. 83–98.

LuperFoy, S. (1996) "Machine Interpretation of Bilingual Dialogue," *Interpreting* 1 (2): 213–33.

Mack, G. (2002) "New Perspectives and Challenges for Interpretation: The Example of Television," in Garzone and Viezzi (eds) (2002), pp. 203–13.

Mackintosh, J. (1983) "Relay Interpretation: An Exploratory Study," MA dissertation, Birkbeck College, University of London.

—— (1985) "The Kintsch and van Dijk Model of Discourse Comprehension and Production Applied to the Interpretation Process," *Meta* 30 (1): 37–43.

—— (1995) "A Review of Conference Interpretation: Practice and Training," *Target* 7 (1): 119-33.

—— (1999) "Interpreters Are Made Not Born," *Interpreting* 4 (1): 67–80.

MacWhinney, B. (1997) "Simultaneous Interpretation and the Competition Model," in Danks *et al.* (eds) (1997), pp. 215–32.

Marcos, L.R. (1979) "Effects of Interpreters on the Evaluation of Psychopathology in Non-English-speaking Patients," *American Journal of Psychiatry* 136 (2): 171–4.

Marzocchi, C. (1998) "The Case for an Institution-specific Component in Interpreting Research," *The Interpreters' Newsletter* No. 8: 51–74.

Mason, I. (2000) "Models and Methods in Dialogue Interpreting Research," in M. Olohan (ed.) *Intercultural Faultlines*, Manchester: St Jerome Publishing.

—— (ed.) (2001) *Triadic Exchanges. Studies in Dialogue Interpreting*, Manchester: St Jerome Publishing.

—— and Stewart, M. (2001) "Interactional Pragmatics, Face and the Dialogue Interpreter," in Mason (ed.) (2001), pp. 51–70.

Matyssek, H. (1989) *Handbuch der Notizentechnik für Dolmetscher*, Heidelberg: Groos.

Maxwell, J.A. (1998) "Designing a Qualitative Study," in Bickman and Rog (eds) (1998), pp. 69–100.

Mazzetti, A. (1999) "The Influence of Segmental and Prosodic Deviations on Source-text Comprehension in Simultaneous Interpretation," *The Interpreters' Newsletter* No. 9: 125–47.

McAllister, R. (2000) "Perceptual Foreign Accent and its Relevance for Simultaneous Interpreting," in Englund Dimitrova and Hyltenstam (eds) (2000), pp. 45–63.

McDonough, J. and McDonough, S. (1997) *Research Methods for English Language Teachers*, London: Arnold.

McIntire, M.L. (ed.) (1984) *New Dialogues in Interpreter Education. Proceedings of the Fourth National Conference of Interpreter Trainers Convention*, Silver Spring, MD: RID Publications.

—— and Sanderson, G.R. (1995) "Bye-bye! Bi-bi!: Questions of Empowerment and Role," in RID (1995), pp. 94–118.

Mead, P. (1999) "Interpreting: The Lexicographers' View," *The Interpreters' Newsletter* No. 9: 199–209.

—— (2000) "Control of Pauses by Trainee Interpreters in their A and B Languages," *The Interpreters' Newsletter* No. 10: 89–102.

—— (2001) "Research on Interpreting by Students at SSLiMIT, University of Bologna (Italy)," *The Interpreters' Newsletter* No. 11: 119–29.

—— (2002) "Exploring Hesitation in Consecutive Interpreting: An Empirical Study," in Garzone and Viezzi (eds) (2002), pp. 73–82.

Mesa, A.-M. (2000) "The Cultural Interpreter: An Appreciated Professional," in Roberts *et al.* (eds) (2000), pp. 67–79.

Metzger, M. (1999) *Sign Language Interpreting: Deconstructing the Myth of Neutrality*, Washington, DC: Gallaudet University Press.

—— (2000) "Interactive Role-plays as a Teaching Strategy," in Roy (ed.) (2000c), pp. 83–108.

Meyer, B. (2002) "Medical Interpreting: Some Salient Features," in Garzone and Viezzi (eds) (2002), pp. 159–69.

Mikkelson, H. (1996) "Community Interpreting: An Emerging Profession," *Interpreting* 1 (1): 125–9.

—— (1998) "Towards a Redefinition of the Role of the Court Interpreter," *Interpreting* 3 (1): 21–46.

—— (1999) "The Professionalization of Community Interpreting," *Journal of Interpretation* 1999: 119–33.

—— (2000) *Introduction to Court Interpreting*, Manchester: St Jerome Publishing.

—— (2000/01) "Interpreter Ethics: A Review of the Traditional and Electronic Literature," *Interpreting* 5 (1): 49–56.

Miles, M.B. and Huberman, A.M. (1994) *Qualitative Data Analysis: An Expanded Sourcebook*, 2nd edn, Thousand Oaks, London and New Delhi: Sage.

Mizuno, A. (1999) "Shifts of Cohesion and Coherence in Simultaneous Interpretation from English into Japanese," *Interpreting Research* 8 (2): 31–41.

Monacelli, C. (2002) "Interpreters for Peace," in Garzone and Viezzi (eds) (2002), pp. 181–93.

Morris, R. (1989) "Court Interpretation: The Trial of Ivan John Demjanjuk," *The Interpreters' Newsletter* No. 2: 27–37.

—— (1990) "Interpretation at the Demjanjuk Trial," in Bowen and Bowen (eds) (1990), pp. 101–7.

—— (1995) "The Moral Dilemmas of Court Interpreting," *The Translator* 1 (1): 25–46.

—— (2000) "Plus ça Change . . . ? Community Interpreters at the End of the Twentieth Century," in Roberts *et al.* (eds) (2000), pp. 243–64.

Moser, B. (1978) "Simultaneous Interpretation: A Hypothetical Model and its Practical Application," in Gerver and Sinaiko (eds) (1978), pp. 353–68.

Moser, P. (1996) "Expectations of Users of Conference Interpretation," *Interpreting* 1 (2): 145–78.

Moser-Mercer, B. (1985) "Screening Potential Interpreters," *Meta* 30 (1): 97–100.

—— (1992) "Terminology Documentation in Conference Interpretation," *Terminologie et Traduction* 2/3. 285–303.

—— (1994a) "Paradigms Gained or the Art of Productive Disagreement," in Lambert and Moser-Mercer (eds) (1994), pp. 17–23.

—— (1994b) "Aptitude Testing for Conference Interpreting: Why, When and How," in Lambert and Moser-Mercer (eds) (1994), pp. 57–68.

—— (1996) "Quality in Interpreting: Some Methodological Issues," *The Interpreters' Newsletter* No. 7: 43–55.

—— (1997) "Beyond Curiosity: Can Interpreting Research Meet the Challenge?" in Danks *et al.* (eds) (1997), pp. 176–205.

—— (1997/2002) "Process Models in Simultaneous Interpretation," in Pöchhacker and Shlesinger (eds) (2002), pp. 149–61.

—— (2000) "The Rocky Road to Expertise in Interpreting: Eliciting Knowledge from Learners," in M. Kadric, K. Kaindl and F. Pöchhacker (eds) (2000) *Translations-wissenschaft. Festschrift für Mary Snell-Hornby zum 60. Geburtstag*, Tübingen: Stauffenburg, pp. 339–52.

—— and Setton, R. (2000) "The Geneva (ETI) Perspective on Interpretation Research," *Conference Interpretation and Translation* 2: 49–56.

—— Lambert, S., Darò, V. and Williams, S. (1997) "Skill Components in Simultaneous Interpreting," in Gambier *et al.* (eds) (1997), pp. 133–48.

—— Künzli, A. and Korac, M. (1998) "Prolonged Turns in Interpreting: Effects on Quality, Physiological and Psychological Stress (Pilot Study)," *Interpreting* 3 (1): 47–64.

—— Frauenfelder, U.H., Casado, B. and Künzli, A. (2000) "Searching to Define Expertise in Interpreting," in Englund Dimitrova and Hyltenstam (eds) (2000), pp. 107–31.

Mouzourakis, P. (1996) "Videoconferencing: Techniques and Challenges," *Interpreting* 1 (1): pp. 21–38.

—— (2000) "Interpretation Booths for the Third Millennium," *Communicate!* March–April 2000 (http://www.aiic.net/ViewPage.cfm/page131.htm).

Munday, J. (2001) *Introducing Translation Studies: Theories and Applications*, London and New York: Routledge.

Napier, J. (2002) *Sign Language Interpreting: Linguistic Coping Strategies*, Coleford: Douglas McLean.

Nida, E.A. and Taber, C.R. (1969) *The Theory and Practice of Translation*, Leiden: Brill.

Niska, H. (1995) "Just Interpreting: Role Conflicts and Discourse Types in Court Interpreting," in M. Morris (ed.) *Translation and the Law*, Amsterdam and Philadelphia: Benjamins, pp. 293–316.

—— [*et al.*] (1999) "Quality Issues in Remote Interpreting," in Álvarez Lugrís and Fernández Ocampo (eds) (1999), pp. 109–21.

—— (2002) "Community Interpreter Training: Past, Present, Future," in Garzone and Viezzi (eds) (2002), pp. 133–44.

Nord, C. (1997) *Translating as a Purposeful Activity*, Manchester: St Jerome Publishing.

NUPIT (2001) "What Do Interpreters and Translators Talk about among Themselves? A Survey of Employment Conditions among Interpreters and Translators," London: NUPIT/MSF.

Oléron, P. and Nanpon, H. (1965) "Récherches sur la traduction simultanée," *Journal de Psychologie Normale et Pathologique* 62 (1): 73–94.

—— (1965/2002) "Research into Simultaneous Translation," in Pöchhacker and Shlesinger (eds) (2002), pp. 43–50.

Ong, W.J. (1982) *Orality and Literacy: The Technologizing of the Word*, London and New York: Methuen.

Ozolins, U. (2000) "Communication Needs and Interpreting in Multilingual Settings: The International Spectrum of Response," in Roberts *et al.* (eds) (2000), pp. 21–33.

Padilla, P., Bajo, M.T., Cañas, J.J. and Padilla, F. (1995) "Cognitive Processes of Memory in Simultaneous Interpretation," in Tommola (ed.) (1995), pp. 61–71.

Page, J. (1993) "In the Sandwich or on the Side? Cultural Variability and the Interpreter's Role," *Journal of Interpretation* 6: 107–25.

Paneth, E. (1957/2002) "An Investigation into Conference Interpreting," in Pöchhacker and Shlesinger (eds) (2002), pp. 31–40.

—— (1990) "The Future of Projected Interpretation," *The Interpreters' Newsletter* No. 3: 38–40.

Paradis, M. (1994) "Toward a Neurolinguistic Theory of Simultaneous Translation: The Framework," *International Journal of Psycholinguistics* 9 (3): 319–35.

—— (2000) "Prerequisites to a Study of Neurolinguistic Processes involved in Simultaneous Interpreting. A Synopsis," in Englund Dimitrova and Hyltenstam (eds) (2000), pp. 17–24.

Patrie, C.J. (1995) "A Confluence of Diverse Relationships: Interpreter Education and Educational Interpreting," in RID (1995), pp. 3–18.

—— and Mertz, J. (1997) *An Annotated Bibliography on Interpretation*, Washington, DC: Gallaudet University.

Penney, C. and Sammons, S. (1997) "Training the Community Interpreter: The Nunavut Arctic College Experience," in Carr *et al.* (eds) (1997), pp. 65–76.

Peper, E. and Gibney, K.H. (1999) "Psychophysiological Basis for Discomfort during Sign Language Interpreting," *Journal of Interpretation* 1999: 11–18.

Petsche, H., Etlinger, S.C. and Filz, O. (1993) "Brain Electrical Mechanisms of Bilingual Speech Management: An Initial Investigation," *Electroencephalography and Clinical Neurophysiology* 86: 385–94.

Pippa, S. and Russo, M. (2002) "Aptitude for Conference Interpreting: A Proposal for a Testing Methodology Based on Paraphrase," in Garzone and Viezzi (eds) (2002), pp. 245–56.

Pöchhacker, F. (1992) "The Role of Theory in Simultaneous Interpreting," in Dollerup and Loddegaard (eds) (1992), pp. 211–20.

—— (1993) "From Knowledge to Text: Coherence in Simultaneous Interpreting," in Gambier and Tommola (eds) (1993), pp. 87–100.

—— (1994a) *Simultandolmetschen als komplexes Handeln*, Tübingen: Gunter Narr.

—— (1994b) "Simultaneous Interpretation: 'Cultural Transfer' or 'Voice-over Text'?" in Snell-Hornby *et al.* (eds) (1994), pp. 169–78.

—— (1994c) "Quality Assurance in Simultaneous Interpreting," in Dollerup and Lindegaard (eds) (1994), pp. 233–42.

—— (1995a) "Simultaneous Interpreting: A Functionalist Perspective," *Hermes. Journal of Linguistics* 14: 31–53.

—— (1995b) "Slips and Shifts in Simultaneous Interpreting," in Tommola (ed.) (1995), pp. 73–90.

—— (1999) "Teaching Practices in Simultaneous Interpreting," *The Interpreters' Newsletter* No. 9: 157–76.

—— (2000a) *Dolmetschen. Konzeptuelle Grundlagen und deskriptive Untersuchungen*, Tübingen: Stauffenburg.

—— (2000b) "The Community Interpreter's Task: Self-perception and Provider Views," in Roberts *et al.* (eds) (2000), pp. 49–65.

—— (2002) "Researching Interpreting Quality: Models and Methods," in Garzone and Viezzi (eds) (2002), pp. 95–106.

—— and Kadric, M. (1999) "The Hospital Cleaner as Healthcare Interpreter: A Case Study," *The Translator* 5 (2): 161–78.

—— and Shlesinger, M. (eds) (2002) *The Interpreting Studies Reader*, London and New York: Routledge.

Pollitt, K. (1997) "The State We're In: Some Thoughts on Professionalisation, Professionalism and Practice among the UK's Sign Language Interpreters," *Deaf Worlds* 13 (3): 21–6.

Poyatos, F. (1987/2002) "Nonverbal Communication in Simultaneous and Consecutive Interpretation: A Theoretical Model and New Perspectives," in Pöchhacker and Shlesinger (eds) (2002), pp. 235–46.

Prillwitz, S. (2001) *Empirische Studien zu Angeboten für Gehörlose im Fernsehen und ihre Rezeption*, Kiel: ULR.

Puebla Fortier, J. (1997) "Interpreting for Health in the United States," in Carr *et al.* (eds) (1997), pp. 165–77.

Putsch, R.W. (1985) "Cross-cultural Communication: The Special Case of Interpreters in Health Care," *Journal of the American Medical Association* 254 (23): 3344–8

Rabin, C. (1958) "The Linguistics of Translation," in Smith (ed.) (1958), pp. 123–45.

Repa, J. (1991) "Training and Certification of Court Interpreters in a Multicultural Society," *Meta* 36 (4): 595–605

Riccardi, A. (1996) "Language-specific Strategies in Simultaneous Interpreting," in Dollerup and Appel (eds) (1996), pp. 213–22.

—— (2002) "Evaluation in Interpretation: Macrocriteria and Microcriteria," in Hung (ed.) (2002), pp. 115–26.

RID (1995) *A Confluence of Diverse Relationships. Proceedings of the Thirteenth National Convention of the Registry of Interpreters for the Deaf, August 10–14, 1993*, Silver Spring, MD: RID Publications.

Rinne, J.O., Tommola, J., Laine, M., Krause, B.J., Schmidt, D., Kaasinen, V., Teräs, M., Sipilä, H. and Sunnari, M. (2000) "The Translating Brain: Cerebral Activation Patterns during Simultaneous Interpreting," *Neuroscience Letters* 294: 85–8.

Roberts, R.P. (ed.) (1981) *L'interprétation auprès des tribunaux. Actes du mini-colloque tenu les 10 et 11 avril 1980 à l'Université d'Ottawa*, Ottawa: University of Ottawa Press.

—— (1997) "Community Interpreting Today and Tomorrow," in Carr *et al.* (eds) (1997), pp. 7–26.

—— (2000) "Interpreter Assessment Tools for Different Settings," in Roberts *et al.* (eds) (2000), pp. 103–20.

—— (2002) "Community Interpreting: A Profession in Search of its Identity," in Hung (ed.) (2002), pp. 157–75.

—— and Tayler, M. (1990) "Development of Legal Interpreter Education in New Jersey," in Bowen and Bowen (eds) (1990), pp. 70–80.

—— Carr, S.E., Abraham, D. and Dufour, A. (eds) (2000) *The Critical Link 2: Interpreters in the Community. Selected Papers from the Second International Conference on Interpreting in Legal, Health and Social Service Settings, Vancouver, BC, Canada, 19–23 May 1998*, Amsterdam and Philadelphia: John Benjamins.

Robson, C. (1993) *Real World Research: A Resource for Social Scientists and Practitioner–Researchers*, Oxford and Cambridge, MA: Blackwell.

Roland, R.A. (1999) *Interpreters as Diplomats*, Ottawa: University of Ottawa Press.

Rosenberg, B.A. (2002) "A Quantitative Discourse Analysis of Community Interpreting," in *Translation: New Ideas for a New Century. Proceedings of the XVI FIT Congress*, Paris: FIT, pp. 222–6.

Roy, C.B. (1984) "Response to Etilvia Arjona on Curriculum Design," in McIntire (ed.) (1984), pp. 36–42.

—— (1993/2002) "The Problem with Definitions, Descriptions and the Role Metaphors of Interpreters," in Pöchhacker and Shlesinger (eds) (2002), pp. 345–53.

—— (1996) "An Interactional Sociolinguistic Analysis of Turn-taking in an Interpreted Event," *Interpreting* 1 (1): 39–67.

—— (2000a) *Interpreting as a Discourse Process*, Oxford: Oxford University Press.

—— (2000b) "Training Interpreters – Past, Present, and Future," in Roy (ed.) (2000c), pp. 1–14.

—— (ed.) (2000c) *Innovative Practices for Teaching Sign Language Interpreters*, Washington, DC: Gallaudet University Press.

Rozan, J.-F. (1956) *La prise de notes en interprétation consécutive*, Geneva: Georg.

Russo, M. (1993) "Testing Aptitude for Simultaneous Interpretation: Evaluation of the First Trial and Preliminary Results," *The Interpreters' Newsletter* No. 5: 68–71.

—— (1995) "Self-Evaluation: The Awareness of One's Own Difficulties as a Training Tool for Simultaneous Interpretation," *The Interpreters' Newsletter* No. 6: 75–85.

Sabatini, E. (2000/01) "Listening Comprehension, Shadowing and Simultaneous Interpretation of Two 'Non-standard' English Speeches," *Interpreting* 5 (1): 25–48.

Salevsky, H. (1987) *Probleme des Simultandolmetschens. Eine Studie zur Handlungsspezifik*, Berlin: Akademie der Wissenschaften der DDR.

—— (1993) "The Distinctive Nature of Interpreting Studies," *Target* 5 (2): 149–67.

Sanz, J. (1931) "Le travail et les aptitudes des interprètes parlementaires," *Anals d'Orientació Professional* 4: 303–18.

Sawyer, D.B. (2001) "The Integration of Curriculum and Assessment in Interpreter Education: A Case Study," doctoral dissertation, University of Mainz (http://archimed.uni-mainz.de/pub/2001/0097/diss.pdf).

Scheffer, T. (1997) "Dolmetschen als Darstellungsproblem. Eine ethnographische Studie zur Rolle der Dolmetscher in Asylanhörungen," *Zeitschrift für Soziologie* 26 (3): 159–80.

Schiffrin, D., Tannen, D. and Hamilton, H.E. (eds) (2001) *The Handbook of Discourse Analysis*, Oxford and Malden, MA: Blackwell.

Schjoldager, A. (1995/2002) "An Exploratory Study of Translational Norms in Simultaneous Interpreting: Methodological Reflections," in Pöchhacker and Shlesinger (eds) (2002), pp. 301–11.

—— (1996) "Assessment in Simultaneous Interpreting," in Dollerup and Appel (eds) (1996), pp. 187–95.

Schleiermacher, F. (1813/1997) "On the Different Methods of Translating," in D. Robinson (ed.) *Western Translation Theory*, Manchester: St Jerome Publishing, pp.225–38.

Schmitz, B. (1998) *Pragmatikbasiertes Maschinelles Dolmetschen*, Heidelberg: Groos.

Schweda Nicholson, N. (1989) "Documentation and Text Preparation for Simultaneous Interpretation," in Hammond (ed.) (1989), pp. 163–82.

—— (1990) "Consecutive Note-taking for Community Interpretation," in Bowen and Bowen (eds) (1990), pp. 136–45.

—— (1994) "Professional Ethics for Court and Community Interpreters," in D.L. Hammond (ed.) *Professional Issues for Translators and Interpreters*, Philadelphia: John Benjamins, pp. 79–97.

Seal, B.C. (1998) *Best Practices in Educational Interpreting*, Boston, MA: Allyn and Bacon.

Seleskovitch, D. (1962) "L'Interprétation de Conférence," *Babel* 8 (1): 13–18.

—— (1968) *L'interprète dans les conférences internationales: problèmes de langage et de communication*, Paris: Minard Lettres Modernes.

—— (1975) *Langage, langues et mémoire. Étude de la prise de notes en interprétation consécutive*, Paris: Minard Lettres Modernes.

—— (1975/2002) "Language and Memory: A Study of Note-taking in Consecutive Interpreting," in Pöchhacker and Shlesinger (eds) (2002), pp. 121–9.

—— (1976) "Interpretation, a Psychological Approach to Translating," in Brislin (ed.) (1976b), pp. 92–116.

—— (1978a) *Interpreting for International Conferences*, Washington, DC: Pen and Booth.

—— (1978b) "Language and Cognition," in Gerver and Sinaiko (eds) (1978), pp. 333–41.

—— (1991) "De la pratique de l'interprétation a la traductologie," in M. Lederer and F. Israël (eds) *La liberté en traduction*, Paris: Didier Érudition, pp. 289–98.

—— (1999) "The Teaching of Simultaneous Interpretation in the Course of the Last 50 Years," *Interpreting* 4 (1): 55–66.

—— and Lederer, M. (1984) *Interpréter pour traduire*, Paris: Didier Érudition.

—— and Lederer, M. (1989) *Pédagogie raisonnée de l'interprétation*, Paris/Brussels: Didier Érudition/OPOCE.

—— and Lederer (1995) *A Systematic Approach to Teaching Interpretation* (trans. J. Harmer), Silver Spring, MD: Registry of Interpreters for the Deaf.

Setton, R. (1994) "Experiments in the Application of Discourse Studies to Interpreter Training," in Dollerup and Lindegaard (eds) (1994), pp. 183–98.

—— (1998/2002) "Meaning Assembly in Simultaneous Interpretation," in Pöchhacker and Shlesinger (eds) (2002), pp. 179–202.

—— (1999) *Simultaneous Interpretation: A Cognitive-pragmatic Analysis*, Amsterdam and Philadelphia: John Benjamins.

—— (2003a) "Words and Sense: Revisiting Lexical Processes in Interpreting," *Forum* 1 (1): 139–68.

—— (2003b) "Models of the Interpreting Process," in A. Collados Aís and J.A. Sabio Pinilla (eds) *Avances en la investigación sobre interpretación*, Granada: Comares, pp. 29–89.

Shackman, J. (1984) *The Right To Be Understood: A Handbook on Working with, Employing and Training Community Interpreters*, Cambridge: National Extension College.

Shannon C.E. and Weaver, W. (1949) *The Mathematical Theory of Communication*, Urbana, IL: University of Illinois Press.

Shiryayev, A. (1979) *Sinkhronniy perevod. Deyatelnost sinkhronnogo perevodchika i metodika prepodavaniya sinkhronnogo perevoda* [Simultaneous Interpretation: The Activity of a Simultaneous Interpreter and Methods of Teaching Simultaneous Interpretation], Moscow: Voyenizdat.

Shlesinger, M. (1989a) "Extending the Theory of Translation to Interpretation: Norms as a Case in Point," *Target* 1 (1): 111–16.

—— (1989b) "Simultaneous Interpretation as a Factor in Effecting Shifts in the Position of Texts on the Oral–Literate Continuum," MA thesis, Tel Aviv University.

—— (1991) "Interpreter Latitude vs. Due Process. Simultaneous and Consecutive Interpretation in Multilingual Trials," in S. Tirkkonen-Condit (ed.) *Empirical Research in Translation and Intercultural Studies*, Tübingen: Gunter Narr, pp. 147–55.

—— (1994) "Intonation in the Production and Perception of Simultaneous Interpretation," in Lambert and Moser-Mercer (eds) (1994), pp. 225–36.

—— (1995a) "Stranger in Paradigms: What Lies Ahead for Simultaneous Interpreting Research? *Target* 7 (1): 7–28.

—— (1995b) "Shifts in Cohesion in Simultaneous Interpreting," *The Translator* 1 (2): 193–214.

—— [*et al.*] (1997) "Quality in Simultaneous Interpreting," in Gambier *et al.* (eds) (1997), pp. 123–31.

—— (1998). "Corpus-based Interpreting Studies as an Offshoot of Corpus-based Translation Studies," *Meta* 43 (4): 486–93.

—— (1999) "Norms, Strategies and Constraints: How Do We Tell Them Apart?" in Álvarez Lugrís and Fernández Ocampo (eds) (1999), pp. 65–77.

—— (2000a) "Strategic Allocation of Working Memory and Other Attentional Resources," PhD dissertation, Bar-Ilan University.

—— (2000b) "Interpreting as a Cognitive Process: How Can We Know What Really Happens?" in Tirkkonen-Condit and Jääskeläinen (eds) (2000), pp. 3–15.

—— (2002) "Choosing a Research Topic," *Conference Interpretation and Translation* 4: 25–36.

Shreve, G.M. and Diamond, B.J. (1997) "Cognitive Processes in Translation and Interpreting: Critical Issues," in Danks *et al.* (eds) (1997), pp. 233–51.

Shuttleworth, M. and Cowie, M. (1997) *Dictionary of Translation Studies*, Manchester: St Jerome Publishing.

Smith, A.H. (ed.) (1958) *Aspects of Translation*, Studies in Communication 2, London: Secker and Warburg.

Snedecor, G.W. and Cochran, W.G. (1980) *Statistical Methods*, 7th edn, Ames, IA: Iowa State University Press.

Snell-Hornby, M. (1988) *Translation Studies – An Integrated Approach*, Amsterdam: John Benjamins.

—— Pöchhacker, F. and Kaindl, K. (eds) (1994) *Translation Studies – An Interdiscipline*, Amsterdam and Philadelphia: John Benjamins.

—— Hönig, H.G., Kussmaul, P. and Schmitt, P.A. (eds) (1998) *Handbuch Translation*, Tübingen: Stauffenburg.

Snelling, D. [*et al.*] (1997) "On Media and Court Interpreting," in Gambier *et al.* (eds) (1997), pp. 187–206.

Stauffer, L.K., Burch, D.D. and Boone, S.E. (1999) "A Study of the Demographics of Attendees at the 1997 Biennial Convention of the Registry of Interpreters for the Deaf, Inc.," *Journal of Interpretation* 1999: 105–16.

Steiner, B. (1998) "Signs from the Void: The Comprehension and Production of Sign Language on Television," *Interpreting* 3 (2): 99–146.

Steiner, G. (1975) *After Babel: Aspects of Language and Translation*, London: Oxford University Press.

Stenzl, C. (1983) "Simultaneous Interpretation: Groundwork Towards a Comprehensive Model," MA thesis, Birkbeck College, University of London.

—— (1989) "From Theory to Practice and from Practice to Theory," in Gran and Dodds (eds) (1989), pp. 23–6.

Stewart, D.A., Schein, J.D. and Cartwright, B.E. (1998) *Sign Language Interpreting: Exploring Its Art and Science*, Boston, MA: Allyn and Bacon.

Stoll, C. (2000) "New Technologies in Conference Interpretation: Interpreting and Videoconferences," in F. Austermühl and D. Apollon (eds) *Humanities Education and the Challenge of e-Learning*, Bergen: University of Bergen, pp. 211–21.

—— (2002) "Terminologiesysteme für Simultandolmetscher," in F. Mayer, K.-D. Schmitz and J. Zeumer (eds) *eTerminology. Akten des Symposiums Köln, 12.–13. April 2002*, Deutscher Terminologie Tag e.V., pp. 31–42.

Straniero Sergio, F. (1999) "The Interpreter on the (Talk) Show," *The Translator* 5 (2): 303–26.

Strong, M. and Rudser, S.F. (1985) "An Assessment Instrument for Sign Language Interpreters," *Sign Language Studies* 49: 344–62.

—— (1992) "The Subjective Assessment of Sign Language Interpreters," in Cokely (ed.) (1992b), pp. 1–14.

Sunnari, M. (1995) "Processing Strategies in Simultaneous Interpreting: 'Saying It All' vs. Synthesis," in Tommola (ed.) (1995), pp. 109–19.

Tannen, D. (1982) "The Oral/Literate Continuum in Discourse," in D. Tannen (ed.) *Spoken and Written Language: Exploring Orality and Literacy*, Norwood, NJ: Ablex, pp. 1–16.

Tate, G. and Turner, G.H. (1997/2002) "The Code and the Culture: Sign Language Interpreting – In Search of the New Breed's Ethics," in Pöchhacker and Shlesinger (eds) (2002), pp. 373–83.

Taylor, C. (1989) "Primary and Secondary Orality in Teaching Interpreting Technique," in J.M. Dodds (ed.) *Aspects of English. Miscellaneous Papers for English Teachers and Specialists*, Udine: Campanotto, pp. 93–102.

Taylor Torsello, C. [*et al.*] (1997) "Linguistics, Discourse Analysis and Interpretation," in Gambier *et al.* (eds) (1997), pp. 167–86.

Tebble, H. (1998) *Medical Interpreting – Improving Communication with Your Patients*, Geelong/Melbourne: Language Australia/Deakin University.

—— (1999) "The Tenor of Consultant Physicians: Implications for Medical Interpreting," *The Translator* 5 (2): 179–200.

Thieme, K., Hermann, A. and Glässer, F. (1956) *Beiträge zur Geschichte des Dolmetschens*, Munich: Isar.

Thiéry, C. (1978) "True Bilingualism and Second-language Learning," in Gerver and Sinaiko (eds) (1978), pp. 145–53.

—— (1990) "The Sense of Situation in Conference Interpreting," in Bowen and Bowen (eds) (1990), pp. 40–3.

Tijus, C.A. (1997) "Understanding for Interpreting, Interpreting for Understanding," in Gambier *et al.* (eds) (1997), pp. 29–48.

Tirkkonen-Condit, S. and Jääskeläinen, R. (eds) (2000) *Tapping and Mapping the Processes of Translation and Interpreting*, Amsterdam and Philadelphia: John Benjamins.

Tissi, B. (2000) "Silent Pauses and Disfluencies in Simultaneous Interpretation: A Descriptive Analysis," *The Interpreters' Newsletter* No. 10: 103–27.

Titscher, S., Meyer, M., Wodak, R. and Vetter, E. (2000) *Methods of Text and Discourse Analysis*, London, Thousand Oaks and New Delhi: Sage.

Tommola, J. (ed.) (1995) *Topics in Interpreting Research*, Turku: University of Turku, Centre for Translation and Interpreting.

—— (1999) "New Trends in Interpreting Research: Going Psycho – or Neuro?" in Álvarez Lugrís and Fernández Ocampo (eds) (1999), pp. 321–30.

—— (2003) "Estimating the Transfer of Semantic Information in Interpreting," in Collados Aís *et al.* (eds) (2003), pp. 125–46.

—— and Helevä, M. (1998) "Language Direction and Source Text Complexity: Effects on Trainee Performance in Simultaneous Interpreting," in L. Bowker, M. Cronin, D. Kenny and J. Pearson (eds) *Unity in Diversity? Current Trends in Translation Studies*, Manchester: St Jerome Publishing, pp. 177–86.

—— and Lindholm, J. (1995) "Experimental Research on Interpreting: Which Dependent Variable?" in Tommola (ed.) (1995), pp. 121–33.

Toury, G. (1978/2000) "The Nature and Role of Norms in Translation," in Venuti (ed.) (2000), pp. 198–211.

—— (1995) *Descriptive Translation Studies and Beyond*, Amsterdam and Philadelphia: John Benjamins.

Treisman, A.M. (1965) "The Effects of Redundancy and Familiarity on Translating and Repeating Back a Foreign and a Native Language," *British Journal of Psychology* 56: 369–79.

Tseng, J. (1992) "Interpreting as an Emerging Profession in Taiwan – a Sociological Model," MA thesis, Fu Jen Catholic University, Taipeh.

Tulving, E. and Craik, F.I.M. (eds) (2000) *The Oxford Handbook of Memory*, Oxford: Oxford University Press.

Turner, G.H. (2001) "The Bilingual, Bimodal Courtroom: A First Glance," in Harrington and Turner (2001), pp. 124–51.

UN (2001) "Remote Interpretation," *The Interpreters' Newsletter* No. 11: 163–80.

Van Besien, F. (1999) "Anticipation in Simultaneous Interpretation," *Meta* 44 (2): 250–9.

van Dijk, T.A. (ed.) (1997a) *Discourse as Structure and Process. Discourse Studies: A Multidisciplinary Introduction*, vol. 1, London, Thousand Oaks and New Delhi: Sage.

—— (ed.) (1997b) *Discourse as Social Interaction. Discourse Studies: A Multidisciplinary Introduction*, vol. 2, London, Thousand Oaks and New Delhi: Sage.

—— and Kintsch, W. (1983) *Strategies of Discourse Comprehension*, New York: Academic Press.

van Hoof, H. (1962) *Théorie et pratique de l'interprétation*, Munich: Max Hueber.

Venuti, L. (ed.) (2000) *The Translation Studies Reader*, London and New York: Routledge.

Vermeer, H.J. (1989/2000) "Skopos and Commission in Translational Action," in Venuti (ed.) (2000), pp. 221–32.

—— (1992) *Skizzen zu einer Geschichte der Translation*, Frankfurt: Verlag für Interkulturelle Kommunikation.

Viaggio, S. (1991) "Teaching Beginners to Shut Up and Listen," *The Interpreters' Newsletter* No. 4: 45–58.

—— (1996) "The Pitfalls of Metalingual Use in Simultaneous Interpreting," *The Translator* 2 (2): 179–98.

Vidrine, J. (1984) "An Historical Overview of Interpreter-training Programs," in McIntire (ed.) (1984), pp. 317–26.

Viezzi, M. (1990) "Sight Translation, Simultaneous Interpretation and Information Retention," in Gran and Taylor (eds) (1990), pp. 54–60.

Vuorikoski, A. (1993) "Simultaneous Interpretation – User Experience and Expectations," in C. Picken (ed.) *Translation – the Vital Link: Proceedings of the XIIIth World Congress of FIT*, vol. 1, London: Institute of Translation and Interpreting, pp. 317–27.

Wadensjö, C. (1993/2002) "The Double Role of a Dialogue Interpreter," in Pöchhacker and Shlesinger (eds) (2002), pp. 355–70.

—— (1998) *Interpreting as Interaction*, London and New York: Longman.

—— (1999) "Telephone Interpreting and the Synchronization of Talk in Social Interaction," *The Translator* 5 (2): 247–64.

—— (2001) "Interpreting in Crisis: The Interpreter's Position in Therapeutic Encounters," in Mason (ed.) (2001), pp. 71–85.

Wahlster, W. (ed.) (2000) *Verbmobil: Foundations of Speech-to-Speech Translation*, Berlin: Springer.

Weber, W.K. (1990) "The Importance of Sight Translation in an Interpreter Training Program," in Bowen and Bowen (eds) (1990), pp. 44–52.

Wiegand, C. (2000) "Role of the Interpreter in the Healing of a Nation: An Emotional View," in Roberts *et al.* (eds) (2000), pp. 207–18.

Williams, J. and Chesterman, A. (2002) *The Map: A Beginner's Guide to Doing Research in Translation Studies*, Manchester: St Jerome Publishing.

Wilss, W. (1978) "Syntactic Anticipation in German–English Simultaneous Interpreting," in Gerver and Sinaiko (eds) (1978), pp. 343–52.

—— (1999) *Translation and Interpreting in the 20th Century: Focus on German*, Amsterdam and Philadelphia: John Benjamins.

Winston, E.A. and Monikowski, C. (2000) "Discourse Mapping: Developing Textual Coherence Skills in Interpreters," in Roy (ed.) (2000c), pp. 15–66.

Wirl, J. (1958) *Grundsätzliches zur Problematik des Dolmetschens und des Übersetzens*, Vienna: Wilhelm Braumüller.

Wong, F.K. (1990) "Court Interpreting in a Multiracial Society – the Malaysian Experience," in Bowen and Bowen (eds) (1990), pp. 108–16.

Yagi, S.M. (1999) "Computational Discourse Analysis for Interpretation," *Meta* 44 (2): 268–79.

Zeier, H. (1997) "Psychophysiological Stress Research," *Interpreting* 2 (1/2): 231–49.

Zimman, L. (1994) "Intervention as a Pedagogical Problem in Community Interpreting," in Dollerup and Lindegaard (eds) (1994), pp. 217–24.

Zimmer, J. (1989) "ASL/English Interpreting in an Interactive Setting," in Hammond (ed.) (1989), pp. 225–31.

Internet links

(All sites last accessed on 20 April 2003)

Bibliographic collections

AIIC Bibliography on Interpretation
  → http://www.aiic.net/en/prof/research/default.htm
Conference Interpreting Research Information Network (CIRIN, formerly IRN)
  → http://perso.wanadoo.fr/daniel.gile/
Bibliography on Court & Legal Interpreting (R. Morris)
  → http://www.aiic.net/ViewPage.cfm?page_id=235
International Bibliography of Sign Language
  → http://www.sign-lang.uni-hamburg.de/bibweb/
Research in Medical Interpretation – Bibliography (E. Hardt, NCIHC)
  → http://www.ncihc.org/NCIHC_Bibliography.pdf

Journals (Publisher)

Babel (FIT/John Benjamins, Amsterdam)
  → http://www.benjamins.nl/cgi-bin/t_seriesview.cgi?series=babel
CIRIN Bulletin (Daniel Gile, Paris)
  → http://perso.wanadoo.fr/daniel.gile/Bulletin[26].htm
Communicate! (AIIC, Geneva)
  → http://www.aiic.net/ViewIssues.cfm
The Critical Link (Diana Abraham, Toronto)
  → http://www.criticallink.org/English/newsletters.htm
Forum (Presses de la Sorbonne Nouvelle/KSCI)
  → http://ksci.or.kr/ksci-e/main-k.htm
Interpretation Studies (Japan Association of Interpretation Studies)
  → http://www.cl.aoyama.ac.jp/~someya/10-JAIS/
The Interpreters' Newsletter (SSLMIT, Trieste)
  → http://www.sslmit.units.it
Interpreting (John Benjamins, Amsterdam)
  → http://www.benjamins.com/cgi-bin/t_seriesview.cgi?series=INTP

Journal of Interpretation (RID)
  → http://www.rid.org/pubs.html
Meta (Presses Universitaires de Montréal)
  → http://www.pum.umontreal.ca/revues/meta.html
  → http://www.erudit.org/revue/meta
Target (John Benjamins, Amsterdam)
  → http://www.benjamins.com/cgi-bin/t_seriesview.cgi?series=Target
The Translator (St Jerome, Manchester)
  → http://www.stjerome.co.uk/journal.html

International associations and institutions

AIIC – International Association of Conference Interpreters
  → http://www.aiic.net
CIUTI – International Permanent Conference of University Institutes of Translators and Interpreters
  → http://www-gewi.kfunigraz.ac.at/ciuti/
EFSLI – European Forum of Sign Language Interpreters
  → http:://www.efsli.org.uk
EST – European Society for Translation Studies
  → http.//est.utu.fi
FIT – International Federation of Translators
  → http://www.fit-ift.org
SCIC – Joint Interpreting and Conference Service, European Commission
  → http://europa.eu.int/comm/scic

National associations and centers (academic and professional)

Aarhus Centre for Interpreting Research
  → http://www.sprog.asb.dk/tolk
ATA – American Translators Association
  → http://www.atanet.org
CHIA – California Healthcare Interpreters Association
  → http://www.chia.ws
CIT – Conference of Interpreter Trainers (US)
  → http://www.cit-asl.org
IoL – Institute of Linguists (UK)
  → http://www.iol.org.uk (> NRPSI)
JAIS – Japan Association for Interpretation Studies
  → http://www.jais-org.net
KSCI – Korean Society of Conference Interpretation
  → http://ksci.or.kr
MMIA – Massachusetts Medical Interpreters Association
  → http://www.mmia.org

NAATI – National Accreditation Authority for Translators and Interpreters (Australia)
  → http://www.naati.com.au
NCIHC – National Council on Interpretation in Health Care (US)
  → http://www.ncihc.org
NAJIT – National Association of Judiciary Interpreters and Translators (US)
  → http://www.najit.org
RID – Registry of Interpreters for the Deaf (US, and Canada)
  → http://www.rid.org

Author index

Page numbers in *italics* indicate the passage(s) with the most detailed reference to an author and his or her work. First names are usually found where authors are first mentioned in the text.

Subject index

Page numbers in *italics* refer to the most detailed reference(s) to the subject.

bottom-up (processing) 101, 118
British Sign Language 18, 145–6
broadcast interpreting 15, 146, 162, 172;
    see also media interpreting; TV
    interpreting
Brussels 171–2; *see also* EU
BSL *see* British Sign Language
burnout 173
business interpreting 14, 28, 200

Canada 15, 37, 41, 45, 88, 148, 155, 165,
    236
case study *63–4*, 78, 149–52, 156–7, 178,
    209
certification 29, 79, 161, *165*, 189
CE(T)RA Chair 39–40
channel 19–22, *92–3*; capacity 116, 127;
    interpreter as 147
China 43, 197, 200
Chinese 131, 134, 157, 182, 203;
    publications 40, 43
chuchotage 19; *see also* whispered interpreting
chunking 118, 124, 133, 183; *see also*
    segmentation
CIRIN (Conference Interpreting Research
    Information Network) 40, 234
CIT (Conference of Interpreter Trainers)
    179, 190–2, 235
CIUTI (Conference of University-level
    Translator and Interpreter Schools) *31*,
    179, 190–2, 197, 235
C-language 21
clients 12, 16, 18, 30, 59, 89, 148–9, 152,
    154–5, 165, 173–4, 190; *see also* primary
    parties; users
cloze *119–20*, 131, 181, 183, 185
code (language as) 17–18, 54, *92–3*;
    switching 55–6; 92; manual 138;
    mixing 157
code of ethics 29, 79, 87, 147, 161, *163–6*,
    189; *see also* AIIC; RID
cognition 60, 65, 73, 118, 203; embodied
    203; situated 178, 203
cognitive apprenticeship 178
cognitive information processing skills 53,
    55, 73, 83
cognitive load 99, 117, 123, 133, 171; *see
    also* input, load
cognitive processing 38, 56, *73–6*, 78, 88,
    104, 108, 113, *121*, 137, 168, 182; *see
    also* information processing; process(ing)
    models
cognitive science(s) 42, *49–50*, 56–7, 72–4,
    80–1, 100, 102, 113, *118*, 125, 137,

142, 203
coherence 58, *140*, 143, 156–7
cohesion 58, 131, *140*, 143, 146, 153;
    logical 153; *see also* textuality
colonial empire 86, 162
communication 10, 12–16, 18, 22, 25, 28,
    50, 53, 56, 58–9, 69, 77–9, 85, *88–95*,
    108, 132, 137–8, 150–2, 154, 169, 174,
    179, 200–2; cross-cultural 59; face-to-
    face 79, *90–1*, 133, 139, 144, 151;
    facilitator 148; intercultural 37, 50,
    186, 200, 202; models 54, *92–5*; modes
    163; nonverbal 150; value orientation
    167
communicative effect 12, 57, *144–7*, 153
communicative needs 59, 77, 157
communicative situation 56, 143, 155,
    171; *see also* context; situation
community(-based) interpreting *15–17*,
    25–6, 30, 37, 39, *40–1*, 44, 79, 87–8,
    161–4, 173, 180, 182, 186, 199, 202; *see
    also* dialogue interpreting; liaison
    interpreting; settings, community(-
    based)
community interpreter(s) 29–30, 41,
    162–4, 171, 173–4, 179–80, 182,
    188–9; *see also* dialogue interpreter(s)
competence 90, 146–7, *165–7*, 177, 180–1,
    186, 188; communicative 145; cultural
    154, 167, 180; linguistic 104, 115, 143,
    154, 180, 182
completeness 141, 153–5, 157, 163, 165
comprehension 57, 68, 95–6, 98, 101–2,
    104, 108, *118–20*, 123–7, 131–3, 142,
    144–6, 167, 181–3; *see also*
    understanding
compression 132, 134–5
computer aided/assisted interpreting 23,
    170
concurrent operations 98, 101, 104; *see also*
    attention; simultaneity
condensation 134–5
conduit model 147
Conference Interpretation and Translation
    (journal) 43
conference interpreters *28*, 30, *32–5*, 59,
    69, 71, 81, 113, 116, 125, 127–8, 151,
    153, *160–2*, 164, 166, 169–74, 188–90,
    200, 202, 235; *see also* AIIC
conference interpreting *16–17*, 19–21,
    25–6, *28–9*, 31–3, 36–8, 40, 53, 56, 59,
    64, 68–9, 78, 81, *87*, 89, 127, 133, 138,
    146–7, 149, 160, 162, 165–6, *171–4*,
    200; *see also* settings, conference